# Beginning ARKit for iPhone and iPad

## Augmented Reality App Development for iOS

Wallace Wang

Apress®

*Beginning ARKit for iPhone and iPad: Augmented Reality App Development for iOS*

Wallace Wang
San Diego, CA, USA

ISBN-13 (pbk): 978-1-4842-4101-1          ISBN-13 (electronic): 978-1-4842-4102-8
https://doi.org/10.1007/978-1-4842-4102-8

Library of Congress Control Number: 2018962490

Managing Director, Apress Media LLC: Welmoed Spahr
Acquisitions Editor: Aaron Black
Development Editor: James Markham
Coordinating Editor: Jessica Vakili

Cover image designed by Freepik (www.freepik.com)

Distributed to the book trade worldwide by Springer Science+Business Media New York, 233 Spring Street, 6th Floor, New York, NY 10013. Phone 1-800-SPRINGER, fax (201) 348-4505, e-mail orders-ny@springer-sbm.com, or visit www.springeronline.com. Apress Media, LLC is a California LLC and the sole member (owner) is Springer Science + Business Media Finance Inc (SSBM Finance Inc). SSBM Finance Inc is a **Delaware** corporation.

For information on translations, please e-mail rights@apress.com, or visit http://www.apress.com/rights-permissions.

Apress titles may be purchased in bulk for academic, corporate, or promotional use. eBook versions and licenses are also available for most titles. For more information, reference our Print and eBook Bulk Sales web page at http://www.apress.com/bulk-sales.

Any source code or other supplementary material referenced by the author in this book is available to readers on GitHub via the book's product page, located at www.apress.com/978-1-4842-4101-1. For more detailed information, please visit http://www.apress.com/source-code.

Printed on acid-free paper

*This is book is dedicated to everyone who has an idea for an app but didn't know what to do first or how to get started. First, believe in your idea. Second, trust that you have intelligence to achieve your dream even if you don't know how you'll get there. Third, keep learning and improving your skills all the time. Fourth, stay focused. Success will come one day as long as you persist and never give up on yourself.*

# Table of Contents

# About the Author

**Wallace Wang** has written dozens of computer books over the years, beginning with ancient MS-DOS programs like WordPerfect and Turbo Pascal, migrating to writing books on Windows programs like Visual Basic and Microsoft Office, and finally switching to Swift programming for Apple products like the Macintosh and iPhone.

When he's not helping people discover the joys of programming, he performs stand-up comedy and appears on two radio shows on KNSJ in San Diego (`http://knsj.org`) called "Notes From the Underground" (with Dane Henderson, Jody Taylor, and Kristen Yoder) and "Laugh In Your Face Radio" (with Chris Clobber, Sarah Burford, and Ikaika Patria).

He also writes a screenwriting blog called "The 15 Minute Movie Method" (`http://15minutemoviemethod.com`) and a blog about the latest cat news on the Internet called "Cat Daily News" (`http://catdailynews.com`).

# About the Technical Reviewer

**Wesley Matlock** is a published author of books about iOS technologies. He has more than 20 years of development experience in several different platforms. He first started doing mobile development on the Compaq iPaq in the early 2000s. Today, Wesley enjoys developing on the iOS platform and bringing new ideas to life for Major League Baseball in the Denver Metro area.

# CHAPTER 1

# Understanding Augmented Reality and ARKit

You may have heard of virtual reality (VR), but there's a similar innovation that's appearing on mobile devices like the iPhone and iPad that's called augmented reality (AR). Although they may rely on similar technology, virtual reality and augmented reality offer vastly different uses in everyday life.

Virtual reality works by forcing users to strap a device around their head like an alien facehugger. Such VR headsets completely isolate the user from his or her surroundings and immerses the user in a completely fictional world. NASA uses virtual reality to train astronauts to explore the surface of Mars, while American football teams are experimenting with virtual reality to train quarterbacks to re-experience plays without actually going out on a field and risking physical injury. By practicing skills in a virtual reality world, users can safely make mistakes and learn from them without any physical consequences.

The huge drawback with virtual reality is that to use it, you must be in a safe place such as in a home or office. Because VR headsets isolate you from your surroundings, using virtual reality essentially blindfolds you. You can't use virtual reality while driving, walking, or operating a

© Wallace Wang 2018
W. Wang, *Beginning ARKit for iPhone and iPad*,
https://doi.org/10.1007/978-1-4842-4102-8_1

vehicle of any kind. Because you need to wear a VR headset, you can only use virtual reality wherever you can safely stand or sit without worrying about interference from outside elements such as other people or moving vehicles. For that reason, virtual reality's uses are limited to fixed locations where users can remain safe while they immerse themselves in another world.

On the other hand, augmented reality is designed to interact with the world around you. Augmented reality lets you view the real world but with additional information overlaid over reality to help you better understand what you're looking at.

For example, a measuring cup is a simple version of augmented reality. By pouring liquid in a transparent cup with measurement units printed on the outside, you can accurately measure the amount of any liquid in the cup, as shown in Figure 1-1. Without the measurement units printed on the outside of the transparent cup, you would never know exactly how much liquid the cup contains.

***Figure 1-1.*** *A measuring cup is a simple version of augmented reality*

Hunters use a similar type of augmented reality when aiming a rifle. The scope magnifies the view of whatever the hunter may be looking at, and crosshairs etched in the lens shows the hunter exactly where the rifle's bullet will hit, as shown in Figure 1-2.

***Figure 1-2.*** *A hunting scope is another form of static augmented reality*

Both the measuring cup and rifle scope represent simple, but fixed, types of augmented reality. A measuring cup can only measure amounts of liquids poured into that cup and a rifle scope can only magnify a target. Computers have helped make augmented reality more versatile so it can show information as the real world around you changes.

In the early days of aviation, pilots had to glance at an instrument panel to get information on their speed, direction, and location. Unfortunately, glancing down at the instrument panel means taking your eyes off the real world around you, even for a moment. Such brief glances away from the outside world can be dangerous because it takes your eyes off any possible threats or obstacles nearby. In war time, these obstacles could be enemy planes trying to shoot you down, while in peace time, these obstacles could be buildings or other planes that you need to avoid. That's why modern planes offer a form of augmented reality known as a heads-up display (HUD).

A heads-up display displays flight information projected directly on the cockpit glass. A pilot can turn off the heads-up display to get a clean view of the outside world, or turn on the heads-up display to see the real world and crucial flight information at the same time, as shown in Figure 1-3.

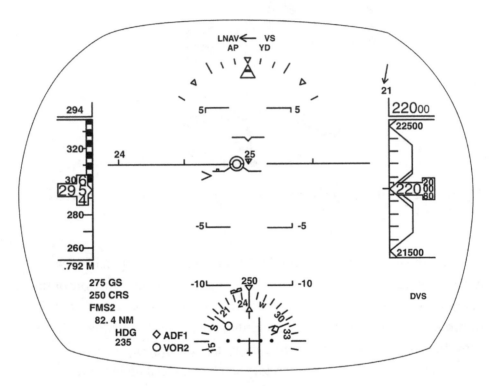

***Figure 1-3.*** *An airplane heads-up display offers a more sophisticated form of augmented reality*

Unlike the fixed information displayed by a measuring cup or a rifle scope, an airplane's heads-up display can display constantly changing information such as altitude and speed. Because heads-up displays are simply projections on a cockpit window, a computer can display different types of information depending on the pilot's need. The ability to display dynamic, changing data and choose which type of data to display makes augmented reality far more useful and versatile than the fixed type of information displayed by crude augmented reality devices like a measuring cup or a hunter's rifle scope.

# Augmented Reality on Mobile Devices

The heads-up display in airplanes made flying easier for pilots. Unfortunately, such heads-up displays were expensive and bulky. That's why only large passenger jets like the Boeing 737 or military aircraft like the F-14 were initial users of heads-up displays. As computers got smaller, lighter, and less expensive, the technology behind augmented reality became available in mobile devices like the iPhone and iPad.

Three elements have made augmented reality possible on iOS devices:

- Powerful processors

- High resolution cameras

- High-resolution displays

The processors used in the iPhone and iPad now rival the power of desktop processors. An iPhone that you can buy today offers more processing power than a desktop computer sold just a few years ago. Even more remarkable is that the processor used in today's iPhone and iPad far surpasses the power that early mainframe and minicomputers once offered. With each passing year, the processor used in the iPhone and iPad gets closer to matching the processing power of desktop computers. In some cases, the processor used in the iPhone and iPad actually exceeds the processing power of desktop computers.

Augmented reality needs fast processing power, especially when dealing with changing information. However, the second element that makes augmented reality possible on mobile devices are the built-in cameras available on iOS devices. In the early days, cameras on mobile

5

phones could only capture poor quality images. Today's camera on the iPhone and iPad now rivals dedicated digital cameras of just a few years ago. Many professional photographers and even filmmakers use the iPhone camera instead of expensive, dedicated digital or film cameras. The high quality resolution of today's mobile cameras have also helped make augmented reality possible.

Finally, the displays on mobile devices also offer high resolution. Not only can the iPhone and iPad screens display sharp images of the real world around you, but they can also display augmented reality data on the screens as well. The combination of fast and small processors and high-resolution cameras and displays has made augmented reality possible on mobile devices such as the iPhone and iPad. Combine these features with motion tracking and iOS devices have all the technical capabilities necessary to display augmented reality on an iPhone or iPad.

One of the earliest uses for augmented reality appeared with the game Pokemon GO. Instead of limiting the game to a virtual cartoon world trapped within the confines of your screen, Pokemon GO lets players hunt for cartoon Pokemon characters in the real world. By simply holding up your iPhone or iPad, you could aim your iOS device's camera at the ground, in a tree, or on a couch to look for cartoon Pokemon characters, as shown in Figure 1-4.

**Figure 1-4.** *Pokemon GO displays cartoon Pokemon characters overlaid on the real world*

# Introducing ARKit

With the technical capabilities available in the latest iOS devices, augmented reality was ready for mobile devices. The big problem was tackling the complexity of creating apps that could use augmented reality. To create an augmented reality app, you had to create your own algorithms for detecting objects in the real world and displaying virtual objects in that image. That also meant tracking camera positioning and movement of the iOS device itself. Because of this complexity, augmented reality was possible, but too difficult for most developers to use.

7

That's why Apple created ARKit as a software framework to make creating augmented reality apps much simpler. ARKit takes care of the complexity of making augmented reality so you can focus on the actual use of your app, such as displaying cartoon monsters on the screen like Pokemon GO or displaying data on the screen like a pilot's heads-up display.

Apple didn't invent augmented reality, nor did they create ARKit on their own. Instead, Apple has been buying augmented reality companies over the years and incorporating these other companies' technologies into a unified framework called ARKit specifically designed to help iOS developers create augmented reality apps.

One of Apple's major augmented reality acquisitions happened in 2015 when they acquired a German augmented reality company called Metaio. To this day you can still search for "Metaio" on search engines like Google or Bing and find old videos and images showing Metaio's technology in action, much of which will continue being integrated into Apple's ARKit framework.

IKEA initially used Metaio's technology to create their augmented reality app that allowed you to place furniture to see how it would look in your own home. By aiming your camera at the floor, you can place a virtual image of furniture in your home so you can see how a piece of furniture might look before you buy it and bring it home. You can download the IKEA Place app and try it out in your house, as shown in Figure 1-5.

**Figure 1-5.** *IKEA Place is an augmented reality app that lets you place virtual furniture in the real world*

Ferrari used Metaio's augmented reality technology to let prospective buyers view a Ferrari in the showroom, but use augmented reality to display that car in different colors. By simply pointing an iPhone or iPad at a Ferrari in the showroom, you could change the color on that car to see what color you might like best, even if that particular color car wasn't available to examine physically in the showroom.

Since many car enthusiasts want to know what's inside a car, Ferrari's augmented reality app also let users aim an iPhone or iPad at a car and view the internal features such as what the engine looks like, as shown in Figure 1-6.

***Figure 1-6.*** *Ferrari's augmented reality app lets users view the internal features of a car*

The Berlin Wall Memorial created an interesting augmented reality app with Metaio's technology that let you point an iPhone or iPad at a static image such as a window in a boarded-up building that bordered the Berlin Wall. Then the augmented reality app would show a historical video showing how people climbed out of that specific window in their attempt to escape East Berlin and make it to freedom in West Berlin.

You could also use this app to view different parts of Berlin and the app would display a video showing what that part of Berlin looked like during the time when the Berlin Wall still existed, as shown in Figure 1-7. Such uses of augmented reality helped turn the Berlin Wall Memorial from a museum filled with static images and places to a visually dynamic display that helped make history seem to occur right before your eyes.

***Figure 1-7.*** *Augmented reality shows tourists what Berlin looked like back in the 1960s*

Augmented reality will likely become common in advertising. Pepsi used augmented reality as a promotional prank by displaying a camera and a screen on a popular London bus stop. While people waited for the bus, the screen displayed augmented reality showing a tiger walking down the sidewalk, a giant robot attacking the city, a meteor crashing into the ground, and UFOs floating above the sky, as shown in Figure 1-8.

***Figure 1-8.*** *Pepsi used augmented reality as a promotional gimmick*

Just as air forces around the world rely on heads-up displays for their pilots, so will soldiers on the ground soon rely on similar heads-up displays to help them identify targets around them. The U.S. Army is developing Tactical Augmented Reality (TAC) where soldiers will wear smart glasses so they can see enhanced views of the world around them, including night vision and identification of possible targets, as shown in Figure 1-9.

***Figure 1-9.*** *Soldiers of the future may wear smart glasses with heads-up displays to identify possible targets*

The Disney Corporation is experimenting with augmented reality to create interactive coloring books. As a child colors an image, they can view that image as a three-dimensional character standing on the pages right in front of them, as shown in Figure 1-10.

***Figure 1-10.*** *Augmented reality can create interactive coloring books*

Games, advertising, heads-up displays, and interactive books are just some of the many possibilities that augmented reality offers. To this day, Apple continues acquiring augmented reality companies to improve its augmented reality plans, such as ARKit. In 2016, Apple acquired Flyby Media, an augmented reality company that focused on spatial recognition. Flyby Media's technology would let augmented reality devices understand distances between mobile devices and real-world objects around them.

In 2017, Apple acquired SensoMotoric Instruments, a company that specialized in eye tracking technology that could be used for virtual and augmented reality glasses. That same year, Apple acquired VRvana, a company that specialized in mixed reality headsets. In 2018, Apple acquired Akonia Holographics, a startup that advertised that they made "holographic reflective and waveguide optics for transparent display elements in smart glasses".

By tracking Apple's latest augmented reality acquisitions, you can see what new features will eventually come to ARKit on iOS devices like the iPhone and iPad, and in future devices like smart glasses or heads-up displays for cars. ARKit will continue growing in features while making augmented reality accessible to all Swift and Objective-C developers who want to add augmented reality in their own iOS apps. By learning ARKit now, you can create augmented reality apps now and in the future.

---

**Note**    Augmented reality is best suited for mobile devices with a camera such as the iPhone and iPad. That means ARKit is designed for creating iOS apps but is not designed to work with Apple's other operating systems, such as MacOS, tvOS, or watchOS.

---

# System Requirements for ARKit

Since augmented reality requires processing power, cameras, and high-resolution displays, you can only create and run ARKit apps on modern iOS devices. That means ARKit apps can only run on the iPhone 6s/6s Plus or higher along with the iPad Pro. Older iOS devices such as the iPhone 5s or iPad mini won't be able to run ARKit apps. As people abandon older iOS devices in favor of newer models, this restriction won't be much of a problem but for now, be aware that any ARKit apps you create may not run on some people's older iOS devices.

To create apps, you need to use Apple's free Xcode compiler. When creating ordinary iOS apps, you can test them on the Simulator program that lets your Macintosh mimic different iPhone and iPad models such as the iPhone 4s. When creating iOS apps that use ARKit, you will not be able to test your apps on the Simulator program. Instead, you'll need a physical iOS device such as an iPhone 6s or newer, or iPad Pro that you'll need to connect to your Macintosh through its USB cable. You can only test ARKit apps through a physical device because you need to use the camera in a real iOS device.

Finally, to create iOS apps that use ARKit, you can choose between Apple's two official programming languages—Swift and Objective-C. While many older apps were written in Objective-C, Swift is Apple's programming language of the future. Not only is Swift just as powerful as Objective-C, but it's also faster and far easier to learn. Although you can use Objective-C to create ARKit apps, it's far better to focus solely on Swift to create ARKit apps. Swift will only continue to grow in popularity, while Objective-C will continue decreasing in popularity over time as more developers embrace Swift. Because the future of Apple development is Swift and not Objective-C, this book focuses exclusively on Swift to create ARKit apps.

To create augmented reality apps in this book, you'll need a Macintosh and a copy of Xcode 10 or greater. You'll also need an iOS device such as an iPhone or iPad that you can connect to your Macintosh through its USB cable. To take full advantage of all the latest features of ARKit, your iOS device should also be running iOS 12 or later.

# Summary

The true potential of augmented reality and ARKit in particular is yet to be realized. Unlike virtual reality, which requires the purchase of a dedicated VR headset, augmented reality can be used on ordinary iPhones and iPads that many people already own. Also unlike virtual reality, augmented reality lets you use it wherever you happen to be as you interact with the real world around you.

Games like Pokemon GO have helped introduce augmented reality to the public just as video games helped introduce people to early personal computers. Beyond the entertainment value of augmented reality, more people and companies will start seeing and using augmented reality for useful applications.

One simple use for augmented reality involves directions. By viewing your surroundings through an iPhone or iPad screen, you can see streets and buildings. With augmented reality, you will soon be able to see colored pathways showing you the fastest way to walk to your destination along with street names and business names overlaid over roads and storefronts.

When you want to use augmented reality, it's as easy as pulling out your iPhone or iPad. When you're done using augmented reality, just put your iPhone or iPad away. (To use virtual reality, you have to buy a dedicated virtual reality headset and strap it over your face, cutting off your view of your surroundings. When you're done with virtual reality, you still have to lug around the virtual reality headset or store it somewhere, which makes virtual reality less convenient to use than augmented reality.)

Augmented reality will gradually become commonplace on every iPhone and iPad. Eventually, smart glasses will appear that will display augmented reality without the need to hold an iPhone or iPad in the air. The future of augmented reality is coming faster than you think. By learning how to create augmented reality apps today using ARKit, you'll be ready for the future, whatever form it may take.

# CHAPTER 2

# Getting to Know ARKit

Augmented reality works by tracking the real world through a camera. By identifying solid objects in the real world such as floors, tables, and walls, augmented reality can then accurately place virtual objects on the scene that create the illusion of actually being there. Even if the virtual object is nothing more than a cartoon Pokémon character, augmented reality must overlay that virtual object so the virtual object doesn't get cut in half by furniture, walls, or tables.

Since creating algorithms for detecting objects in the real world can be difficult even for experienced programmers, Apple created a software framework called ARKit, which provides much of the basic needs of any augmented reality app. By using ARKit, you can create augmented reality apps by focusing on the unique features of your app rather than on the details of detecting, displaying, and tracking virtual objects in the real world.

ARKit acts as a platform for you to develop your own augmented reality apps. To help you get familiar using ARKit, Xcode provides a simple augmented reality project that you can compile and run on any compatible iOS device physically connected to your Macintosh through its USB cable. To create this ARKit sample app, follow these steps:

1. Start Xcode. (Make sure you're using Xcode 10 or greater.)

2. Choose File ➤ New ➤ Project. Xcode asks you to choose a template, as shown in Figure 2-1.

© Wallace Wang 2018
W. Wang, *Beginning ARKit for iPhone and iPad*,
https://doi.org/10.1007/978-1-4842-4102-8_2

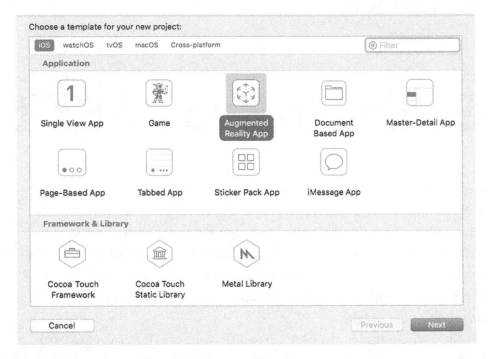

***Figure 2-1.*** *Choosing an Xcode project template*

3.  Click the Augmented Reality App icon and click
    the Next button. Xcode asks for a product name,
    organization name, organization identifiers, and
    content technology, as shown in Figure 2-2.

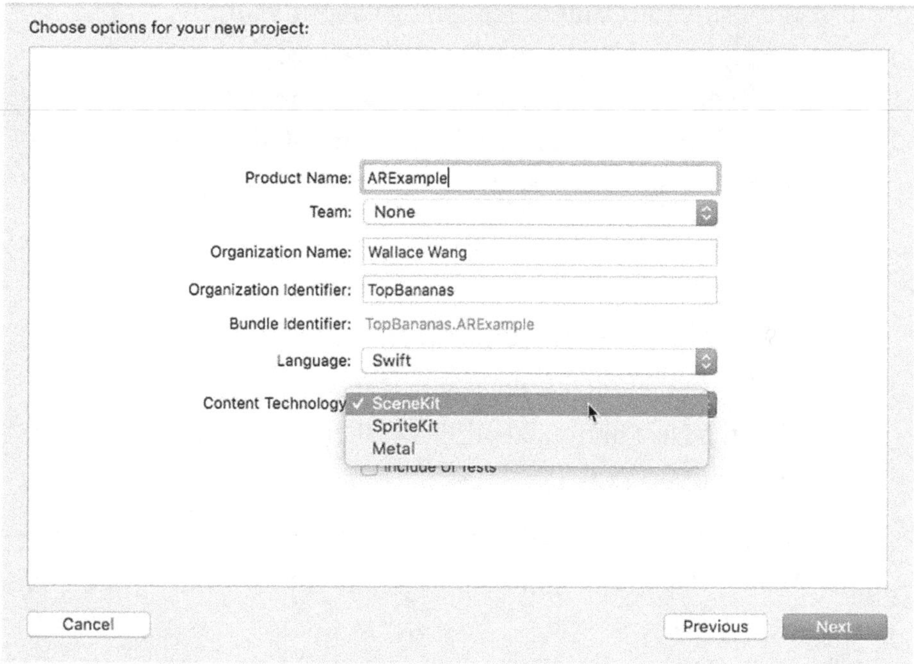

**Figure 2-2.** *Defining the options for an augmented reality project*

4.  Click in the Product Name text field and type
    a descriptive name for your project, such as
    ARExample. (The exact name does not matter.)

---

**Note**   The organization name and identifier can be any text such as
your name or company name. The organization identifier is typically
the website address of your company spelled backwards, such as
com.microsoft.

---

5.   Make sure the Content Technology popup menu displays SceneKit. SpriteKit and Metal give you more versatility at the expense of more complexity. For the purposes of this book, all augmented reality apps will rely on SceneKit.

6.   Make sure the Include Unit Tests and Include UI Tests check boxes are not checked since we won't be using these features in any of the apps created in this book.

7.   Click the Next button. Xcode asks where you want to store your project.

8.   Choose a folder and click the Create button. Xcode creates an augmented reality project that's ready to run.

9.   Connect your iPhone or iPad to your Macintosh using its USB cable.

10.  Click on the popup menu near the top of Xcode window that displays the device to run your project on, as shown in Figure 2-3.

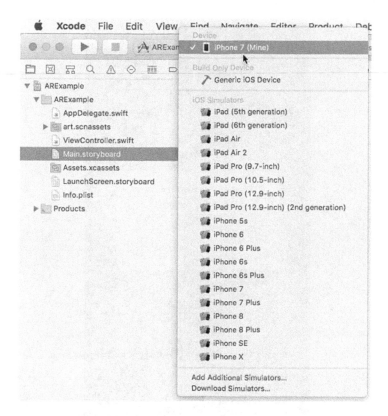

***Figure 2-3.*** *Defining the target to run the project on*

11. Choose your iOS device, such as an iPhone or iPad.

12. Click the Run button or choose Product ➤ Run.
A dialog appears, asking if you want to allow your
project to access the iOS device's camera, as shown
in Figure 2-4.

**Figure 2-4.** *Apps must always ask for permission to access an iOS device's camera*

---

**Note**    Xcode may ask for your password to allow your app to access additional libraries. To grant access, type your password and click the Allow button.

---

13.    Your project appears on your iOS device. Notice that a cartoon airplane appears, as shown in Figure 2-5. Each time you run this project, point your iOS device in a different direction. Whatever direction your iOS device's camera points at is where the

cartoon airplane will appear. Move your iOS
device around and you'll be able to see the cartoon
airplane from different angles.

**Figure 2-5.** *Viewing the virtual airplane through an iPhone screen*

14. Click the Stop button in Xcode or choose Product ➤
Stop.

# Understanding the Swift Source Code

By creating a project using the Augmented Reality App template, you can
create a working augmented reality app without writing or modifying a
single line of code. To better understand how to use ARKit, let's dissect the
Swift code so you can understand exactly what's happening.

Your entire augmented reality project consists of several files, but the
ViewController.swift file contains all the Swift code you need to add
augmented reality to any project. First, notice that the ViewController.
swift file imports three software frameworks: UIKit (defines the user

25

interface), SceneKit (defines the 3D animation used to create virtual images), and ARKit (links to the ARKit augmented reality library).

```
import UIKit
import SceneKit
import ARKit
```

---

**Note**    SceneKit is Apple's framework for creating 3D animation, but two other options are SpriteKit and Metal. If you choose either of these options, your project would need to import the SpriteKit or Metal framework instead of SceneKit.

---

Next, you must define the `ViewController` class as the `ARSCNViewDelegate`:

```
class ViewController: UIViewController, ARSCNViewDelegate {
```

Now you need to create a scene for displaying a virtual image. To do this, you need to create an IBOutlet. The name of this IBOutlet can be anything you wish, but the Augmented Reality App template names this IBOutlet `sceneView` and it represents an `ARSCNView` object:

```
@IBOutlet var sceneView: ARSCNView!
```

Within the `viewDidLoad` method, you need to define four items. First, you must set the `ViewController` class to its own `ARSCNViewDelegate`:

```
// Set the view's delegate
sceneView.delegate = self
```

Second, you can display statistics on the screen that let you know information such as frames per second (fps):

```
// Show statistics such as fps and timing information
sceneView.showsStatistics = true
```

Third, you need to define the actual image to display on the augmented reality scene. Remember, the scene is defined by the IBOutlet named sceneView:

```
// Create a new scene
let scene = SCNScene(named: "art.scnassets/ship.scn")!
```

If you click on the art.scnassets folder in Xcode, you can see two graphic files called ship.scn and texture.png, as shown in Figure 2-6.

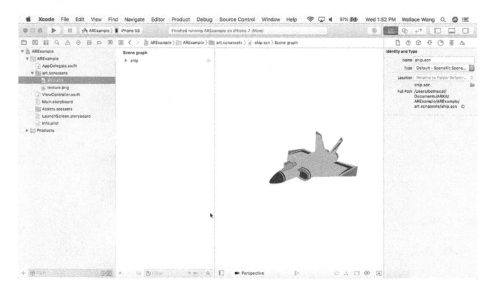

**Figure 2-6.** *The contents of the art.scnassets folder*

The ship.scn file represents a SceneKit image (notice the .scn file extension). Another type of graphic image you can use with ARKit is the COLLADA (COLLAborative Design Activity) file, which has the .dae file extension. Nearly all 3D authoring tools, such as SketchUp, can export files to the .dae format, which is an open standard for storing 3D images.

The ship.scn file defines the 3D shape of the plane. The texture.png graphic file defines the image that gets applied on the ship.scn image to display different colors or patterns. In most cases, you'll need both a 3D image

27

(a .scn or .dae file) and a texture (a .png file) that wraps around the 3D image and provides the "skin" or outside graphics for that 3D image. If you click on the texture.png file, you can see what it looks like, as shown in Figure 2-7.

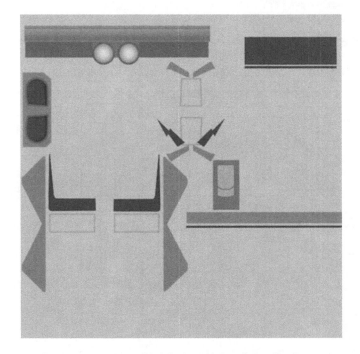

***Figure 2-7.*** *The texture.png file defines the "skin" of a 3D image*

Fourth, after defining the 3D image with a variable name (scene), you need to put this 3D image into the actual scene view:

```
// Set the scene to the view
sceneView.scene = scene
```

In the viewWillAppear method, you need two additional lines of Swift code. The first line turns on the iOS device's tracking to measure the location and angle you aim the iOS device's camera:

```
// Create a session configuration
let configuration = ARWorldTrackingConfiguration()
```

The second line runs the actual augmented reality session:

```
// Run the view's session
sceneView.session.run(configuration)
```

# Understanding the User Interface

The user interface for the Augmented Reality App Template consists of a single view in a storyboard. On that view is an ARSCNView object that fills the entire view, as shown in Figure 2-8. This ARKit SceneKit View allows SceneKit 3D images to appear on the user interface.

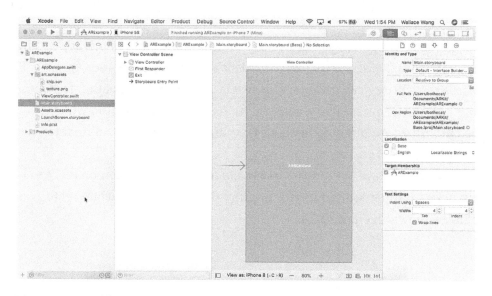

***Figure 2-8.*** *The ARKit SceneKit View defines where to display the 3D image on the user interface*

Every augmented reality app must access the iOS device's camera. However, every app must first ask for permission to use the camera. To ask for permission to access the camera, your app must define a privacy setting for the camera. You can view this camera privacy setting in the Info.plist file, as shown in Figure 2-9.

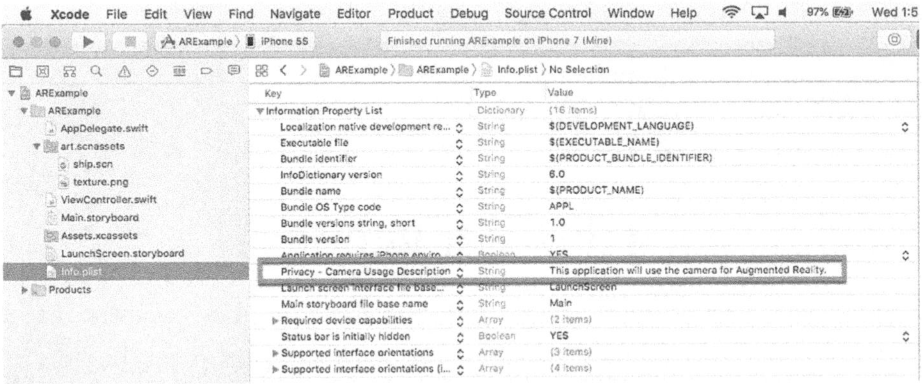

***Figure 2-9.*** *The Info.plist file defines the privacy setting for the iOS device camera*

The text that appears in the Value column of the camera privacy setting will appear in the dialog that asks the user's permission for your app to access the iOS device's camera. This text is simply an explanation for why your app needs access to the camera, such as "This application will use the camera for Augmented Reality." You can always change this text to something else if you wish.

The second line in the Info.plist file that every augmented reality app needs is the Required Device Capabilities setting. It must be set to arkit, as shown in Figure 2-10.

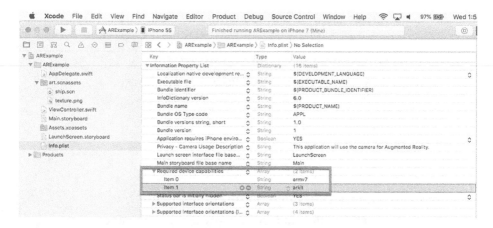

***Figure 2-10.*** *The Info.plist file defines the hardware requirements for an iOS device to run augmented reality apps*

This setting in the `Info.plist` file makes sure your app will only attempt to run on an iOS device with the proper hardware capable of running ARKit such as an iPhone 6s or higher, or an iPad Pro or higher.

# Creating Augmented Reality with the Single View App Template

The Augmented Reality App template provides the basic Swift code needed to display augmented reality. Rather than use the Augmented Reality App template, you can create an augmented reality app using the simple Single View App template instead. By creating an augmented reality app through the Single View App template, you can get a better idea what code you need to write and what user interface elements you need to give any app augmented reality capabilities.

1. Start Xcode. (Make sure you're using Xcode 10 or greater.)

2. Choose File ➤ New ➤ Project. Xcode asks you to choose a template (see Figure 2-1).

3. Click the Single View App icon and click the Next button. Xcode asks for a product name, organization name, organization identifiers, and content technology (see Figure 2-2). Make sure all check boxes are clear for additional options such as Use Core Data or Include Unit Tests.

4. Click in the Product Name text field and type a descriptive name for your project, such as ARExample2. (The exact name does not matter, but make sure it's different from the project you created using the Augmented Reality App template.)

5. Click the Next button. Xcode asks where you want to store your project.

6. Choose a folder and click the Create button. Xcode creates a basic iOS project that's ready to run.

At this point, you have a basic iOS app with no augmented reality features. To add augmented reality to an app, we need to write Swift code, modify the user interface, and define settings in the Info.plist file to allow access to the camera and run only on ARKit-compatible iOS devices such as the iPad Pro or iPhone 6s and higher.

First, we need to make sure our iOS app can access the ARKit framework and use the camera. To do this, we need to modify the Info.plist file.

1. Click the Info.plist file in the Navigator pane. Xcode displays a list of keys, types, and values.

2. Click the disclosure triangle to expand the Required Device Capabilities category to display Item 0.

3. Move the mouse pointer over Item 0 to display a plus (+) icon.

4.  Click this plus (+) icon to display a blank Item 1.

5.  Type arkit under the Value category in the Item
    1 row (see Figure 2-10).

6.  Move the mouse pointer over the last row to display
    a plus (+) icon.

7.  Click on the plus (+) icon to create a new row.
    A popup menu appears.

8.  Choose Privacy – Camera Usage Description, as
    shown in Figure 2-11.

***Figure 2-11.*** *The Privacy – Camera Usage Description line lets your*
*app access an iOS device's camera*

9. Type AR needs to use the camera under the Value
   category in the Privacy – Camera Usage Description
   row.

With "arkit" and "Privacy – Camera Usage Description" defined in the
Info.plist file, our app can now access ARKit and use an iOS device's
camera. The next step is to modify the ViewController.swift file and
write Swift code to display augmented reality.

1. Click on the ViewController.swift file in the
   Navigator pane of Xcode.

2. Add the following two lines under the Import UIKit
   line, as follows:

```
import SceneKit
import ARKit
```

3. Modify the class ViewController line to add the
   ARSCNViewDelegate as follows:

```
class ViewController: UIViewController,
ARSCNViewDelegate {
```

4. At the bottom of the ViewController.swift file,
   add the viewWillAppear and viewWillDisappear
   functions as follows:

```
override func viewWillAppear(_ animated: Bool) {
    super.viewWillAppear(animated)

    let configuration =
    ARWorldTrackingConfiguration()

    sceneView.session.run(configuration)
}
```

```
override func viewWillDisappear(_ animated: Bool) {
    super.viewWillDisappear(animated)

    sceneView.session.pause()
}
```

In this code, we're referencing `sceneView`, which hasn't been defined yet. This `sceneView` variable name will represent the user interface view that displays augmented reality in our app. The user interface object that displays augmented reality is called ARKit Scene View.

To add the ARKit Scene View object, we need to drag it to the `Main.storyboard` file and create an IBOutlet for it in the `ViewController.swift` file. To do this, follow these steps:

1. Click on the Main.storyboard file in the Navigator pane of Xcode. Xcode displays an iOS device on the storyboard screen that you can change by clicking View As at the bottom of the storyboard screen, as shown in Figure 2-12.

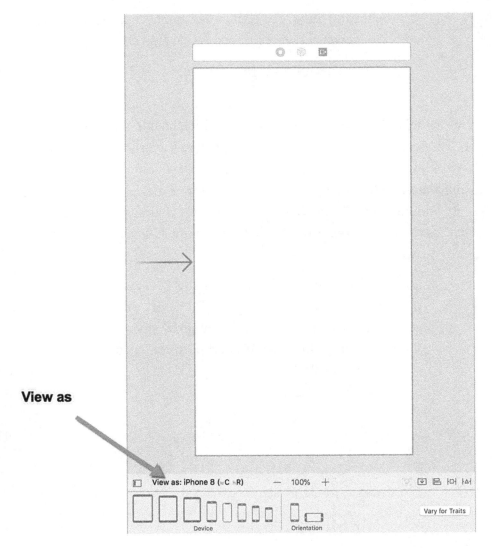

**Figure 2-12.**  *The View As option lets you choose different iOS devices for a storyboard*

2.  Click the Object Library icon to display the Object Library window, as shown in Figure 2-13.

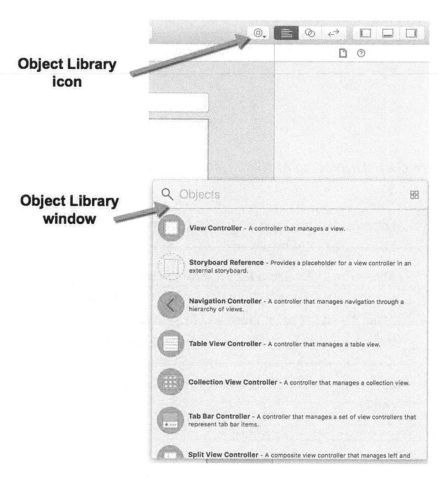

**Figure 2-13.**  *The Object Library icon opens the Object Library window*

3.  Click in the search field at the top of the Object Library window and type ARKit. The Object Library window displays all ARKit objects available, as shown in Figure 2-14.

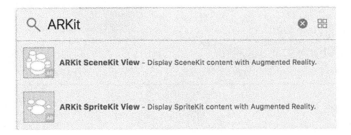

*Figure 2-14.* *Displaying ARKit objects in the Object Library window*

4.  Drag the ARKit SceneKit View from the Object
    Library on to the storyboard.

5.  Resize the ARKit SceneKit View on the storyboard,
    as shown in Figure 2-15. The exact size and position
    of the ARKit SceneKit View isn't important but
    make it large enough because the size of the ARKit
    SceneKitView defines how large the image will
    appear when viewed through the iOS device's
    camera.

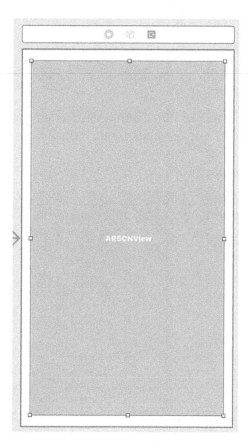

**Figure 2-15.** *Resizing the ARKit SceneKit View*

6.  Click on the ARKit SceneKit View to select it and
    then choose Editor ➤ Resolve AutoLayout Issues
    ➤ Reset to Suggested Constraints. Xcode adds
    constraints to keep your ARKit SceneKit View
    properly aligned no matter which size or orientation
    the user holds the iOS device.

7.  Click the Show Assistant Editor icon, as shown in
    Figure 2-16, or choose View ➤ Assistant Editor ➤ Use
    Assistant Editor. Xcode displays the ViewController.
    swift file side by side with the storyboard.

39

**Show Assistant Editor icon**

***Figure 2-16.*** *The Show Assistant Editor icon lets you view a storyboard and Swift controller file at the same time*

8.  Move the mouse over the ARKit SceneKIt View, hold down the Control key, and drag the mouse underneath the class `ViewController` line, as shown in Figure 2-17.

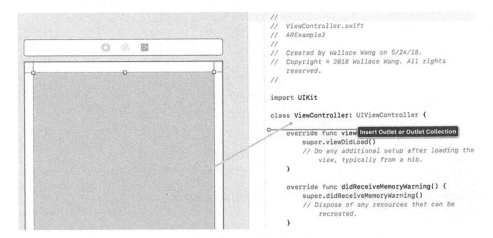

***Figure 2-17.*** *Control-dragging from the ARKit SceneKit View to the ViewController.swift file*

9.  Release the Control key and the mouse. Xcode displays a popup menu to define a name for the IBOutlet, as shown in Figure 2-18.

**Figure 2-18.**  *Defining a name for an IBOutlet*

10.  Click in the Name field, type sceneView, and press Return. Xcode creates an IBOutlet in the ViewController.swift file as follows:

**@IBOutlet var** sceneView: ARSCNView!

11.  Click the Use Standard Editor icon or choose View ➤ Standard Editor ➤ Use Standard Editor.

12.  Click the ViewController.swift file in the Navigator pane. Xcode displays the Swift code stored in the ViewController.swift file.

13.  Edit the viewDidLoad function as follows:

```
override func viewDidLoad() {
    super.viewDidLoad()

    sceneView.delegate = self
    sceneView.showsStatistics = true
    let scene = SCNScene(named: "")!
    sceneView.scene = scene
}
```

These code changes essentially duplicate the ARKit iOS template. However, we still need an object to place in our augmented reality view. When we created an augmented reality app from the augmented reality template, that template included a ship.scn file, where the .scn file extension stands for SceneKit.

What we need initially are files stored in the .dae COLLADA file format, which stands for COLLAborative Design Activity. This file format is used as a standard file format for sharing graphic designs for three-dimensional programs.

To find .dae COLLADA files, visit your favorite search engine and look for ".dae public domain" files that you can download. (For the artistically-inclined, you can create your own three-dimensional objects using graphics editors, such as the free Blender program available at `www.blender.org`.) Most COLLADA files consist of a .dae file that defines the shape of the object and a texture file that defines the outer design of that shape. Two sites that offer free (and paid) COLLADA files include Free3D (`https://free3d.com`) and TurboSquid (`www.turbosquid.com`).

Once you've downloaded a .dae COLLADA file along with any accompanying texture files, you must create a special scnassets folder to store those images. To create an scnassets folder, follow these steps:

1. Choose File ➤ New ➤ File. Xcode displays different file templates.

2. Click iOS at the top of the template window and scroll down to click on the SceneKit Catalog icon under the Resource category, as shown in Figure 2-19.

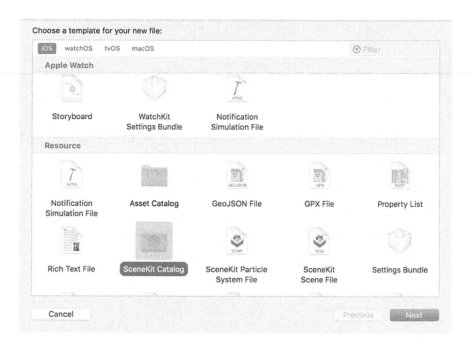

***Figure 2-19.*** *Choosing the SceneKit Catalog icon*

3.  Click the Next button. Xcode asks where you want to store this folder.

4.  Click the Create button. Xcode creates a SceneKit Asset Catalog.scnassets folder in the Navigator pane.

5.  Click on the SceneKit Asset Catalog.scnassets folder and press Return. Xcode highlights the entire folder name, as shown in Figure 2-20.

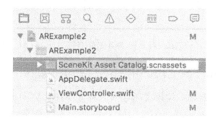

***Figure 2-20.*** *Changing the name of the SceneKit Assets Catalog folder*

6.  Change the name of the folder to art.scnassets and
    press Return.

Now that we've written the bulk of the Swift code needed in the
ViewController.swift file and designed the user interface to display
augmented reality through the ARKit SceneKit View, the last step is to
import a .dae file and its texture file into the .scnassets folder you created
in the Xcode Navigator pane.

To do add 3D images to Xcode, follow these steps:

1.  Drag and drop the .dae and accompanying texture
    file image from the Finder window to the scnassets
    folder, as shown in Figure 2-21.

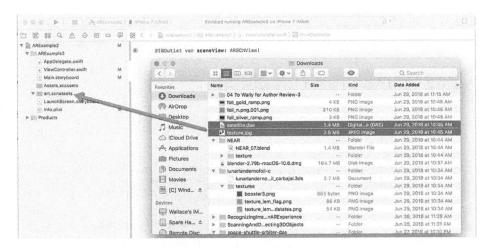

***Figure 2-21.***  *Drag and drop a .dae and texture file from the Finder*
*window to the scnassets folder in Xcode*

2.  Click on the .dae file in the scnassets folder to select it.

3.  Choose Editor ➤ Convert to SceneKit scene file
    format (.scn). A dialog appears, asking you to verify
    you want to convert the .dae file to a .scn file, as
    shown in Figure 2-22.

**Convert this document to SCN format?**

SceneKit scene documents (.scn) are not compatible with some applications. Convert anyway?

Duplicate          Cancel          Convert

*Figure 2-22.* *Xcode asks for confirmation to convert the .dae file to an .scn file*

4.  Click the Convert button. Xcode converts your .dae file to an .scn file.

5.  (Optional) Click on the .scn file and press Return to edit the filename to something simple and descriptive.

6.  Edit the following line in the viewDidLoad function to include the name of your .scn file. If your .scn file was named satellite.scn, the code would look like this:

```
let scene = SCNScene(named: "art.scnassets/
satellite.scn")!
```

This Swift code will load the .dae file (converted to an .scn file) into your augmented reality view. However, there's still one last step. With most .dae files, there's an accompanying texture file that defines the outer appearance or "skin" of the three-dimensional object. The final step is to apply this texture or "skin" to the .scn file. To do this, follow these steps:

1.  Click on the .scn file in your scnassets folder displayed in the Navigator pane. Xcode displays your image as a general shape but with no outer appearance.

2.  Click the Show Scene Graph View icon near the bottom of the Xcode window, as shown in Figure 2-23. Xcode displays the Scene Graph View.

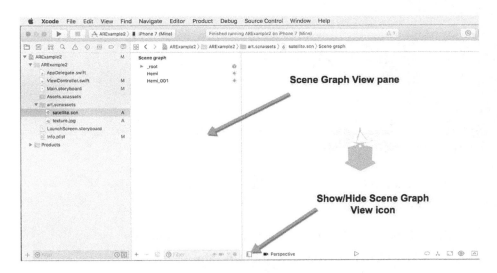

***Figure 2-23.*** *The Show Scene Graph View icon*

3.  Click on each item displayed in the Scene Graph
    View pane and then click on the Show the Material
    Inspector icon, as shown in Figure 2-24. Or choose
    View ➤ inspectors ➤ Show Material Inspector.

***Figure 2-24.*** *The Show Material Inspector icon*

4.  Click on the Diffuse popup menu and choose the
    name of your texture file, such as `texture.jpg`, as
    shown in Figure 2-25.

***Figure 2-25.*** *The Diffuse popup menu lets you choose the texture image*

If your original .dae file came with two or more texture files, you may need to include those multiple texture files in the scnassets folder and use the Diffuse popup menu to select each appropriate texture file for different parts of your three-dimensional object.

Now attach an iOS device to your Macintosh through its USB cable and click the Run icon or choose Product ➤ Run. You should now see your .scn file displayed over the image captured by your iOS device's camera.

# Summary

While it's possible to create augmented reality apps on your own, it's far simpler to rely on Apple's ARKit framework. ARKit takes care of the details of managing a camera and real-world objects around you to combine reality with virtual images.

The simplest way to create an augmented reality app is to start with the Augmented Reality template when creating a new iOS project. However, you can also add augmented reality features to an existing app. First, you must import the ARKit framework along with a graphics framework such as SceneKit. Next you must create an ARKit SceneKit View on your app's user interface to view the actual augmented reality image. Finally, you must import a three-dimensional image into Xcode and convert it to an .scn SceneKit file.

When you want an app focused on augmented reality, it's best to create a new project using the Augmented Reality project template. When you want to add augmented reality features to an existing app, you can easily do so at any time as well.

Now that you have a basic idea how to create an augmented reality app and the various steps you need to follow to create augmented reality, it's time to go into more detail about the specific parts of the different augmented reality features available through ARKit.

# CHAPTER 3

# World Tracking

Augmented reality works by tracking the real world through a camera. By identifying solid objects in the real world such as floors, tables, and walls, augmented reality can then accurately place virtual objects on the scene that create the illusion of actually being there. Even if the virtual object is nothing more than a cartoon Pokémon character, augmented reality must overlay that virtual object so the virtual object feels like it's part of the real world seen through a camera.

To identify the location of both real and virtual objects, ARKit uses a coordinate system where the x-axis points left and right, the y-axis points up and down, and the z-axis points toward and away from the camera, as shown in Figure 3-1.

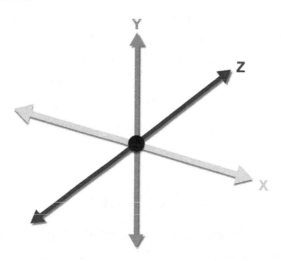

***Figure 3-1.*** *Defining the x-, y-, and z-axes for the ARKit coordinate system*

© Wallace Wang 2018
W. Wang, *Beginning ARKit for iPhone and iPad*,
https://doi.org/10.1007/978-1-4842-4102-8_3

To place virtual objects in the real world, ARKit uses a technique called *visual-inertial odometry,* which is just a fancy way of recognizing solid objects in the real world (such as walls and tabletops) and the current position of the camera (the iOS device) in relation to objects in the real world. With this information, ARKit can place objects on real-world items such as floors or desks, or at a fixed distance from the camera's current location, such as two meters in front of you and a half meter to your left.

Identifying real-life objects seen through a camera is known as *world tracking.* World tracking accuracy works best in good lighting with multiple, contrasting objects that can be easily spotted such as a chair and a table in a room. World tracking accuracy can suffer in dim or poor lighting or when viewing objects that are not easy to identify such as a solid wall or road with no other contrasting objects.

Think of how you identify objects in the real world. It's easy to identify a lamp on a table because you can see both the lamp's entire outline and the table surface and edges. If someone just showed you a close up of a lamp or table surface, you might not know whether you're looking at a wall or a floor. As a general rule, if it's easy for a person to identify objects in an image, it's easy for ARKit to identify the shape of those objects too.

Besides identifying object boundaries, another key to accuracy depends on the user holding the camera steady. This gives ARKit time to accurately map out its surroundings. If the user moves the camera around too quickly or in erratic movements, ARKit will have a harder time accurately identifying real-world objects in the same way you might have trouble identifying objects if shown a video of someone moving a camera rapidly in all directions.

# Displaying the World Origin

Every augmented reality app needs to import the ARKit framework and a graphics framework to display virtual objects such as SceneKit, SpriteKit, or Metal like this:

```
import ARKit
import SceneKit
```

Once your app imports the ARKit framework and a graphics framework like SceneKit, the next step is to use the ARWorldTrackingConfiguration class like this:

```
let configuration = ARWorldTrackingConfiguration()
```

AR world tracking needs to take place inside an ARKit SceneKit View (ARSCNView), which you must add to your app's user interface. You must create an IBOutlet inside this ARSCNView such as:

```
@IBOutlet var sceneView: ARSCNView!
```

Now you need to run AR world tracking within this ARSCNView like this:

```
sceneView.session.run(configuration)
```

At this point, you would normally display a virtual object in the ARSCNView such as a cartoon airplane or chair. For this exercise, we're going to display the world origin that ARKit uses. These world origin coordinates will let you see the x-, y-, and z-axes that define where ARKit places virtual objects. Displaying the world origin is handy to debug your app and make sure it displays virtual objects exactly where you want them. To see how to display the world origin in an augmented reality app, follow these steps:

1. Start Xcode. (Make sure you're using Xcode 10 or greater.)

2. Choose File ➤ New ➤ Project. Xcode asks you to choose a template.

3. Click the iOS category.

4. Click the Single View App icon and click the Next button. Xcode asks for a product name, organization name, organization identifiers, and content technology.

5.   Click in the Product Name text field and type a descriptive name for your project, such as World Tracking. (The exact name does not matter.)

6.   Make sure the Content Technology popup menu displays SceneKit.

7.   Click the Next button. Xcode asks where you want to store your project.

8.   Choose a folder and click the Create button. Xcode creates an iOS project.

First, let's modify the Info.plist file to allow access to the camera and to use ARKit by following these steps:

1.   Click the Info.plist file in the Navigator pane. Xcode displays a list of keys, types, and values.

2.   Click the disclosure triangle to expand the Required Device Capabilities category to display Item 0.

3.   Move the mouse pointer over Item 0 to display a plus (+) icon.

4.   Click this plus (+) icon to display a blank Item 1.

5.   Type arkit under the Value category in the Item 1 row.

6.   Move the mouse pointer over the last row to display a plus (+) icon.

7.   Click on the plus (+) icon to create a new row. A popup menu appears.

8.   Choose Privacy – Camera Usage Description.

9.   Type AR needs to use the camera under the Value category in the Privacy – Camera Usage Description row.

Now that our app can access the camera and use ARKit, let's add an ARKit SceneKit View to the `Main.storyboard` file so our app can display images from the camera. To add an ARKit SceneKit View to your user interface, follow these steps:

1.  Click on the `Main.storyboard` file in the Navigator pane of Xcode. Xcode displays an iOS device on the storyboard screen that you can change by clicking View As at the bottom of the storyboard screen.

2.  Click the Object Library icon to display the Object Library window.

3.  Click in the search field at the top of the Object Library window and type `ARKit`. The Object Library window displays all ARKit objects available.

4.  Drag the ARKit SceneKit View from the Object Library on to the storyboard.

5.  Resize the ARKit SceneKit View on the storyboard. The exact size and position of the ARKit SceneKit View isn't important, but make it large enough because the size of the ARKit SceneKit View defines how large the image will appear when viewed through the iOS device's camera.

6.  Click on the ARKit SceneKit View to select it and then choose Editor ➤ Resolve AutoLayout Issues ➤ Reset to Suggested Constraints. Xcode adds constraints to keep your ARKit SceneKit View properly aligned no matter which size or orientation the user holds the iOS device.

7.  Click the Show Assistant Editor icon, or choose
    View ➤ Assistant Editor ➤ Use Assistant Editor.
    Xcode displays the `ViewController.swift` file side
    by side with the storyboard.

8.  Move the mouse over the ARKit SceneKit View,
    hold down the Control key, and drag the mouse
    underneath the class ViewController line.

9.  Release the Control key and the mouse. Xcode displays
    a popup menu to define a name for the IBOutlet.

10. Click in the Name field and type `sceneView` and
    press Return. Xcode creates an IBOutlet in the
    `ViewController.swift` file as follows:

    ```
    @IBOutlet var sceneView: ARSCNView!
    ```

11. Click the Use Standard Editor icon or choose
    View ➤ Standard Editor ➤ Use Standard Editor.

12. Click the `ViewController.swift` file in the
    Navigator pane. Xcode displays the Swift code
    stored in the `ViewController.swift` file.

13. Edit the `ViewController.swift` file as follows:

    ```swift
    import UIKit
    import SceneKit
    import ARKit

    class ViewController: UIViewController,
    ARSCNViewDelegate {

        @IBOutlet var sceneView: ARSCNView!

        override func viewDidLoad() {
            super.viewDidLoad()
    ```

```
        sceneView.delegate = self
        sceneView.showsStatistics = true
        sceneView.debugOptions = [ARSCNDebugOptions.
        showWorldOrigin]
    }

    override func viewWillAppear(_ animated: Bool) {
        super.viewWillAppear(animated)

        let configuration =
        ARWorldTrackingConfiguration()
        sceneView.session.run(configuration)
    }

}
```

The main difference between this app and the previous augmented reality apps we've built is this single line:

```
sceneView.debugOptions = [ARSCNDebugOptions.showWorldOrigin]
```

This line tells Xcode to display the world origin coordinate system that will consist of red line (x-axis), green line (y-axis), and blue line (z-axis). To see the world origin coordinates in an augmented reality view, follow these steps:

1. Connect your iOS device to your Macintosh through its USB cable.

2. Click on the Set the Active Scheme popup menu and choose the iOS device you've connected to your Macintosh, as shown in Figure 3-2.

**Set the Active Scheme**

*Figure 3-2.* *The Set the Active Scheme popup menu*

3. Click on the Run button or choose Product ➤ Run. (The first time you run this app, you'll need to grant it access to the camera.)

4. Turn and aim your iOS camera until you spot the colored world coordinates floating in midair, as shown in Figure 3-3.

***Figure 3-3.*** *Viewing the world coordinate system through an iOS device camera*

5. Click the Stop button or choose Product ➤ Stop.

ARKit displays the world origin coordinate system where your iOS device appears as soon as the app runs. That's why you may need to step back to see the world coordinate system floating before your eyes the moment your app starts running.

# Resetting the World Origin

Each time you run an augmented reality app, it defines the world coordinates at the current location of the iOS device. Of course, you may not want the world coordinate system to appear only where you're currently holding your iOS device when the app runs. That's why ARKit gives you the option to reset the world coordinate system so you can move your iOS device to a new location and reset the world location to the new position of your iOS device.

To reset world coordinates, we'll need a UIButton for the user to tap. Then we'll need to write an IBAction method to reset the world coordinates to the current position of the iOS device. To create a UIButton and write an IBAction method to reset world tracking coordinates, follow these steps:

1.  Click on the Main.storyboard file in the Navigator pane.

2.  Resize the ARSCNView so there's a blank space between the bottom of the ARSCNView and the bottom of the iOS device screen.

3.  Click the Object Library icon to open the Object Library window.

4.  Type UIButton. The Object Library window displays the UIButton, as shown in Figure 3-4.

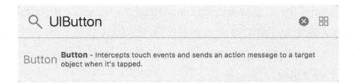

Figure 3-4.  *Finding the UIButton in the Object Library*

5.   Drag the UIButton underneath the ARSCNView.

6.   Resize the width of the UIButton.

7.   Double-click on the UIButton to highlight its caption and type a new caption, such as Reset. Your user interface should look similar to Figure 3-5.

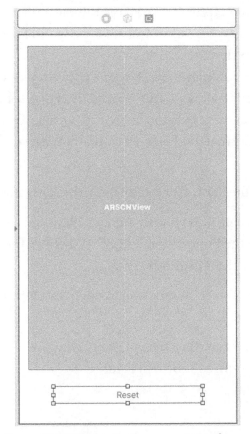

Figure 3-5.  *Adding a UIButton to the user interface*

8.  Hold down the Shift key and click on the
    ARSCNView object. Handles should now appear
    around both the ARSCNView and the UIButton.

9.  Choose Editor ➤ Resolve AutoLayout Issues ➤
    Reset to Suggested Constraints under the All Views
    in View Controller category. Xcode adds constraints
    for both the ARSCNView and the UIButton.

10. Click the Assistant Editor icon or choose View ➤
    Assistant Editor ➤ Show Assistant Editor. Xcode
    displays the ViewController.swift file and the
    storyboard side by side.

11. Move the mouse over the UIButton on the
    storyboard, hold down the Control key, and
    drag the mouse underneath the IBOutlet in the
    ViewController.swift file, as shown in
    Figure 3-6.

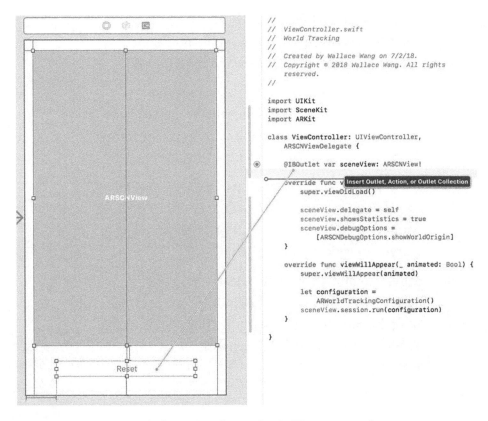

```
//
//  ViewController.swift
//  World Tracking
//
//  Created by Wallace Wang on 7/2/18.
//  Copyright © 2018 Wallace Wang. All rights
      reserved.
//

import UIKit
import SceneKit
import ARKit

class ViewController: UIViewController,
    ARSCNViewDelegate {

    @IBOutlet var sceneView: ARSCNView!

    override func v[Insert Outlet, Action, or Outlet Collection]
        super.viewDidLoad()

        sceneView.delegate = self
        sceneView.showsStatistics = true
        sceneView.debugOptions =
            [ARSCNDebugOptions.showWorldOrigin]
    }

    override func viewWillAppear(_ animated: Bool) {
        super.viewWillAppear(animated)

        let configuration =
            ARWorldTrackingConfiguration()
        sceneView.session.run(configuration)
    }

}
```

*Figure 3-6.    Control-dragging from the UIButton to the ViewController.swift file*

12.    Release the Control key and the mouse. Xcode displays a popup menu.

13.    Click on the Connection popup menu and choose Action, as shown in Figure 3-7.

*Figure 3-7.    Creating an IBAction method*

14.  Click in the Name field, type resetButton, and press Return.

15.  Click in the Type popup menu and choose UIButton.

16.  Click the Connect button. Xcode displays a blank IBAction method.

17.  Click the Standard Editor icon or choose View ➤ Standard Editor ➤ Show Standard Editor. If Xcode does not display the ViewController.swift file, click on the ViewController.swift file in the Navigator pane.

18.  Edit the IBAction resetButton function as follows:

```
@IBAction func resetButton(_ sender: UIButton) {
    sceneView.session.pause()
    sceneView.session.run(configuration, options:
    [.resetTracking])
}
```

19.  Move the let configuration = ARWorldTracking Configuration line underneath the IBOutlet line, as follows:

```
@IBOutlet var sceneView: ARSCNView!

let configuration = ARWorldTrackingConfiguration()
```

The entire ViewController.swift file should look like this:

```
import UIKit
import SceneKit
import ARKit
```

```
class ViewController: UIViewController,
ARSCNViewDelegate {

    @IBOutlet var sceneView: ARSCNView!

     let configuration = ARWorldTrackingConfiguration()

    @IBAction func resetButton(_ sender: UIButton) {
        sceneView.session.pause()
        sceneView.session.run(configuration, options:
        [.resetTracking])
    }

    override func viewDidLoad() {
        super.viewDidLoad()

        sceneView.delegate = self
        sceneView.showsStatistics = true
        sceneView.debugOptions = [ARSCNDebugOptions.
        showWorldOrigin]
    }

    override func viewWillAppear(_ animated: Bool) {
        super.viewWillAppear(animated)

        sceneView.session.run(configuration)
    }

}
```

20. Connect an iOS device to your Macintosh with its USB cable.

21. Click the Run button or choose Product ➤ Run. When the app runs, step back to see the x-, y-, and x-axes world coordinates floating in the air.

22.   Move to a new location and tap the Reset button on the iOS screen.

23.   Step back and you'll see the x-, y-, and z-axes world coordinates in the location of your iOS device when you tapped the Reset button.

24.   Click the Stop button or choose Product ➤ Stop.

# Displaying Shapes at Coordinates

Displaying the world origin lets you see where you can define virtual objects to appear in your augmented reality view. By specifying x, y, and z coordinates, you can display virtual objects appear in relation to the current position of the user's iOS device. Besides displaying virtual objects like spaceships or dinosaurs, the simplest virtual objects ARKit can display at specific coordinates are shapes like spheres, boxes, and planes.

To create a shape, you must start by creating a node based on the SCNNode class like this:

```
let node = SCNNode()
```

At this point, you need to define a shape for the node. SceneKit provides boxes, planes, spheres, toruses, and other shapes, so let's choose a sphere and define its radius as 0.05 meters like this:

```
node.geometry = SCNSphere(radius: 0.05)
```

To make the sphere visible, let's give it a color. To do this, we need to define the node's material that defines its outer surface such as:

```
node.geometry?.firstMaterial?.diffuse.contents = UIColor.
yellow
```

These three lines of Swift code create a node, define the geometry of that node as a sphere, and then color the outside surface of that sphere with yellow. Now the only remaining task is to place that node at a specific location based on the world origin. To do this, we need to define the node's position like this:

```
node.position = SCNVector3(0,0,0)
```

Since the node needs an x, y, and z coordinate, the position of the node must be defined by three specific values as well. Defining the x, y, and z positions as 0 means that the node will appear at the world origin where the x-, y-, and z-axes intersect.

After defining a geometric shape, its dimensions, its color, and its position, the final step is to add that node to the existing scene so it actually appears in the augmented reality view. To do this, you just need one final line of code as follows:

```
sceneView.scene.rootNode.addChildNode(node)
```

This line of code adds the node (the sphere) to the root node of the augmented reality scene. The root node defines the hierarchy of items displayed in an augmented reality view. To see how this code works to display a yellow sphere at the world origin, follow these steps:

1. Modify the World Tracking project or create a new project identical to the World Tracking project except give it a name of Node Placement.

2. Modify the ViewController.swift file so the code looks like this:

```
import UIKit
import SceneKit
import ARKit
```

```swift
class ViewController: UIViewController,
ARSCNViewDelegate {

    @IBOutlet var sceneView: ARSCNView!

    let configuration = ARWorldTrackingConfiguration()

    override func viewDidLoad() {
        super.viewDidLoad()
        // Do any additional setup after loading the
        view, typically from a nib.
        sceneView.delegate = self
        sceneView.showsStatistics = true
        sceneView.debugOptions = [ARSCNDebugOptions.
        showWorldOrigin]
        showShape()
    }

    override func viewWillAppear(_ animated: Bool) {
        super.viewWillAppear(animated)

        sceneView.session.run(configuration)
    }

    @IBAction func resetButton(_ sender: UIButton) {
        sceneView.session.pause()
        sceneView.session.run(configuration, options:
        [.resetTracking])
        showShape()
    }

    func showShape() {
        let node = SCNNode()
        node.geometry = SCNSphere(radius: 0.05)
```

```
node.geometry?.firstMaterial?.diffuse.contents
= UIColor.yellow
node.position = SCNVector3(0,0,0)
sceneView.scene.rootNode.addChildNode(node)
```

    }

}

3.  Connect an iOS device to your Macintosh through
    its USB cable.

4.  Click the Run button or choose Product ➤ Run.
    A yellow sphere appears at the world origin, as
    shown in Figure 3-8.

**Figure 3-8.**  *Displaying a yellow sphere at the world origin*

5.  Move your iOS device to a new location and tap the Reset button. Notice that the world coordinates now appear in a different location with a yellow sphere at the origin.

6.  Click the Stop button or choose Product ➤ Stop.

Making a yellow sphere appear at the origin is fine, but you can experiment with different values for the x, y, and z coordinates of the sphere besides 0,0,0. Try modifying the following line of code with different values for the node's position, such as:

```
node.position = SCNVector3(0.2, -0.4, 0.1)
```

Remember, these values define meters so if you choose too large a value, such as 10 meters, the yellow sphere will appear too far away to see within the augmented reality view, so experiment with low values such as -0.4 or 0.2.

# Adding and Removing Multiple Objects

In the previous app example, we displayed the world origin, which appears at the current iOS device's location. Then we displayed a yellow sphere at a specific location. Unfortunately, defining x, y, and z coordinates for the yellow sphere remains fixed in code. If we want the yellow sphere to appear in another location, or if we want to display additional yellow spheres, we can't do that.

For more versatility, let's put an Add button on the user interface. Each time the user taps the Add button, it will add a new yellow sphere. Of course, adding multiple yellow spheres won't look any different if all the spheres share the same x, y, and z coordinates, so let's also add three sliders that let us define new x, y, and z coordinates for a sphere before adding it to the augmented reality view.

To do this, we'll need to resize the height of the ARKit SceneKit View and add three UISliders at the bottom along with three labels to identify which axis each slider defines. To do this, follow these steps:

1. Click the Main.storyboard file in the Navigator pane.

2. Resize the height of the ARKit SceneKit View to make more room near the bottom.

3. Add a new UIButton next to the existing Reset button and give this new UIButton a caption name of Add.

4. Add three UISliders.

5. Add three labels and modify the captions to display X, Y, and Z. Your user interface should look similar to Figure 3-9.

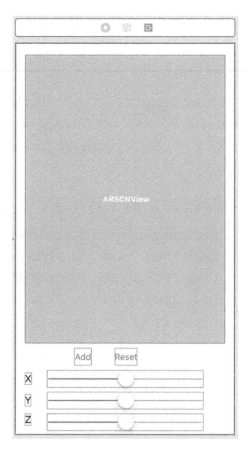

***Figure 3-9.*** *Redesigning the user interface with three sliders*

This completes the user interface changes. Let's add constraints by choosing Edit ➤ Select All (or pressing Command+A). Then choose Editor ➤ Resolve Auto Layout Issues ➤ Reset to Suggested Constraints. Xcode adds constraints to your labels, buttons, and sliders.

Now we need to modify this user interface in two ways. First, we need to define the minimum and maximum values for the slider along with a default value. Second, we need to connect the three sliders to our ViewController.swift file as IBOutlets. In addition, we also need to connect the Add button as an IBAction method.

To define the minimum and maximum values for each slider, follow these steps:

1.   Click on each slider.

2.   Click the Show Attributes Inspector icon or choose View ➤ Inspectors ➤ Show Attributes inspector. Xcode displays the Attributes Inspector pane.

3.   Change the Value property to 0.

4.   Change the Minimum property to -1.

5.   Change the Maximum property to 1, as shown in Figure 3-10. This lets you choose a value of -1 meter to 1 meter for defining a coordinate for placing a sphere in the augmented reality view.

***Figure 3-10.***  *Modifying the properties of a slider*

6.   Make sure you change the Value, Minimum, and Maximum properties identically for all three sliders.

Now that we've defined the slider values, we need to connect all three sliders and the Add button to the `ViewController.swift` file. To do this, follow these steps:

1.   Click on the Assistant Editor icon or choose View ➤ Assistant Editor ➤ Show Assistant Editor. Xcode displays the `ViewController.swift` file side by side with the `Main.storyboard` file.

2.  Click on each slider, hold down the Control key, and drag the mouse to the ViewController.swift file under the existing IBOutlet, as shown in Figure 3-11.

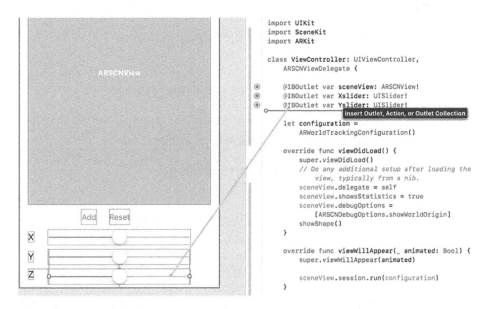

*Figure 3-11.* *Creating an IBOutlet for a slider*

3.  Release the Control key and the mouse. A popup menu appears.

4.  Click in the Name text field and type a descriptive name such as Xslider, Yslider, or Zslider. You should create three IBOutlets that represent the x, y, and z coordinates as follows:

```
@IBOutlet var Xslider: UISlider!
@IBOutlet var Yslider: UISlider!
@IBOutlet var Zslider: UISlider!
```

5.  Click on the Add button, hold down the Control key, and drag the mouse near the bottom of the ViewController.swift file to create an IBAction method.

6.  Release the Control key and the mouse. A popup menu appears.

7.  Click in the Connection popup menu and choose Action.

8.  Click in the Name text field and type addButton.

9.  Click in the Type popup menu and choose UIButton.

10. Click the Connect button. Xcode creates an IBAction method.

11. Edit this addButton  IBAction method like this:

```
@IBAction func addButton(_ sender: UIButton) {
    showShape()
}
```

12. Modify the showShape() function like this:

```
func showShape() {

    let node = SCNNode()

    node.geometry = SCNSphere(radius: 0.05)

    node.geometry?.firstMaterial?.diffuse.contents
    = UIColor.yellow

    node.position = SCNVector3(Xslider.
    value,Yslider.value,Zslider.value)
```

```
        node.name = "sphere"
        sceneView.scene.rootNode.addChildNode(node)
    }
```

The showShape() function creates yellow spheres
that are placed in the augmented reality view based
on the x, y, and z coordinates defined by the three
sliders (Xslider, Yslider, and Zslider) on the user
interface. The first step to creating a virtual object is
to define a node:

**let** node = SCNNode()

SCNNode defines a SceneKit node where a node
simply represents a virtual object. Once we've
defined a node, we need to define an actual object to
appear. SceneKit offers several different geometric
shapes to choose, but for this example, we'll use a
sphere and define its radius as 0.05 meters:

node.geometry = SCNSphere(radius: 0.05)

The geometry property defines the node's shape,
which is a sphere. To make that object visible, we
need to define its material. For this example, we'll
choose the color yellow and diffuse it across the
entire surface of the sphere:

node.geometry?.firstMaterial?.diffuse.
contents = UIColor.yellow

Next, we need to define the node's position, which
requires an x, y, and z floating point value. Rather
than define fixed values, we'll retrieve the values
from the three sliders on the user interface:

```
node.position = SCNVector3(Xslider.value,
Yslider.value,Zslider.value)
```

Each time we add a new node (sphere), let's give it a name. This name will be important later when we need to remove all spheres from the augmented reality view. The name can be anything so just call it sphere:

```
node.name = "sphere"
```

Finally, we need to add this node to the root node. ARKit organizes everything displayed as a hierarchy where every augmented reality view comes with a single root node. Each time you create a new object to display in an augmented reality view, that new object is a node that becomes a child node to the root node. Every augmented reality view contains one root node and zero or more child nodes:

```
sceneView.scene.rootNode.addChildNode(node)
```

13.   Modify the resetButton function like this:

```
@IBAction func resetButton(_ sender: UIButton) {
    sceneView.session.pause()

    sceneView.scene.rootNode.enumerateChildNodes {
    (node, _) in
        if node.name == "sphere" {
          node.removeFromParentNode()
        }
    }
    sceneView.session.run(configuration, options:
    [.resetTracking])
}
```

This `resetButton` function first pauses the current augmented reality session, then it checks each child node. If the name of that child node happens to be `sphere`, then it removes that node from the root node.

This `if` statement to check if a node's name is `sphere` is important because, when the app displays the world origin, that's also a child node connected to the root node. Suppose you just had the following code:

```
sceneView.scene.rootNode.enumerateChildNodes { (node, _) in
    node.removeFromParentNode()
}
```

This code would remove all nodes from the root node, including the world origin. By only removing nodes named `sphere`, we can keep the world origin displayed while removing all yellow spheres displayed in the augmented reality view.

The complete `ViewController.swift` file should look like this:

```
import UIKit
import SceneKit
import ARKit

class ViewController: UIViewController, ARSCNViewDelegate {

    @IBOutlet var sceneView: ARSCNView!
    @IBOutlet var Xslider: UISlider!
    @IBOutlet var Yslider: UISlider!
    @IBOutlet var Zslider: UISlider!

    let configuration = ARWorldTrackingConfiguration()

    override func viewDidLoad() {
        super.viewDidLoad()
        // Do any additional setup after loading the view,
        typically from a nib.
        sceneView.delegate = self
```

```swift
        sceneView.showsStatistics = true
        sceneView.debugOptions = [ARSCNDebugOptions.
        showWorldOrigin]
    }

    override func viewWillAppear(_ animated: Bool) {
        super.viewWillAppear(animated)

        sceneView.session.run(configuration)
    }

    @IBAction func addButton(_ sender: UIButton) {
        showShape()
    }

    @IBAction func resetButton(_ sender: UIButton) {
        sceneView.session.pause()

        sceneView.scene.rootNode.enumerateChildNodes { (node, _) in
            if node.name == "sphere" {
              node.removeFromParentNode()
            }
        }
        sceneView.session.run(configuration, options:
        [.resetTracking])
    }

    func showShape() {
        let node = SCNNode()
        node.geometry = SCNSphere(radius: 0.05)
        node.geometry?.firstMaterial?.diffuse.contents =
        UIColor.yellow
        node.position = SCNVector3(Xslider.value,
        Yslider.value,Zslider.value)
```

```
    node.name = "sphere"
    sceneView.scene.rootNode.addChildNode(node)
  }

}
```

Attach an iOS device to your Macintosh through a USB cable and then
click the Run button or choose Product ➤ Run. After a few moments, step
back and you should see the world origin appear. Move the sliders left or right
and then tap the Add button. Your app should display a yellow sphere at the
x, y, and z coordinates defined by the three sliders, as shown in Figure 3-12.

***Figure 3-12.*** *Displaying multiple yellow spheres*

You can repeat this process of changing the slider values and tapping the Add button to keep adding more yellow spheres. Move your iOS device to a new location and tap the Reset button. Your app will remove all yellow spheres and display the world origin at the current location of your iOS device.

# Summary

In this chapter, you learned how to display a world origin for debugging purposes in helping you verify that your app is placing objects correctly in an augmented reality view. Once your app is finished, you'll need to remove the code that makes the world origin appear each time your app displays its augmented reality view.

The world origin helps you position objects by defining its x, y, and z coordinates. To display items in an augmented reality view, you need to create a node and define a shape for that node, such as a sphere, box, or torus. Next, you need to define an object's appearance, such as yellow or red, along with its size.

To make augmented reality more versatile, you can reset the world origin based on a new location the user may hold an iOS device. This ability to reset the world origin lets your app display virtual objects wherever the user decides to move and point an iOS device.

In the next chapter, we go into more details about creating geometric shapes and applying different textures to a shape beyond solid colors.

# CHAPTER 4

# Working with Shapes

In the previous chapter, we used a debugging option that allowed our augmented reality app to display the world origin, which showed the x-, y-, and z-axes based on the iOS device's current location. Based on this world origin, we can place virtual objects in the augmented reality view by defining its x, y, and z coordinates.

ARKit offers another debugging option, called *feature points*. Like the world origin, you'll only use feature points to debug your app. When it's time to ship your app, you'll remove both the world origin and feature points from appearing.

To make feature points appear, modify the debugOptions line like this:

```
sceneView.debugOptions = [ARSCNDebugOptions.showWorldOrigin,
ARSCNDebugOptions.showFeaturePoints]
```

This line tells Xcode to display both the world origin (.showWorldOrigin) and feature points (.showFeaturePoints).

In our previous app, we could create yellow spheres along with the world origin, and then reset tracking to make the world origin appear in the new current location of the iOS device. Generally when you reset tracking and delete any existing virtual objects (such as our yellow spheres), you'll also want to remove anchors.

Anchors define the position of virtual objects in an augmented reality view. Our previous app just removed the virtual objects from view, but once we delete the yellow sphere, we also don't need to know the sphere's previous position or anchor anymore, so we should delete that as well.

© Wallace Wang 2018
W. Wang, *Beginning ARKit for iPhone and iPad*,
https://doi.org/10.1007/978-1-4842-4102-8_4

To make anchors of virtual objects disappear, we just need to modify the session.run line when we reset world tracking like this:

```
sceneView.session.run(configuration, options: [.resetTracking,
.removeExistingAnchors])
```

This code resets the world origin (.resetTracking) and removes any invisible anchors defining the position of virtual objects (.removeExistingAnchors).

To see how to make feature points appear (and delete invisible anchor points of the yellow spheres), modify the previous app's code so the entire ViewController.swift file looks like this:

```swift
import UIKit
import SceneKit
import ARKit

class ViewController: UIViewController, ARSCNViewDelegate {

    @IBOutlet var sceneView: ARSCNView!
    @IBOutlet var Xslider: UISlider!
    @IBOutlet var Yslider: UISlider!
    @IBOutlet var Zslider: UISlider!

    let configuration = ARWorldTrackingConfiguration()

    override func viewDidLoad() {
        super.viewDidLoad()
        // Do any additional setup after loading the view,
        typically from a nib.
        sceneView.delegate = self
        sceneView.showsStatistics = true
        sceneView.debugOptions = [ARSCNDebugOptions.
        showWorldOrigin, ARSCNDebugOptions.showFeaturePoints]
    }
```

```swift
override func viewWillAppear(_ animated: Bool) {
    super.viewWillAppear(animated)

    sceneView.session.run(configuration)
}

@IBAction func addButton(_ sender: UIButton) {
    showShape()
}

@IBAction func resetButton(_ sender: UIButton) {
    sceneView.session.pause()

    sceneView.scene.rootNode.enumerateChildNodes { (node, _) in
        if node.name == "sphere" {
          node.removeFromParentNode()
        }
    }
    sceneView.session.run(configuration, options:
    [.resetTracking, .removeExistingAnchors])
}

func showShape() {
    let node = SCNNode()
    node.geometry = SCNSphere(radius: 0.05)
    node.geometry?.firstMaterial?.diffuse.contents =
    UIColor.yellow
    node.position = SCNVector3(Xslider.value,Yslider.
    value,Zslider.value)
    node.name = "sphere"
    sceneView.scene.rootNode.addChildNode(node)
}

}
```

Click the Run button or choose Product ➤ Run with an iOS device connected to your Macintosh through its USB cable. When the app runs, you'll see feature points displayed as yellow dots that show you when ARKit detects surfaces of objects in the real world. The more dots that appear, the better ARKit detects that surface.

If you point an augmented reality app at a clearly visible surface, such as a table top, along with contrasting neighboring objects like a vertical wall and horizontal floor, you'll see more feature point dots appear, as shown in Figure 4-1. If you point the camera at the same area but from a different angle, you can see how ARKit displays fewer feature points, meaning it doesn't recognize the nearby area as well.

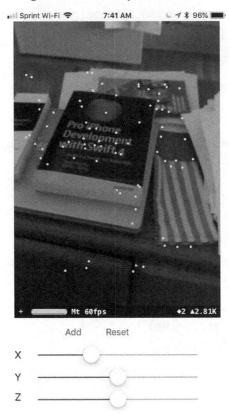

***Figure 4-1.*** *Feature points show how ARKit recognizes surfaces in the real world*

Click the Stop button or choose Product ➤ Stop to stop your app from running.

# Displaying Different Geometric Shapes

Geometric shapes are the simplest types of virtual objects you can display in an augmented reality view. In the previous chapter, we created a sphere, but SceneKit actually offers several different types of geometric shapes to use. Each geometric shape may require you to specify different dimensions.

For example, you can create a sphere by defining its radius, but to create a box, you need to define its width, height, and depth. The different geometric shapes available are:

- SCNFloor

- SCNBox

- SCNCapsule

- SCNCone

- SCNCylinder

- SCNPlane

- SCNPyramid

- SCNTorus

- SCNTube

All of these geometric shapes work alike in that you can define a color for their surface, as UIColor.blue or UIColor.red. By combining multiple geometric shapes, you can create simple virtual objects that appear within an augmented reality view.

To create a sphere, we just needed to define its radius like this:

```
node.geometry = SCNSphere(radius: 0.05)
```

To create a box, we need to define its height, width, and length, as shown in Figure 4-2. In addition, you can also define the edges of the box to make them sharp or round. To modify the corner of a box, you need to define its chamfer radius. A radius of zero creates a sharp edge while non-zero values create a rounded edge. The higher the value, the rounder the edge.

To see how to display a box instead of a sphere, follow these steps:

1. Click on the `ViewController.swift` file of the current app that displays three sliders for defining the x, y, and z coordinates of a shape.

2. Move the cursor to the front of the `node.geometry = SCNSphere(radius: 0.05)` line and type //, which turns the line into a comment. That means the text appears visible but won't affect your app in any way. As soon as you type // in front of the line, Xcode dims the code like this:

   ```
   // node.geometry = SCNSphere(radius: 0.05)
   ```

3. Type underneath this line the following code:

   ```
   node.geometry = SCNBox(width: 0.1, height: 0.2, length: 0.1, chamferRadius: 0)
   ```

4. Replace where text `"sphere"` with `"shape"` in two places like this:

   ```
   if node.name == "shape" {
       node.removeFromParentNode()
   }
   ```

   and

   ```
   node.name = "shape"
   ```

5.  Connect an iOS device to your Macintosh through its USB cable.

6.  Click the Run button or choose Product ➤ Run.

7.  Adjust the x, y, and z sliders to change the location of the shape.

8.  Tap the Add button to see a yellow box appear in the augmented reality view, as shown in Figure 4-2.

***Figure 4-2.***  *Displaying a box in augmented reality*

9.  Click the Stop button or choose Product ➤ Stop.

Notice that the chamferRadius is zero, which creates a sharp edge. If the chamferRadius is non-zero, this will create a more rounded edge. Change this value to 0.05 to create a rounded edge, as shown in Figure 4-3.

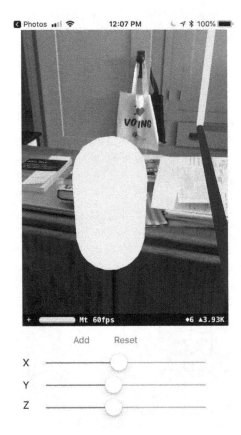

***Figure 4-3.***  *Displaying a box with rounded edges*

Try defining different shapes with their dimensions as follows:

- node.geometry = SCNSphere(radius: 0.05)

- node.geometry = SCNBox(width: 0.1, height: 0.2, length: 0.1, chamferRadius: 0.05)

- node.geometry = SCNTorus(ringRadius: 0.2, pipeRadius: 0.05)

- node.geometry = SCNTube(innerRadius: 0.08, outerRadius: 0.1, height: 0.2)

- node.geometry = SCNCapsule(capRadius: 0.06, height: 0.4)

- node.geometry = SCNCylinder(radius: 0.04, height: 0.3)

- node.geometry = SCNCone(topRadius: 0, bottomRadius: 0.05, height: 0.2)

- node.geometry = SCNPyramid(width: 0.2, height: 0.4, length: 0.2)

- node.geometry = SCNPlane(width: 0.2, height: 0.3)

Remember, just use one of these lines in your code at a time, not all of them. By experimenting with different shapes and dimensions, you can see how to create geometric objects of any size, as shown in Figure 4-4.

**Figure 4-4.**  *Displaying a torus*

Besides displaying a yellow color, try other colors such as brown, cyan, darkGray, gray, green, lightGray, magenta, orange, purple, red, or white like this:

```
node.geometry?.firstMaterial?.diffuse.contents = UIColor.purple
```

# Displaying Text

Besides displaying geometric shapes in augmented reality, you can also display text. When displaying text you can define a string to display along with the text's font, size, and color.

The first part to creating text is to define the string you want to display and its extrusion depth. The extrusion depth defines the thickness of the letters. An extrusion depth of zero creates a flat appearance while a non-zero value for the extrusion depth creates a thickness that makes letters visible when viewed from the side. To define a string and an extrusion depth, you need to use code like this:

```
let text = SCNText(string: "Hello", extrusionDepth: 1)
```

At this point, we've created text but we can't see it. Just as we applied a color to a geometric shape like making a sphere yellow or red, we need to choose a color for text as well. To do that, we need to define a material class like this:

```
let material = SCNMaterial()
```

Next, we need to choose a color for the material and diffuse it across the entire surface like this:

```
material.diffuse.contents = UIColor.orange
```

Finally, we need to apply this material color on the text itself. We can actually apply multiple materials to text where each item appears in an array. Since we're just defining a single color, the array only contains the material color:

```
text.materials = [material]
```

Now that we've defined text and its outer appearance, the next step is to place that text in the augmented reality view as a node. That involves defining a node, the node's x, y, and z coordinates, and its scale that defines a node's width, height, and depth:

```
let node = SCNMaterial()
node.position = SCNVector3(Xslider.value, Yslider.value,
Zslider.value)
node.scale = SCNVector3(0.01, 0.01, 0.01)
```

89

Finally, we need to define the node's geometry as the text we defined using SCNText like this:

```
node.geometry = text
```

Finally, we need to add this node to the root node of the augmented reality scene:

```
sceneView.scene.rootNode.addChildNode(node)
```

To see how this code works to display orange text at x, y, and z coordinates you specify, follow these steps:

1.  Modify the World Tracking project or create a new project identical to the World Tracking project except give it a different name such as Node Placement Text.

2.  Modify the ViewController.swift file so the code looks like this:

    ```swift
    import UIKit
    import SceneKit
    import ARKit

    class ViewController: UIViewController,
    ARSCNViewDelegate {

        @IBOutlet var sceneView: ARSCNView!
        @IBOutlet var Xslider: UISlider!
        @IBOutlet var Yslider: UISlider!
        @IBOutlet var Zslider: UISlider!

        let configuration = ARWorldTrackingConfiguration()

        override func viewDidLoad() {
            super.viewDidLoad()
    ```

```swift
    // Do any additional setup after loading the
    view, typically from a nib.
    sceneView.delegate = self
    sceneView.showsStatistics = true
    sceneView.debugOptions = [ARSCNDebugOptions.
    showWorldOrigin, ARSCNDebugOptions.
    showFeaturePoints]
}

override func viewWillAppear(_ animated: Bool) {
    super.viewWillAppear(animated)

    sceneView.session.run(configuration)
}

@IBAction func addButton(_ sender: UIButton) {
    showShape()
}

@IBAction func resetButton(_ sender: UIButton) {
    sceneView.session.pause()

    sceneView.scene.rootNode.enumerateChildNodes {
    (node, _) in
        if node.name == "shape" {
            node.removeFromParentNode()
        }
    }
    sceneView.session.run(configuration, options:
    [.resetTracking, .removeExistingAnchors])
}

func showShape() {
```

```
let text = SCNText(string: "Hello",
extrusionDepth: 1)

let material = SCNMaterial()
material.diffuse.contents = UIColor.orange
text.materials = [material]

let node = SCNNode()
node.position = SCNVector3(Xslider.value,
Yslider.value, Zslider.value)
node.scale = SCNVector3(0.01, 0.01, 0.01)
node.geometry = text
node.name = "shape"

sceneView.scene.rootNode.addChildNode(node)
    }

}
```

3. Connect an iOS device to your Macintosh through its USB cable.

4. Click the Run button or choose Product ➤ Run.

5. Tap the Add button. Orange text appears where you defined the x, y, and z coordinates, as shown in Figure 4-5.

**Figure 4-5.** *Displaying text in augmented reality*

6.   Click the Stop button or choose Product ➤ Stop.

Try experimenting with different text and extrusion depth along with different colors.

# Adding Textures to Shapes

In the examples we've created so far, we've simply used solid colors to color the geometric shapes we've added to our augmented reality view. However, you can apply graphic images to the surface of geometric shapes. This can create interesting visual effects such as showing shapes as planets or boxes that looks like they're made out of bricks.

You can find public domain texture images from various sites on the Internet by searching for "texture images" in your favorite search engine. Such a search will help you find texture images of all varieties, as shown in Figure 4-6.

***Figure 4-6.*** *Finding texture images on the Internet*

Once you download one or more texture images, you need to add the texture image to your Xcode project by following these steps:

1.  Modify the current Xcode project you used to display text or create a new project that allows the use of the camera to display an augmented reality view. (This should be the Xcode project you created earlier for this chapter.)

2.  Drag the texture image to the navigator pane of your Xcode project. A window appears, displaying different options for adding a file, as shown in Figure 4-7.

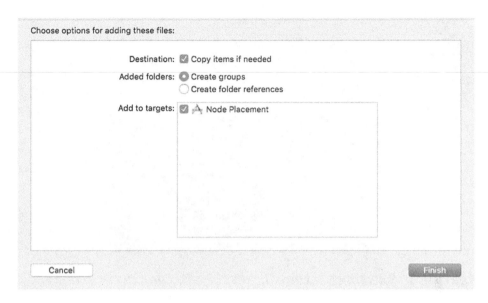

Choose options for adding these files:

Destination: ☑ Copy items if needed

Added folders: ⦿ Create groups
⦾ Create folder references

Add to targets: ☑ Ⓐ Node Placement

Cancel                                                  Finish

*Figure 4-7.* *Adding a file to an Xcode project*

3. Make sure the Copy Items if Needed check box is selected and then click the Finish button.

4. Click on the stexture file you just added in the Navigator pane. Xcode displays the contents of that texture image, as shown in Figure 4-8.

***Figure 4-8.*** *Selecting a texture file displays its contents in Xcode*

Once you've added a texture image to your Xcode project, the final step is to define that texture image to appear on the surface of a geometric shape such as a sphere, box, or pyramid. First, define the geometric shape separately like this:

```
let sphere = SCNSphere(radius: 0.05)
```

Next, define a material for the sphere. We'll need to first create a material then assign the texture image to that material contents. Finally, we'll need to apply the material to the sphere like this:

```
let material = SCNMaterial()
material.diffuse.contents = UIImage(named: "earth.jpg")
sphere.materials = [material]
```

In this example, the texture image is called earth.jpg but you'll need to change this to the name of your specific image file, including the file extension such as .jpg.

After defining a sphere and its material (the texture image), the final step is to create a node, assign that node's geometry to the sphere, and position that node in the augmented reality view like this:

```
let node = SCNNode()
node.geometry = sphere
node.position = SCNVector3(Xslider.value,Yslider.value,Zslider.value)
```

To edit the ViewController.swift file, follow these steps:

1. Click on the ViewController.swift file in the Navigator pane.

2. Edit the contents of the ViewController.swift file so it looks like the following:

```
import UIKit
import SceneKit
import ARKit

class ViewController: UIViewController,
ARSCNViewDelegate {

    @IBOutlet var sceneView: ARSCNView!
    @IBOutlet var Xslider: UISlider!
    @IBOutlet var Yslider: UISlider!
    @IBOutlet var Zslider: UISlider!

    let configuration = ARWorldTrackingConfiguration()

    override func viewDidLoad() {
        super.viewDidLoad()
        // Do any additional setup after loading the
        view, typically from a nib.
        sceneView.delegate = self
```

```
        sceneView.showsStatistics = true
        sceneView.debugOptions = [ARSCNDebugOptions.
        showWorldOrigin, ARSCNDebugOptions.
        showFeaturePoints]
    }

    override func viewWillAppear(_ animated: Bool) {
        super.viewWillAppear(animated)

        sceneView.session.run(configuration)
    }

    @IBAction func addButton(_ sender: UIButton) {
        showShape()
    }

    @IBAction func resetButton(_ sender: UIButton) {
        sceneView.session.pause()

        sceneView.scene.rootNode.enumerateChildNodes {
        (node, _) in
            if node.name == "shape" {
                node.removeFromParentNode()
            }
        }
        sceneView.session.run(configuration, options:
        [.resetTracking, .removeExistingAnchors])
    }
```

```
func showShape() {
    let sphere = SCNSphere(radius: 0.05)
    let material = SCNMaterial()
    material.diffuse.contents = UIImage(named:
    "earth.jpg")
    sphere.materials = [material]

    let node = SCNNode()
    node.geometry = sphere
    node.position = SCNVector3(Xslider.
    value,Yslider.value,Zslider.value)
    node.name = "shape"
    sceneView.scene.rootNode.addChildNode(node)

}

}
```

3. Connect an iOS device to your Macintosh with its USB cable.

4. Click the Run button or chose Product ➤ Run.

5. Use the sliders to define an x, y, and z coordinate for your sphere and tap the Add button. The sphere appears covered in the texture file you specified, as shown in Figure 4-9.

***Figure 4-9.*** *Displaying a texture file over a geometric shape*

6.    Click the Stop button or choose Product ➤ Stop in Xcode.

Experiment with different geometric shapes and texture images, such as a pyramid and a wood texture, as shown in Figure 4-10.

```
let pyramid = SCNPyramid(width: 0.04, height: 0.03,
length: 0.04)
let material = SCNMaterial()
material.diffuse.contents = UIImage(named: "wood.jpg")
pyramid.materials = [material]
```

*Figure 4-10.* *You can display different geometric shapes and textures*

# Changing the Transparency of Shapes

Normally when you add a texture or color to a geometric shape, that texture or color appears solid. However, you can define a transparency value between 0 and 1 where 1 creates a solid appearance and 0 essentially makes the texture or color completely invisible, such as:

```
material.transparency = 0.6
```

To see how to change the transparency, follow these steps:

1. Use the Xcode project that displayed a texture over a geometric shape.

2. Click on the ViewController.swift file in the Navigator pane.

3. Add the following line under the line that defines the texture of a geometric shape, such as:

```
material.diffuse.contents = UIImage(named: "wood.jpg")
material.transparency = 0.6
```

Remember to replace "wood.jpg" with the filename and extension of the texture file you're using. The entire ViewController.swift file should look like this:

```
import UIKit
import SceneKit
import ARKit

class ViewController: UIViewController,
ARSCNViewDelegate {

    @IBOutlet var sceneView: ARSCNView!
    @IBOutlet var Xslider: UISlider!
    @IBOutlet var Yslider: UISlider!
    @IBOutlet var Zslider: UISlider!

    let configuration = ARWorldTrackingConfiguration()

    override func viewDidLoad() {
        super.viewDidLoad()
        // Do any additional setup after loading the
        view, typically from a nib.
```

```
        sceneView.delegate = self
        sceneView.showsStatistics = true
        sceneView.debugOptions = [ARSCNDebugOptions.
        showWorldOrigin, ARSCNDebugOptions.
        showFeaturePoints]
    }

    override func viewWillAppear(_ animated: Bool) {
        super.viewWillAppear(animated)

        sceneView.session.run(configuration)
    }

    @IBAction func addButton(_ sender: UIButton) {
        showShape()
    }

    @IBAction func resetButton(_ sender: UIButton) {
        sceneView.session.pause()

        sceneView.scene.rootNode.enumerateChildNodes {
        (node, _) in
            if node.name == "shape" {
              node.removeFromParentNode()
            }
        }
        sceneView.session.run(configuration, options:
        [.resetTracking, .removeExistingAnchors])
    }

    func showShape() {
        //let sphere = SCNSphere(radius: 0.05)
        let pyramid = SCNPyramid(width: 0.04, height:
        0.03, length: 0.04)
```

```
    let material = SCNMaterial()
    material.diffuse.contents = UIImage(named:
    "wood.jpg")
    material.transparency = 0.6
    //material.diffuse.contents = UIImage(named:
    "earth.jpg")
    //sphere.materials = [material]
    pyramid.materials = [material]

    let node = SCNNode()
    node.geometry = pyramid// sphere
    node.position = SCNVector3(Xslider.
    value,Yslider.value,Zslider.value)
    node.name = "shape"
    sceneView.scene.rootNode.addChildNode(node)

  }

}
```

4. Connect an iOS device to your Macintosh with its USB cable.

5. Click the Run button or choose Product ➤ Run.

6. Modify the sliders to define the x, y, and z coordinates of the shape.

7. Tap the Add button. Notice that the shape now appears transparent, as shown in Figure 4-11.

***Figure 4-11.*** *Displaying a geometric shape and texture as transparent*

8.   Click the Stop button or choose Product ➤ Stop.

# Drawing Shapes

By offering different geometric shapes you can customize, ARKit makes it easy to add virtual objects to any augmented reality view. However, what if you want to create a shape that doesn't fit within the confines of a common geometric shape like a box or a sphere? The simplest solution is to draw your own shape.

The simplest type of shape to draw is a plane, which you can create by defining two different sets of points. To draw a shape, you must define a BezierPath object like this:

```
let plane = UIBezierPath()
```

After creating a BezierPath object, the next step is to define a starting set of x and y coordinates such as 0, 0, like this:

```
plane.move(to: CGPoint(x: 0, y: 0))
```

Remember, these x and y coordinates don't define the physical position of the shape in the augmented reality view. After defining a starting point, you can define a second set of x, y coordinates that defines a plane like this:

```
plane.addLine(to: CGPoint(x: 0, y: 0.1))
```

This plane.addLine command tells Xcode to start drawing at the beginning x and y coordinates defined by the plane.move command. Then the plane.addLine command draws a line 0 that points along the x-axis and 0.1 distance that points along the y-axis.

Finally, you need to define the shape as an SCNShape object, which also specifies how thick to make the shape along the z-axis, known as the extrusion depth. To do this, you define the shape name along with its extrusion depth like this:

```
let customShape = SCNShape(path: plane, extrusionDepth: 0.1)
```

After creating a custom shape, the final step is to assign this shape to a node and display this node at specific x, y, and z coordinates like this:

```
let node = SCNNode()
node.geometry = customShape
node.geometry?.firstMaterial?.diffuse.contents =
UIColor.yellow
```

```
node.position = SCNVector3(0,0,0)
sceneView.scene.rootNode.addChildNode(node)
```

This code creates a yellow plane that extends 0.1 points along the z-axis, rises 0.1 points up on the y-axis, and doesn't extend at all along the x-axis, as shown in Figure 4-12.

**Figure 4-12.** *Displaying a plane defined by its distance along the x-, y-, and z-axes*

By adding multiple addLine commands, you can define additional planes on a custom shape. To see how to create a wedge shape, follow these steps:

1. Use the Xcode project that displayed a texture over a geometric shape.

2. Click on the ViewController.swift file in the Navigator pane.

3. Edit the showShape function so the entire ViewController.swift file looks like this:

```swift
import UIKit
import SceneKit
import ARKit

class ViewController: UIViewController,
ARSCNViewDelegate {

    @IBOutlet var sceneView: ARSCNView!
    @IBOutlet var Xslider: UISlider!
    @IBOutlet var Yslider: UISlider!
    @IBOutlet var Zslider: UISlider!

    let configuration = ARWorldTrackingConfiguration()

    override func viewDidLoad() {
        super.viewDidLoad()
        // Do any additional setup after loading the
        view, typically from a nib.
        sceneView.delegate = self
        sceneView.showsStatistics = true
        sceneView.debugOptions = [ARSCNDebugOptions.
        showWorldOrigin, ARSCNDebugOptions.
        showFeaturePoints]
    }
```

```swift
override func viewWillAppear(_ animated: Bool) {
    super.viewWillAppear(animated)

    sceneView.session.run(configuration)
}

@IBAction func addButton(_ sender: UIButton) {
    showShape()
}

@IBAction func resetButton(_ sender: UIButton) {
    sceneView.session.pause()

    sceneView.scene.rootNode.enumerateChildNodes {
    (node, _) in
        if node.name == "shape" {
          node.removeFromParentNode()
        }
    }
    sceneView.session.run(configuration, options:
    [.resetTracking, .removeExistingAnchors])
}

func showShape() {
    let plane = UIBezierPath()
    plane.move(to: CGPoint(x: 0, y: 0))
    plane.addLine(to: CGPoint(x: 0.1, y: 0.1))
    plane.addLine(to: CGPoint(x: 0.1, y: -0.03))
    let customShape = SCNShape(path: plane,
    extrusionDepth: 0.1)

    let node = SCNNode()
    node.geometry = customShape
```

```
        node.geometry?.firstMaterial?.diffuse.contents =
        UIColor.yellow
        node.position = SCNVector3(Xslider.value,
        Yslider.value,Zslider.value)
        node.name = "shape"
        sceneView.scene.rootNode.addChildNode(node)

    }

}
```

4.   Connect an iOS device to your Macintosh through
     its USB cable.

5.   Click the Run button or choose Product ➤ Run.

6.   Tap the Add button when the app runs. A yellow
     wedge appears, as shown in Figure 4-13.

7.   Click the Stop button or choose Product ➤ Stop.

**Figure 4-13.**  *Two addLine commands help define a wedge shape*

The first addLine command defined the left side of the wedge and the second addLine command defined the right side of the wedge:

```
plane.addLine(to: CGPoint(x: 0.1, y: 0.1))
plane.addLine(to: CGPoint(x: 0.1, y: -0.03))
```

By using as many addLine commands as you wish, you can define your own custom three-dimensional shapes that can't be created by common geometric shapes like spheres, boxes, or cones.

111

# Summary

Besides displaying 3D images, ARKit can also display geometric shapes in an augmented reality view. Some common geometric shapes include boxes, spheres, planes, and cylinders. By specifying dimensions and positions, you can make a geometric shape appear anywhere.

After defining the dimensions of a geometric shape, you can modify its appearance by choosing different colors for its surface. For more variety, you can also apply different texture images to cover the surfaces of any geometric shapes you create.

In case no geometric shape matches what you need, you can draw individual lines to create your own virtual objects to display in an augmented reality view. By drawing lines and combining multiple geometric shapes, you can create custom shapes limited only by your imagination.

Colors and textures can give your geometric shapes a distinctive appearance. In the next chapter, we learn other ways to alter the appearance of virtual objects using different lighting sources.

# CHAPTER 5

# Working with Lights

The simplest way to alter the appearance of a virtual object is to change its color or texture. However, a more subtle way to alter the appearance of virtual objects is to change the lighting source. Think of a typical studio that lets a photographer place one or more lights in different positions around a subject. These lights can be bright or dim, and shine at different intensities and colors to highlight an object in different ways.

Augmented reality is no different. To highlight virtual objects in an augmented reality view, you can place one or more light sources at specific x, y, and z coordinates. In addition, you can also define different types of light sources, such as direction, ambient, or spot to create unique visual effects, as shown in Figure 5-1.

*Figure 5-1. Different light types available*

By adding light and customizing the appearance of light through color, intensity, and temperature, you can illuminate virtual objects in unique ways within an augmented reality view.

© Wallace Wang 2018
W. Wang, *Beginning ARKit for iPhone and iPad*,
https://doi.org/10.1007/978-1-4842-4102-8_5

# Using Color, Intensity, and Temperature

Color light can illuminate virtual objects in different ways, especially if the virtual objects display their own colors. While color is an obvious way to change a light, two other ways to change the appearance of light involve temperature and intensity.

Temperature works by multiplying the color value by a color corresponding to the light's temperature. The default value of 6500 represents a pure white light, while lower values (down to a minimum of zero) add a "warmer" yellow or orange effect to the light source. On the other hand, higher values (up to a maximum of 40000) add a "cooler" blue effect.

Intensity modifies light by brightening or dimming the light where a value of 1000 leaves the light unaffected. Lower values dim the light while higher values brighten the light.

To learn how to use light to modify the appearance of virtual objects, let's start by creating a new Xcode project by following these steps:

1.  Start Xcode. (Make sure you're using Xcode 10 or greater.)

2.  Choose File ➤ New ➤ Project. Xcode asks you to choose a template.

3.  Click the iOS category.

4.  Click the Single View App icon and click the Next button. Xcode asks for a product name, organization name, organization identifiers, and content technology.

5.  Click in the Product Name text field and type a descriptive name for your project, such as Light Sources. (The exact name does not matter.)

6. Click the Next button. Xcode asks where you want to store your project.

7. Choose a folder and click the Create button. Xcode creates an iOS project.

Now modify the `Info.plist` file to allow access to the camera and to use ARKit by following these steps:

1. Click the `Info.plist` file in the Navigator pane. Xcode displays a list of keys, types, and values.

2. Click the disclosure triangle to expand the Required Device Capabilities category to display Item 0.

3. Move the mouse pointer over Item 0 to display a plus (+) icon.

4. Click this plus (+) icon to display a blank Item 1.

5. Type `arkit` under the Value category in the Item 1 row.

6. Move the mouse pointer over the last row to display a plus (+) icon.

7. Click on the plus (+) icon to create a new row. A popup menu appears.

8. Choose Privacy – Camera Usage Description.

9. Type **AR needs to use the camera** under the Value category in the Privacy – Camera Usage Description row.

Now it's time to modify the `ViewController.swift` file to use ARKit and SceneKit by following these steps:

1. Click on the `ViewController.swift` file in the Navigator pane.

2.  Edit the ViewController.swift file so it looks like this:

```swift
import UIKit
import SceneKit
import ARKit

class ViewController: UIViewController,
ARSCNViewDelegate {

    let configuration = ARWorldTrackingConfiguration()

    override func viewDidLoad() {
        super.viewDidLoad()
        // Do any additional setup after loading the
        view, typically from a nib.

    }

}
```

To view augmented reality in our app, we need to add the following objects to the Main.storyboard user interface:

- One ARKit SceneKit View (ARSCNView)—For displaying augmented reality with the camera view

- Two UISliders—For controlling the temperature and intensity of the light

- Two UILabels—For identifying the purpose of each slider

- Five UIButtons—For choosing different colors for the light

To design the user interface, click on the Main.storyboard file in the Navigator pane and click on the Object Library button to open the Object Library. Then drag and drop the different user interface items on to the user interface. The user interface should eventually look similar to Figure 5-2.

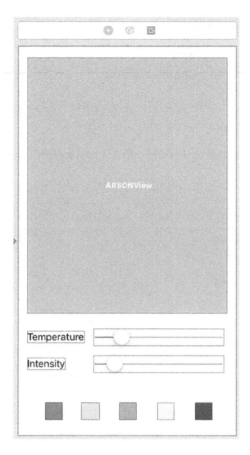

**Figure 5-2.** *Designing the user interface*

After you've designed the user interface, you need to put constraints on those user interface items. To add constraints, choose Editor ➤ Resolve Auto Layout Issues ➤ Reset to Suggested Constraints at the bottom half of the menu under the All Views in Container category.

After adding constraints, the next step is to modify the user interface objects. Double-click on the two UILabels and change their titles to Temperature and Intensity (see Figure 5-2).

Now modify the UISlider next to the Temperature label by following these steps:

1.  Click on the Temperature UISlider.

2.  Click the Attributes Inspector icon or choose View ➤ Inspectors ➤ Show Attributes Inspector.

3.  Type in the Value text field the number 6500.

4.  Type in the Minimum text field 0.

5.  Type in the Maximum text field 40000, as shown in Figure 5-3.

***Figure 5-3.*** *Defining values for the Temperature slider*

6.  Click on the Intensity UISlider.

7.  Type in the Value text field the number 1000.

8.  Type in the Minimum text field 0.

9.  Type in the Maximum text field 10000, as shown in Figure 5-4.

***Figure 5-4.*** *Defining values for the Intensity slider*

Now it's time to modify the UIButtons at the bottom of the screen by resizing each button, removing the title, and displaying a background color. To do this, follow these steps:

1. Click on UIButton.

2. Click on the Size Inspector icon or choose View ➤ Navigators ➤ Show Size Inspector.

3. Type 30 in the Width and Height text fields in the View category, as shown in Figure 5-5.

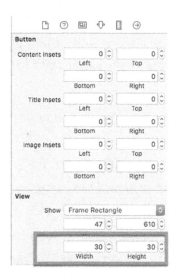

***Figure 5-5.*** *Defining a width and height for the UIButton*

4. Click on the Attributes Inspector icon or choose View ➤ Navigators ➤ Show Attributes Inspector.

5. Delete the title from the UIButton.

6. Click on the Background popup menu under the View category and choose a color, as shown in Figure 5-6.

119

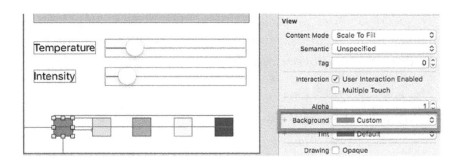

**Figure 5-6.** *Defining a background color for a UIButton*

7. Repeat Steps 2-6 for each UIButton except choose a different color for each UIButton in Step 5. (The specific colors you choose won't matter but make sure you don't choose the same color for two or more UIButtons.)

After designing the user interface, the next step is to connect the user interface items to the Swift code in the ViewController.swift file. To do this, follow these steps:

1. Click the Main.storyboard file in the Navigator pane.

2. Click the Assistant Editor icon or choose View ➤ Assistant Editor ➤ Show Assistant Editor to display the Main.storyboard and the ViewController. swift file side by side.

3. Move the mouse pointer over the ARSCNView, hold down the Control key, and Ctrl-drag under the class ViewController line.

4. Release the Control key and the left mouse button. A popup menu appears.

5.  Click in the Name text field and type sceneView,
    then click the Connect button. Xcode creates an
    IBOutlet as shown here:

```
@IBOutlet var sceneView: ARSCNView!
```

6.  Underneath this IBOutlet, type the following:

```
let showLight = SCNNode()
```

7.  Edit the viewDidLoad function so it looks like this:

```
override func viewDidLoad() {
    super.viewDidLoad()
    // Do any additional setup after loading the
    view, typically from a nib.
    sceneView.delegate = self
    sceneView.showsStatistics = true
    sceneView.debugOptions = [ARSCNDebugOptions.
    showWorldOrigin, ARSCNDebugOptions.
    showFeaturePoints]
}
```

8.  Edit the viewWillAppear function so it looks like this:

```
override func viewWillAppear(_ animated: Bool) {
    super.viewWillAppear(animated)
    showShape()
    lightOn()
    sceneView.session.run(configuration)
}
```

This viewWillAppear function calls on a showShape
and a lightOn function. The showShape function
displays a sphere and the lightOn function defines a
light source.

9.  Type the following underneath the `viewWillAppear` function:

```
func showShape() {
    let sphere = SCNSphere(radius: 0.03)
    sphere.firstMaterial?.diffuse.contents =
    UIColor.white

    let node = SCNNode()
    node.geometry = sphere
    node.position = SCNVector3(0.1, 0, 0)
    sceneView.scene.rootNode.addChildNode(node)
}

func lightOn() {
    showLight.light = SCNLight()
    showLight.light?.type = .omni
    showLight.light?.color = UIColor(white: 0.6,
    alpha: 1.0)
    showLight.position = SCNVector3(0,0,0)
    sceneView.scene.rootNode.addChildNode(showLight)
}
```

10.  Move the mouse pointer over the Temperature UISlider, hold down the Control key, and Ctrl-drag underneath the `lightOn` function.

11.  Release the control key and left mouse button. A popup menu appears.

12.  Click on the Connection popup menu and choose Action.

13.  Click in the Name text field and type `temperatureChange`.

14. Click in the Type popup menu and choose UISlider, then click the Connect button. This creates an IBAction method.

15. Edit this temperatureChange IBAction method as follows:

```
@IBAction func temperatureChange(_ sender:
UISlider) {
    showLight.light?.temperature = CGFloat
    (sender.value)
}
```

16. Move the mouse pointer over the Intensity UISlider, hold down the Control key, and Ctrl-drag underneath the lightOn function.

17. Release the control key and left mouse button. A popup menu appears.

18. Click on the Connection popup menu and choose Action.

19. Click in the Name text field and type intensityChange.

20. Click in the Type popup menu and choose UISlider, then click the Connect button. This creates an IBAction method.

21. Edit this intensityChange IBAction method as follows:

```
@IBAction func intensityChange(_ sender: UISlider) {
    showLight.light?.intensity = CGFloat(sender.
    value)
}
```

22.  Move the mouse pointer over any UIButton, hold down the Control key, and Ctrl-drag at the bottom of the ViewController.swift file right above the last } bracket.

23.  Release the Control key and the left mouse button. A popup menu appears.

24.  Click on the Connection popup menu and choose Action.

25.  Click in the Name text field and type colorButton.

26.  Click in the Type popup menu and choose UIButton, then click the Connect button. This creates an IBAction method.

27.  Edit this colorButton IBAction method as follows:

```
@IBAction func colorButton(_ sender: UIButton) {
    //colorMe.backgroundColor = sender.
    backgroundColor
    showLight.light?.color = sender.
    backgroundColor!

}
```

28.  Move the mouse pointer over another UIButton (not the one you originally used to Ctrl-drag into the ViewController.swift file to create the colorButton IBAction method), hold down the Control key, and Ctrl-drag the mouse over the colorButton IBAction method that you just created until it's highlighted, as shown in Figure 5-7.

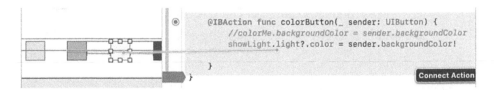

***Figure 5-7.*** *Connecting additional UIButtons to an existing IBAction method*

29. When the entire `colorButton` IBAction method appears highlighted, release the Control key and the left mouse button.

30. Repeat Steps 28-29 for each additional UIButton until all UIButtons are connected to the same `colorButton` IBAction method.

The entire `ViewController.swift` file should look like this:

```
import UIKit
import SceneKit
import ARKit

class ViewController: UIViewController, ARSCNViewDelegate {

    @IBOutlet var sceneView: ARSCNView!

    let configuration = ARWorldTrackingConfiguration()
    let showLight = SCNNode()

    override func viewDidLoad() {
        super.viewDidLoad()
        // Do any additional setup after loading the view,
        typically from a nib.
        sceneView.delegate = self
        sceneView.showsStatistics = true
```

```
        sceneView.debugOptions = [ARSCNDebugOptions.
        showWorldOrigin, ARSCNDebugOptions.showFeaturePoints]
    }

    override func viewWillAppear(_ animated: Bool) {
        super.viewWillAppear(animated)
        showShape()
        lightOn()
        sceneView.session.run(configuration)
    }

    func showShape() {
        let sphere = SCNSphere(radius: 0.03)
        sphere.firstMaterial?.diffuse.contents = UIColor.white

        let node = SCNNode()
        node.geometry = sphere
        node.position = SCNVector3(0.1, 0, 0)
        sceneView.scene.rootNode.addChildNode(node)
    }

    func lightOn() {
        showLight.light = SCNLight()
        showLight.light?.type = .omni
        showLight.light?.color = UIColor(white: 0.6, alpha: 1.0)
        showLight.position = SCNVector3(0,0,0)
        sceneView.scene.rootNode.addChildNode(showLight)
    }

    @IBAction func temperatureChange(_ sender: UISlider) {
        showLight.light?.temperature = CGFloat(sender.value)
    }
```

```
@IBAction func intensityChange(_ sender: UISlider) {
    showLight.light?.intensity = CGFloat(sender.value)
}

@IBAction func colorButton(_ sender: UIButton) {
    showLight.light?.color = sender.backgroundColor!
}
}
```

This app places a light source at the world origin (0, 0, 0) and places a white sphere at (0.1, 0, 0) so it appears on the x-axis. To run this app, follow these steps:

1. Connect an iOS device to your Macintosh through its USB cable.

2. Click the Run button or choose Product ➤ Run.

3. When the app runs, a sphere appears on the x-axis. Click on any of the color buttons at the bottom of the screen to change the light source color.

4. Slide the Temperature and Intensity sliders left and right to see how it alters the appearance of the light, as shown in Figure 5-8.

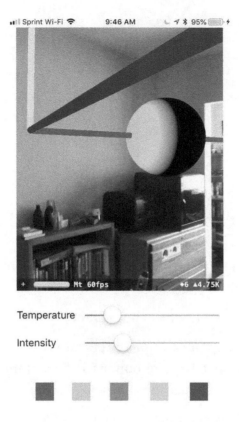

**Figure 5-8.** *Changing the temperature, intensity, and color of a light source*

5.    Click the Stop button or choose Product ➤ Stop.

Try running this app again except in the lightOn function, change the light type from .omni to .directional like this:

```
showLight.light?.type = .directional
```

Also comment out the showLight.position command like this:

```
//showLight.position = SCNVector3(0,0,0)
```

A directional light illuminates virtual objects from the positive z-axis so there's no need to define a position for a directional light. When you run the app with a directional light instead of an omni light, you'll notice a different lighting effect that only illuminates the half of the sphere in the positive z-axis direction, as shown in Figure 5-9.

***Figure 5-9.*** *Using directional light instead of omni light*

# Using a Spotlight

In a theater, people can position one or more spotlights in different locations and aim them at different angles to create interesting visual effects. When you create a spotlight, you need to define its location and angle.

By default, the spotlight aims down the negative z-axis so if you place a spotlight at the world origin (0, 0, 0), then the spotlight will shine down the z-axis away from the user. If a virtual object off the z-axis, the spotlight will miss it completely.

To verify this, rewrite the Swift code in the `ViewController.swift` file and position the spotlight at the world origin (0, 0, 0) like this:

```
showLight.position = SCNVector3(0,0,0)
showLight.light?.type = .spot
```

If you run this code, the spotlight will appear at the world origin (0, 0, 0) and shine down the z-axis, missing the sphere completely, leaving the sphere completely unlit.

To make sure a spotlight shines on a virtual object, you can do one or more of the following:

- Change the spotlight's position relative to any virtual objects you want to illuminate

- Change the angle that the spotlight points

To change the angle that the spotlight points, you need to define the `eulerAngles` property of the spotlight that defines the following axes of rotation:

- Pitch (the x component) is the rotation about the node's x-axis.

- Yaw (the y component) is the rotation about the node's y-axis.

- Roll (the z component) is the rotation about the node's z-axis.

130

To see how the spotlight's position and angle alter the way it shines on virtual objects, follow these steps:

1. Start Xcode. (Make sure you're using Xcode 10 or greater.)

2. Choose File ➤ New ➤ Project. Xcode asks you to choose a template.

3. Click the iOS category.

4. Click the Single View App icon and click the Next button. Xcode asks for a product name, organization name, organization identifiers, and content technology.

5. Click in the Product Name text field and type a descriptive name for your project such as Spotlight. (The exact name does not matter.)

6. Click the Next button. Xcode asks where you want to store your project.

7. Choose a folder and click the Create button. Xcode creates an iOS project.

Now modify the `Info.plist` file to allow access to the camera and to use ARKit by following these steps:

1. Click the `Info.plist` file in the Navigator pane. Xcode displays a list of keys, types, and values.

2. Click the disclosure triangle to expand the Required device capabilities category to display Item 0.

3. Move the mouse pointer over Item 0 to display a plus (+) icon.

4. Click this plus (+) icon to display a blank Item 1.

5.  Type `arkit` under the Value category in the Item 1 row.

6.  Move the mouse pointer over the last row to display a plus (+) icon.

7.  Click on the plus (+) icon to create a new row. A popup menu appears.

8.  Choose Privacy – Camera Usage Description.

9.  Type `AR needs to use the camera` under the Value category in the Privacy – Camera Usage Description row.

Now modify the `ViewController.swift` file to use ARKit and SceneKit by following these steps:

1.  Click on the `ViewController.swift` file in the Navigator pane.

2.  Edit the `ViewController.swift` file so it looks like this:

```swift
import UIKit
import SceneKit
import ARKit

class ViewController: UIViewController,
ARSCNViewDelegate {

    let configuration = ARWorldTrackingConfiguration()

    override func viewDidLoad() {
        super.viewDidLoad()
        // Do any additional setup after loading the
        view, typically from a nib.
    }

}
```

To view the effects of a spotlight in augmented reality within our app, we need to add the following objects to the Main.storyboard user interface:

- One ARKit SceneKit View (ARSCNView)—For displaying augmented reality with the camera view

- Three UISliders—For controlling the pitch, yaw, and roll of the spotlight

- Three UILabels—For identifying the pitch, yaw, and roll sliders

To design the user interface, click on the Main.storyboard file in the Navigator pane and click on the Object Library button to open the Object Library. Then drag and drop the different user interface items on to the user interface. The user interface should eventually look similar to Figure 5-10.

**Figure 5-10.**  *Designing the user interface*

After you've designed the user interface, you need to put constraints on those user interface items. To add constraints, choose Editor ➤ Resolve Auto Layout Issues ➤ Reset to Suggested Constraints at the bottom half of the menu under the All Views in Container category.

After adding constraints, the next step is to modify the user interface objects. Double-click on the three UILabels and change their titles to Pitch (x-axis), Yaw (y-axis), and Roll (z-axis) (see Figure 5-10).

Now modify the UISlider next to the Pitch (x-axis) label by following these steps:

1. Click on the Pitch (x-axis) UISlider.

2. Click the Attributes Inspector icon or choose View ➤ Inspectors ➤ Show Attributes Inspector.

3. Type in the Value text field the number 0.

4. Type in the Minimum text field -360.

5. Type in the Maximum text field 360, as shown in Figure 5-11.

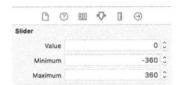

***Figure 5-11.*** *Customizing the UISlider*

6. Repeat Steps 1-5 for the Yaw (y-axis) and Roll (z-axis) UISliders.

After designing the user interface, the next step is to connect the user interface items to the Swift code in the ViewController.swift file. To do this, follow these steps:

1. Click the Main.storyboard file in the Navigator pane.

2. Click the Assistant Editor icon or choose View ➤ Assistant Editor ➤ Show Assistant Editor to display the Main.storyboard and the ViewController.swift file side by side.

3.  Move the mouse pointer over the ARSCNView,
    hold down the Control key, and Ctrl-drag under the
    class ViewController line.

4.  Release the Control key and the left mouse button.
    A popup menu appears.

5.  Click in the Name text field and type sceneView,
    then click the Connect button. Xcode creates an
    IBOutlet as shown here:

```
@IBOutlet var sceneView: ARSCNView!
```

6.  Underneath this IBOutlet, type the following:

```
let configuration = ARWorldTrackingConfiguration()
let showLight = SCNNode()
var currentX : Float = 0
var currentY : Float = 0
var currentZ : Float = 0
```

7.  Edit the viewDidLoad function so it looks like this:

```
override func viewDidLoad() {
    super.viewDidLoad()
    // Do any additional setup after loading the
    view, typically from a nib.
    sceneView.delegate = self
    sceneView.showsStatistics = true
    sceneView.debugOptions = [ARSCNDebugOptions.
    showWorldOrigin, ARSCNDebugOptions.
    showFeaturePoints]
}

override func viewWillAppear(_ animated: Bool) {
    super.viewWillAppear(animated)
```

```
    showShape()
    lightOn()
    sceneView.session.run(configuration)
}
```

This viewWillAppear function calls on a showShape and a lightOn function. The showShape function displays a sphere and the lightOn function defines a light source.

8. Type the following underneath the viewWillAppear function:

```
func showShape() {
    let plane = SCNPlane(width: 0.75, height: 0.75)
    plane.firstMaterial?.diffuse.contents =
    UIColor.yellow

    let node = SCNNode()
    node.geometry = plane
    node.position = SCNVector3(0, 0, -0.3)
    sceneView.scene.rootNode.addChildNode(node)
}

func lightOn() {
    showLight.light = SCNLight()
    showLight.light?.type = .spot
    showLight.light?.color = UIColor(white: 0.6,
    alpha: 1.0)
    showLight.position = SCNVector3(0, 0, 0)
    showLight.eulerAngles = SCNVector3(0, 0, 0)

    sceneView.scene.rootNode.addChildNode(showLight)
}
```

This code creates a yellow plane that appears at -0.03 behind the world origin (0, 0, 0). Then the code creates a spotlight at the world origin aimed at the plane. Even though the spotlight is white, it will shine on the black plane and display yellow because the plane is yellow.

9. Move the mouse pointer over the Pitch (x-axis) UISlider, hold down the Control key, and Ctrl-drag underneath the lightOn function.

10. Release the control key and left mouse button. A popup menu appears.

11. Click on the Connection popup menu and choose Action.

12. Click in the Name text field and type pitchChange.

13. Click in the Type popup menu and choose UISlider, then click the Connect button. This creates an IBAction method.

14. Edit this pitchChange IBAction method as follows:

```
@IBAction func pitchChanged(_ sender: UISlider) {
    currentX = GLKMathDegreesToRadians(sender.value)
    showLight.eulerAngles = SCNVector3(currentX,
    currentY, currentZ)
}
```

15. Move the mouse pointer over the Yaw (y-axis) UISlider, hold down the Control key, and Ctrl-drag underneath the lightOn function.

16. Release the control key and the left mouse button. A popup menu appears.

17.   Click on the Connection popup menu and choose Action.

18.   Click in the Name text field and type yawChange.

19.   Click in the Type popup menu and choose UISlider,
      then click the Connect button. This creates an
      IBAction method.

20.   Edit this yawChange IBAction method as follows:

```
@IBAction func yawChanged(_ sender: UISlider) {
    currentY = GLKMathDegreesToRadians(sender.value)
    showLight.eulerAngles = SCNVector3(currentX,
    GLKMathDegreesToRadians(sender.value), currentZ)
}
```

21.   Move the mouse pointer over the Roll (z-axis)
      UISlider, hold down the Control key, and Ctrl-drag
      underneath the lightOn function.

22.   Release the control key and left mouse button.
      A popup menu appears.

23.   Click on the Connection popup menu and choose Action.

24.   Click in the Name text field and type rollChange.

25.   Click in the Type popup menu and choose UISlider,
      then click the Connect button. This creates an
      IBAction method.

26.   Edit this rollChange IBAction method as follows:

```
@IBAction func rollChanged(_ sender: UISlider) {
    currentZ = GLKMathDegreesToRadians(sender.value)
    showLight.eulerAngles = SCNVector3(currentX,
    currentY, currentZ)
}
```

The entire ViewController.swift file should look like this:

```swift
import UIKit
import SceneKit
import ARKit

class ViewController: UIViewController, ARSCNViewDelegate {

    @IBOutlet var sceneView: ARSCNView!

    let configuration = ARWorldTrackingConfiguration()
    let showLight = SCNNode()
    var currentX : Float = 0
    var currentY : Float = 0
    var currentZ : Float = 0

    override func viewDidLoad() {
        super.viewDidLoad()
        // Do any additional setup after loading the view,
        typically from a nib.
        sceneView.delegate = self
        sceneView.showsStatistics = true
        sceneView.debugOptions = [ARSCNDebugOptions.
        showWorldOrigin, ARSCNDebugOptions.showFeaturePoints]
    }

    override func viewWillAppear(_ animated: Bool) {
        super.viewWillAppear(animated)
        showShape()
        lightOn()
        sceneView.session.run(configuration)
    }

    func showShape() {
        let plane = SCNPlane(width: 0.75, height: 0.75)
        plane.firstMaterial?.diffuse.contents = UIColor.yellow
```

```swift
    let node = SCNNode()
    node.geometry = plane
    node.position = SCNVector3(0, 0, -0.3)
    sceneView.scene.rootNode.addChildNode(node)
}

func lightOn() {
    showLight.light = SCNLight()
    showLight.light?.type = .spot
    showLight.light?.color = UIColor(white: 0.6, alpha: 1.0)
    showLight.position = SCNVector3(0, 0, 0)
    showLight.eulerAngles = SCNVector3(0, 0, 0)

    sceneView.scene.rootNode.addChildNode(showLight)
}

@IBAction func pitchChanged(_ sender: UISlider) {
    currentX = GLKMathDegreesToRadians(sender.value)
    showLight.eulerAngles = SCNVector3(currentX, currentY,
    currentZ)
}

@IBAction func yawChanged(_ sender: UISlider) {
    currentY = GLKMathDegreesToRadians(sender.value)
    showLight.eulerAngles = SCNVector3(currentX,
    GLKMathDegreesToRadians(sender.value), currentZ)
}

@IBAction func rollChanged(_ sender: UISlider) {
    currentZ = GLKMathDegreesToRadians(sender.value)
    showLight.eulerAngles = SCNVector3(currentX, currentY,
    currentZ)
}

}
```

To test this app on an iOS device, follow these steps:.

1.  Connect an iOS device to your Macintosh through a USB cable.

2.  Click the Run button or choose Product ➤ Run.

3.  Slide the Pitch (x-axis), Yaw (y-axis), and Roll (z-axis) sliders left and right to see how the spotlight shines on the plane on different areas. Although the spotlight is white, the plane is yellow so the spotlight appears to be a yellow light, as shown in Figure 5-12.

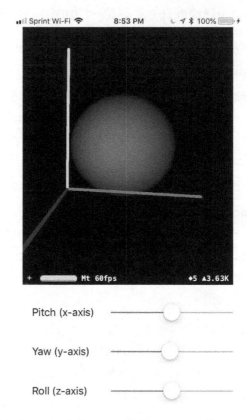

***Figure 5-12.***  *Shining a white spotlight on a yellow plane*

4.  Click the Stop button or choose Product ➤ Stop.

# Summary

In many cases, you can simply display virtual objects through an augmented reality view but if you want to create interesting visual effects, you can define different types of light sources. Think of a theater where you can place multiple lights in different locations and colors to shine on different objects.

By altering the color, intensity, and temperature, you can make a light appear brighter or dimmer. By using a spotlight, you can shine a light in different directions after placing a light anywhere within your augmented reality view.

Experiment with lights and the placement of virtual objects. Lights can give you multiple ways to change the appearance of what users see in your augmented reality app.

# CHAPTER 6

# Positioning Objects

Virtual objects appear in an augmented reality view when you specify their x, y, and z coordinates. Such virtual objects remain fixed in place unless the user resets the world origin so they appear based on the new world origin's location.

However, sometimes you may not want to specify exact coordinates to display a virtual object. Instead, you might want to place one virtual object a specific distance based on the current position of another virtual object. Rather than define exact coordinates, you really want to define relative coordinates such as always placing a second virtual object a fixed distance to the left of another virtual object.

Often times you'll need to combine multiple virtual objects to create a single image, such as a box with a pyramid on top to create a house image. When working with multiple virtual objects that create a single object, relative positioning makes it easy to display all virtual objects correctly so they create a unified visual appearance.

## Defining Relative Positions

Normally when you place a virtual object in an augmented reality view, you need to define two items. First, you need to define the virtual object's x, y, and z coordinates like this:

```
node.position = SCNVector3(0, 0, -0.3)
```

© Wallace Wang 2018
W. Wang, *Beginning ARKit for iPhone and iPad*,
https://doi.org/10.1007/978-1-4842-4102-8_6

This code places a virtual object 0 distance along the x-axis, 0 distance along the y-axis, and -0.3 meters along the z-axis. Once you define the x, y, and z coordinates of a virtual object, the second step is to place that virtual object based on the position of the rootnode like this:

```
sceneView.scene.rootNode.addChildNode(node)
```

The rootnode appears at the world origin (0, 0, 0) so the addChildNode command simply adds a node based on its position of the rootnode.

To learn how to place two virtual objects in an augmented reality view, let's start by creating a new Xcode project by following these steps:

1.  Start Xcode. (Make sure you're using Xcode 10 or greater.)

2.  Choose File ➤ New ➤ Project. Xcode asks you to choose a template.

3.  Click the iOS category.

4.  Click the Single View App icon and click the Next button. Xcode asks for a product name, organization name, organization identifiers, and content technology.

5.  Click in the Product Name text field and type a descriptive name for your project such as Positioning. (The exact name does not matter.)

6.  Click the Next button. Xcode asks where you want to store your project.

7.  Choose a folder and click the Create button. Xcode creates an iOS project.

Now modify the Info.plist to allow access to the camera and to use ARKit by following these steps:

1.  Click the Info.plist file in the Navigator pane. Xcode displays a list of keys, types, and values.

146

2.  Click the disclosure triangle to expand the Required
    Device Capabilities category to display Item 0.

3.  Move the mouse pointer over Item 0 to display a
    plus (+) icon.

4.  Click this plus (+) icon to display a blank Item 1.

5.  Type arkit under the Value category in the Item 1 row.

6.  Move the mouse pointer over the last row to display
    a plus (+) icon.

7.  Click on the plus (+) icon to create a new row. A
    popup menu appears.

8.  Choose Privacy – Camera Usage Description.

9.  Type AR needs to use the camera under the Value
    category in the Privacy – Camera Usage Description
    row.

Now it's time to modify the ViewController.swift file to use ARKit
and SceneKit by following these steps:

1.  Click on the ViewController.swift file in the
    Navigator pane.

2.  Edit the ViewController.swift file so it looks like
    this:

```
import UIKit
import SceneKit
import ARKit

class ViewController: UIViewController,
ARSCNViewDelegate {

    let configuration = ARWorldTrackingConfiguration()
```

```
override func viewDidLoad() {
    super.viewDidLoad()
    // Do any additional setup after loading the
    view, typically from a nib.

}

}
```

To view augmented reality in our app, add a single ARKit SceneKit View (ARSCNView) for displaying augmented reality with the camera view, as shown in Figure 6-1. The exact size of the ARSCNView doesn't matter.

**Figure 6-1.** *The user interface just needs a single ARSCNView*

After you've added a single ARKit SceneView to the user interface, you need to put constraints on those user interface items. To add constraints, choose Editor ➤ Resolve Auto Layout Issues ➤ Reset to Suggested Constraints at the bottom half of the menu under the All Views in Container category.

After designing the user interface, the next step is to connect the user interface items to the Swift code in the `ViewController.swift` file. To do this, follow these steps:

1.  Click the `Main.storyboard` file in the Navigator pane.

2.  Click the Assistant Editor icon or choose View ➤ Assistant Editor ➤ Show Assistant Editor to display the `Main.storyboard` and the `ViewController. swift` file side by side.

3.  Move the mouse pointer over the ARSCNView, hold down the Control key, and Ctrl-drag under the class ViewController line.

4.  Release the Control key and the left mouse button. A popup menu appears.

5.  Click in the Name text field and type sceneView, then click the Connect button. Xcode creates an IBOutlet, as shown here:

    **@IBOutlet var** sceneView: ARSCNView!

6.  Edit the `viewDidLoad` function so it looks like this:

    ```
    override func viewDidLoad() {
        super.viewDidLoad()
        // Do any additional setup after loading the
        view, typically from a nib.
        sceneView.delegate = self
    ```

```
            sceneView.showsStatistics = true
            sceneView.debugOptions = [ARSCNDebugOptions.
            showWorldOrigin, ARSCNDebugOptions.
            showFeaturePoints]
            showShape()
        }
```

7.  Edit the viewWillAppear function so it looks like this:

```
        override func viewWillAppear(_ animated: Bool) {
            super.viewWillAppear(animated)
            sceneView.session.run(configuration)
        }
```

This viewDidLoad function calls on a showShape function. The showShape function displays a sphere.

8.  Type the following underneath the viewWillAppear function:

```
        func showShape() {
            let sphere = SCNSphere(radius: 0.05)
            sphere.firstMaterial?.diffuse.contents =
            UIColor.orange

            let node = SCNNode()
            node.geometry = sphere
            node.position = SCNVector3(0.2, 0.1, -0.1)
            sceneView.scene.rootNode.addChildNode(node)
        }
```

The entire ViewController.swift file should look like this:

```
import UIKit
import SceneKit
import ARKit
```

```swift
class ViewController: UIViewController, ARSCNViewDelegate  {

    @IBOutlet var sceneView: ARSCNView!

    let configuration = ARWorldTrackingConfiguration()

    override func viewDidLoad() {
        super.viewDidLoad()
        // Do any additional setup after loading the view,
        typically from a nib.
        sceneView.delegate = self
        sceneView.showsStatistics = true
        sceneView.debugOptions = [ARSCNDebugOptions.
        showWorldOrigin, ARSCNDebugOptions.showFeaturePoints]
        showShape()
    }

    override func viewWillAppear(_ animated: Bool) {
        super.viewWillAppear(animated)

        sceneView.session.run(configuration)
    }

    func showShape() {
        let sphere = SCNSphere(radius: 0.05)
        sphere.firstMaterial?.diffuse.contents = UIColor.orange

        let node = SCNNode()
        node.geometry = sphere
        node.position = SCNVector3(0.2, 0.1, -0.1)
        sceneView.scene.rootNode.addChildNode(node)
    }

}
```

This app places an orange sphere at (0.2, 0.1, -0.1). To run this app, follow these steps:

1. Connect an iOS device to your Macintosh through its USB cable.

2. Click the Run button or choose Product ➤ Run.

3. When the app runs, an orange sphere appears.

4. Click the Stop button or choose Product ➤ Stop.

Now let's add a second virtual object, such as a green box, except we want it to appear 0.4 meters to the left (the x-axis), 0.3 meters lower (the y-axis), and 0.2 meters in front (the z-axis). To do this, we have to use math.

To make a virtual object appear 0.4 meters to the left of the first virtual object, we need to use a value of -.0.2 (0.2 – 0.4). To make it appear 0.3 meters lower, we need to use a value of -0.2 (0.1 – 0.3), and to make it appear 0.2 meters in front, we need to use a value of 0.1 (-0.1 + 0.2).

Edit the showShape function so it looks like this:

```
func showShape() {
    let sphere = SCNSphere(radius: 0.05)
    sphere.firstMaterial?.diffuse.contents = UIColor.orange

    let box = SCNBox(width: 0.2, height: 0.2, length: 0.2,
    chamferRadius: 0.0)
    box.firstMaterial?.diffuse.contents = UIColor.green
    let boxNode = SCNNode()
    boxNode.geometry = box
    boxNode.position = SCNVector3(-0.2, -0.2, 0.1) //0.4 meters
    to the left (the x-axis), 0.3 meters lower (the y-axis),
    and 0.2 meters in front (the z-axis)
    sceneView.scene.rootNode.addChildNode(boxNode)
```

```
    let node = SCNNode()
    node.geometry = sphere
    node.position = SCNVector3(0.2, 0.1, -0.1)
    sceneView.scene.rootNode.addChildNode(node)
}
```

If you run this modified showShape function, your app should show an orange sphere and a green box. The huge problem with this method of positioning a second virtual object based on the position of another virtual object is that you must calculate the distances between the two virtual objects manually, which makes this method error-prone.

Rather than calculate distances manually and hope you did it right, a far better solution is to simply define the distance you want one virtual object to appear away from another one.

Remember, when you define a position for a node (virtual object), using the SCNVector3 command, you're just defining the virtual object's position based on the rootnode's position, which is the world origin (0, 0, 0) like this:

```
node.position = SCNVector3(0.2, 0.1, -0.1)
sceneView.scene.rootNode.addChildNode(node)
```

Rather than place a virtual object (node) in relation to the rootnode (world origin), you can just place a virtual object in relation to another virtual object. Doing so avoids the hassle of doing the math to determine x, y, and z coordinates solely based on the world origin.

So if we want to place the box 0.4 meters to the left, 0.3 meters lower, and 0.2 meters in front of a virtual object, we can simply use those numbers like this:

```
boxNode.position = SCNVector3(-0.4, -0.3, 0.2)
```

After defining the position of this virtual object, we can then place it relative to another virtual object. Instead of adding the node to the rootnode, we can add it to the other virtual object like this:

```
node.addChildNode(boxNode)
```

Modify the showShape function like this:

```
func showShape() {
    let sphere = SCNSphere(radius: 0.05)
    sphere.firstMaterial?.diffuse.contents = UIColor.orange

    let box = SCNBox(width: 0.2, height: 0.2, length: 0.2,
    chamferRadius: 0.0)
    box.firstMaterial?.diffuse.contents = UIColor.green
    let boxNode = SCNNode()
    boxNode.geometry = box
    boxNode.position = SCNVector3(-0.4, -0.3, 0.2)

    let node = SCNNode()
    node.geometry = sphere
    node.position = SCNVector3(0.2, 0.1, -0.1)
    sceneView.scene.rootNode.addChildNode(node)

    node.addChildNode(boxNode)
}
```

This creates the exact same result of drawing a green box a specific distance from an orange sphere. The big difference is that instead of adding the green box to the rootnode and calculating its distance from the orange sphere, we just added the green box to the orange sphere and defined the distance along the x, y, and z axis to place the green box.

Relative positioning makes it easy to place virtual objects a fixed distance from another virtual object. Initially, you'll need to place one virtual object relative to the rootnode (the world origin of 0, 0, 0), but after that, you can place virtual objects relative to the location of other virtual objects.

# Combining Geometric Shapes

Once you know how to position virtual objects relative to one another, you can easily combine multiple geometric shapes to create interesting objects that you could never create using a single geometric shape. For example, you could create a pyramid on top of a box to create a house object, multiple cylinders with a sphere to create a stick figure, or a plane with a torus to create a basketball hoop.

To see how to use relative positioning to combine multiple geometric shapes together, let's create a snowman. The snowman will consist of three spheres stacked on top of each other with a hat on top, which we'll create with two cylinders.

First, we'll need to create three spheres stacked on top of each other. Let's start with one large sphere that will be positioned relative to the rootnode (the world origin at 0, 0, 0). Then we'll add progressively smaller spheres on top using relative positioning.

The first sphere gets positioned based on the rootnode 0.05 meters on the x-axis, 0.05 on the y-axis, and -0.05 on the z-axis like this:

```
let sphere = SCNSphere(radius: 0.04)
sphere.firstMaterial?.diffuse.contents = UIColor.red

let node = SCNNode()
node.geometry = sphere
node.position = SCNVector3(0.05, 0.05, -0.05)
sceneView.scene.rootNode.addChildNode(node)
```

This creates a red sphere positioned based on the rootnode, which appears at the world origin (0, 0, 0). Now let's create a second sphere in blue that appears on top of the red sphere. Instead of positioning this blue sphere in the augmented reality view by the rootnode (world origin), we'll use relative positioning and place it based on the location of the red sphere.

155

When placing virtual objects relative to another virtual object, you need to use trial and error to define specific distances until the virtual objects appear the way you want in relation to one another.

To place this second, blue sphere on top of the current red sphere, we can use the following code:

```
let middleSphere = SCNSphere(radius: 0.03)
middleSphere.firstMaterial?.diffuse.contents = UIColor.blue
let middleNode = SCNNode()
middleNode.geometry = middleSphere
middleNode.position = SCNVector3(0, 0.06, 0)
node.addChildNode(middleNode)
```

This code creates a sphere with a radius of 0.03 meters and colors it blue. Then it positions it at 0, 0.06, 0 based on the relative position of the red sphere. That means it appears 0.06 meters above the center of the red sphere.

Next, we need to create the third and top sphere. This top sphere has a radius of 0.02 meters and is colored white. We'll place this sphere on top of the middle sphere 0.04 meters above the middle sphere's center like this:

```
let topSphere = SCNSphere(radius: 0.02)
topSphere.firstMaterial?.diffuse.contents = UIColor.white
let topNode = SCNNode()
topNode.geometry = topSphere
topNode.position = SCNVector3(0, 0.04, 0)
middleNode.addChildNode(topNode)
```

Finally, let's add a black hat to the three spheres that make up a virtual snowman. The hat will consist of two cylinders. A wide, flattened cylinder will create the hat brim and a narrower and taller cylinder will make up the rest of the hat. The hat rim needs to be positioned relative to the top sphere like this:

```
let hatRim = SCNCylinder(radius: 0.03, height: 0.002)
hatRim.firstMaterial?.diffuse.contents = UIColor.black
let rimNode = SCNNode()
rimNode.geometry = hatRim
rimNode.position = SCNVector3(0, 0.016, 0)
topNode.addChildNode(rimNode)
```

The radius of the hat rim is 0.03 meters and its height is just 0.002 meters tall. This code colors the cylinder black and places it 0.016 meters above the center of the top sphere.

Finally, we need to complete the hat with a second black cylinder. This cylinder needs to be 0.01 meters above the hat rim with a smaller radius of 0.015 and a taller height of 0.025 meters like this:

```
let hatTop = SCNCylinder(radius: 0.015, height: 0.025)
hatTop.firstMaterial?.diffuse.contents = UIColor.black
let hatNode = SCNNode()
hatNode.geometry = hatTop
hatNode.position = SCNVector3(0, 0.01, 0)
rimNode.addChildNode(hatNode)
```

To see how to create a virtual snowman out of three spheres and two cylinders, follow these steps:

1.  Click the ViewController.swift file in the Navigator pane.

2.  Edit the showShape function so it looks like this:

    ```
    func showShape() {
        let sphere = SCNSphere(radius: 0.04)
        sphere.firstMaterial?.diffuse.contents = UIColor.red
    ```

```swift
let node = SCNNode()
node.geometry = sphere
node.position = SCNVector3(0.05, 0.05, -0.05)
sceneView.scene.rootNode.addChildNode(node)

let middleSphere = SCNSphere(radius: 0.03)
middleSphere.firstMaterial?.diffuse.contents =
UIColor.blue
let middleNode = SCNNode()
middleNode.geometry = middleSphere
middleNode.position = SCNVector3(0, 0.06, 0)
node.addChildNode(middleNode)

let topSphere = SCNSphere(radius: 0.02)
topSphere.firstMaterial?.diffuse.contents =
UIColor.white
let topNode = SCNNode()
topNode.geometry = topSphere
topNode.position = SCNVector3(0, 0.04, 0)
middleNode.addChildNode(topNode)

let hatRim = SCNCylinder(radius: 0.03, height: 0.002)
hatRim.firstMaterial?.diffuse.contents = UIColor.
black
let rimNode = SCNNode()
rimNode.geometry = hatRim
rimNode.position = SCNVector3(0, 0.016, 0)
topNode.addChildNode(rimNode)

let hatTop = SCNCylinder(radius: 0.015, height: 0.025)
hatTop.firstMaterial?.diffuse.contents = UIColor.
black
let hatNode = SCNNode()
hatNode.geometry = hatTop
```

```
        hatNode.position = SCNVector3(0, 0.01, 0)
        rimNode.addChildNode(hatNode)

    }
```

3.  Connect an iOS device to your Macintosh through its USB cable.

4.  Click the Run button or choose Product ➤ Run. Notice that the virtual snowman appears in the augmented reality view, as shown in Figure 6-2.

***Figure 6-2.*** *Three spheres and two cylinders create a virtual snowman*

5.  Click the Stop button or choose Product ➤ Stop

The entire ViewController.swift file should look like this:

```swift
import UIKit
import SceneKit
import ARKit

class ViewController: UIViewController, ARSCNViewDelegate  {

    @IBOutlet var sceneView: ARSCNView!

    let configuration = ARWorldTrackingConfiguration()

    override func viewDidLoad() {
        super.viewDidLoad()
        // Do any additional setup after loading the view,
        typically from a nib.
        sceneView.delegate = self
        sceneView.showsStatistics = true
        sceneView.debugOptions = [ARSCNDebugOptions.
        showWorldOrigin, ARSCNDebugOptions.showFeaturePoints]
        showShape()
    }

    override func viewWillAppear(_ animated: Bool) {
        super.viewWillAppear(animated)

        sceneView.session.run(configuration)
    }
```

```swift
func showShape() {
    let sphere = SCNSphere(radius: 0.04)
    sphere.firstMaterial?.diffuse.contents = UIColor.red

    let node = SCNNode()
    node.geometry = sphere
    node.position = SCNVector3(0.05, 0.05, -0.05)
    sceneView.scene.rootNode.addChildNode(node)

    let middleSphere = SCNSphere(radius: 0.03)
    middleSphere.firstMaterial?.diffuse.contents = UIColor.
blue
    let middleNode = SCNNode()
    middleNode.geometry = middleSphere
    middleNode.position = SCNVector3(0, 0.06, 0)
    node.addChildNode(middleNode)

    let topSphere = SCNSphere(radius: 0.02)
    topSphere.firstMaterial?.diffuse.contents = UIColor.
white
    let topNode = SCNNode()
    topNode.geometry = topSphere
    topNode.position = SCNVector3(0, 0.04, 0)
    middleNode.addChildNode(topNode)

    let hatRim = SCNCylinder(radius: 0.03, height: 0.002)
    hatRim.firstMaterial?.diffuse.contents = UIColor.black
    let rimNode = SCNNode()
    rimNode.geometry = hatRim
    rimNode.position = SCNVector3(0, 0.016, 0)
    topNode.addChildNode(rimNode)
```

```
        let hatTop = SCNCylinder(radius: 0.015, height: 0.025)
        hatTop.firstMaterial?.diffuse.contents = UIColor.black
        let hatNode = SCNNode()
        hatNode.geometry = hatTop
        hatNode.position = SCNVector3(0, 0.01, 0)
        rimNode.addChildNode(hatNode)

    }

}
```

# Summary

When placing virtual objects in an augmented reality view, each virtual object must be assigned to a node and that node needs x, y, and z coordinates to define its location. At least one virtual object needs to be located based on its distance from the rootnode, which represents the world origin (0, 0, 0). After placing at least one virtual object based on the rootnode, you can place additional virtual objects based on either the rootnode or any existing virtual objects.

Placing virtual objects based on the rootnode lets you define their location independent of any other virtual objects. However, if you want one virtual object to appear a fixed distance from a second virtual object, it's easier to use relative positioning. Instead of defining a virtual object based on its location to the rootnode, you define it based on its location to another virtual object.

Without relative positioning, you would have to calculate distances based on the rootnode, which can be inaccurate and cumbersome to do. Relative positioning makes it easy to define virtual objects a fixed distance from one another.

# CHAPTER 7

# Rotating Objects

When you place a virtual object in an augmented reality view, it always appears in its default orientation such as a cylinder or pyramid appearing vertically. However, sometimes you may want a virtual object to appear in a different orientation. To achieve this, you may need to rotate the virtual object around its x-, y-, and z-axes.

Rotating a virtual object involves changing a virtual object's Euler angle around its x-, y-, and z-axes. In addition to learning how to rotate virtual objects around the x-, y-, and z-axes, you'll also learn how Xcode rotates additional virtual objects positioned relative to an existing virtual object. For example, if you create a box and place a pyramid relative to box, rotating the box will also change the position of the pyramid.

## Rotating Objects Using Euler Angles

To rotate a virtual object, you need to define that virtual object's Euler angles like this:

```
node.eulerAngles = SCNVector3(x, y, z)
```

By specifying different values for x, y, and z, `eulerAngles` can define a virtual object's rotation around the x-, y-, and z-axes. When specifying `SCNVector3` values for the x-, y-, and z-axes, make sure you use `Float` values and that you specify the amount of rotation in radians.

© Wallace Wang 2018
W. Wang, *Beginning ARKit for iPhone and iPad*,
https://doi.org/10.1007/978-1-4842-4102-8_7

Since degrees are more familiar for most people to understand, we'll need to convert degrees to radians by relying on GLKit, which provides math libraries including a degree to radian conversion function. First, import GLKit like this:

```
import GLKit
```

Now use the `GLKMathDegreesToRadians` function and specify the rotation in degrees like this:

```
GLKMathDegreesToRadians(degrees)
```

This code converts degrees to radians. Once the degrees have been converted into radians, you can use those radians to define the rotation around the x-, y-, and z-axes.

To learn how to rotate a virtual object in an augmented reality view, let's start by creating a new Xcode project by following these steps:

1. Start Xcode. (Make sure you're using Xcode 10 or greater.)

2. Choose File ➤ New ➤ Project. Xcode asks you to choose a template.

3. Click the iOS category.

4. Click the Single View App icon and click the Next button. Xcode asks for a product name, organization name, organization identifiers, and content technology.

5. Click in the Product Name text field and type a descriptive name for your project, such as Rotation. (The exact name does not matter.)

6.  Click the Next button. Xcode asks where you want to store your project.

7.  Choose a folder and click the Create button. Xcode creates an iOS project.

Now modify the Info.plist to allow access to the camera and to use ARKit by following these steps:

1.  Click the `Info.plist` file in the Navigator pane. Xcode displays a list of keys, types, and values.

2.  Click the disclosure triangle to expand the Required device capabilities category to display Item 0.

3.  Move the mouse pointer over Item 0 to display a plus (+) icon.

4.  Click this plus (+) icon to display a blank Item 1.

5.  Type `arkit` under the Value category in the Item 1 row.

6.  Move the mouse pointer over the last row to display a plus (+) icon.

7.  Click on the plus (+) icon to create a new row. A popup menu appears.

8.  Choose Privacy – Camera Usage Description.

9.  Type **AR Needs to Use the Camera** under the Value category in the Privacy – Camera Usage Description row.

Now it's time to modify the `ViewController.swift` file to use ARKit and SceneKit by following these steps:

1.  Click on the `ViewController.swift` file in the Navigator pane.

2. Edit the ViewController.swift file so it looks like this:

```
import UIKit
import SceneKit
import ARKit
import GLKit

class ViewController: UIViewController,
ARSCNViewDelegate {

let configuration = ARWorldTrackingConfiguration()
    let node = SCNNode()

    var currentX : Float = 0
    var currentY : Float = 0
    var currentZ : Float = 0

    override func viewDidLoad() {
        super.viewDidLoad()
        // Do any additional setup after loading the
        view, typically from a nib.

    }

}
```

To view augmented reality in our app, add the following to the user interface on the Main.storyboard file:

- A single ARKit SceneKit View (ARSCNView)

- Three UILabels

- Three UISliders

The user interface should look similar to Figure 7-1.

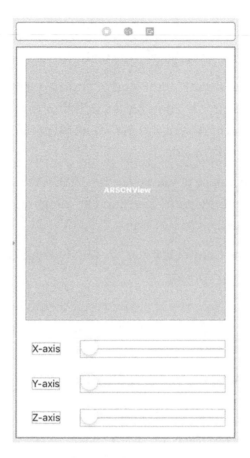

***Figure 7-1.*** *The user interface includes an ARSCNView, three labels, and three sliders*

After you've designed your user interface, you need to put constraints on those user interface items. To add constraints, choose Editor ➤ Resolve Auto Layout Issues ➤ Reset to Suggested Constraints at the bottom half of the menu under the All Views in Container category.

After designing the user interface, the next step is to connect the user interface items to the Swift code in the ViewController.swift file. To do this, follow these steps:

1. Click the Main.storyboard file in the Navigator pane.

2. Click the Assistant Editor icon or choose View ➤ Assistant Editor ➤ Show Assistant Editor to display the Main.storyboard and the ViewController. swift file side by side.

3. Move the mouse pointer over the ARSCNView, hold down the Control key, and Ctrl-drag under the class ViewController line.

4. Release the Control key and the left mouse button. A popup menu appears.

5. Click in the Name text field and type sceneView, then click the Connect button. Xcode creates an IBOutlet, as shown here:

   **@IBOutlet var** sceneView: ARSCNView!

6. Edit the viewDidLoad function so it looks like this:

```
override func viewDidLoad() {
    super.viewDidLoad()
    // Do any additional setup after loading the
    view, typically from a nib.
    sceneView.delegate = self
    sceneView.showsStatistics = true
    sceneView.debugOptions = [ARSCNDebugOptions.
    showWorldOrigin, ARSCNDebugOptions.
    showFeaturePoints]
    showShape()
}
```

7.  Edit the viewWillAppear function so it looks
    like this:

```
override func viewWillAppear(_ animated: Bool) {
    super.viewWillAppear(animated)
    sceneView.session.run(configuration)
}
```

This viewDidLoad function calls on a showShape
function. The showShape function displays a green
pyramid.

8.  Type the following underneath the viewWillAppear
    function:

```
func showShape() {
    let pyramid = SCNPyramid(width: 0.05, height:
    0.1, length: 0.05)
    pyramid.firstMaterial?.diffuse.contents =
    UIColor.green

    node.geometry = pyramid
    node.position = SCNVector3(0.05, 0.05, -0.05)
    sceneView.scene.rootNode.addChildNode(node)
}
```

9.  Click on the top slider (x-axis), hold down the Control
    key, and Ctrl-drag above the last curly bracket at the
    bottom of the ViewController.swift file.

10.  Release the Control key and the left mouse button.
     A popup menu appears.

11.  Click in the Connection popup menu and choose
     Action.

12.  Click in the Name text field and type XChanged.

13.  Click in the Type popup menu and choose UISlider.

14.  Click the Connect button. Xcode creates an
     IBAction method like this:

```
@IBAction func XChanged(_ sender: UISlider) {
    currentX = GLKMathDegreesToRadians(sender.
    value)
    node.eulerAngles = SCNVector3(currentX,
    currentY, currentZ)
}
```

15.  Click on the middle slider (y-axis), hold down the
     Control key, and Ctrl-drag above the last curly bracket
     at the bottom of the ViewController.swift file.

16.  Release the Control key and the left mouse button.
     A popup menu appears.

17.  Click in the Connection popup menu and choose
     Action.

18.  Click in the Name text field and type YChanged.

19.  Click in the Type popup menu and choose UISlider.

20.  Click the Connect button. Xcode creates an
     IBAction method like this:

```
@IBAction func YChanged(_ sender: UISlider) {
    currentY = GLKMathDegreesToRadians(sender.
    value)
    node.eulerAngles = SCNVector3(currentX,
    currentY, currentZ)
}
```

21.  Click on the bottom slider (z-axis), hold down the Control key, and Ctrl-drag above the last curly bracket at the bottom of the ViewController.swift file.

22.  Release the Control key and the left mouse button. A popup menu appears.

23.  Click in the Connection popup menu and choose Action.

24.  Click in the Name text field and type ZChanged.

25.  Click in the Type popup menu and choose UISlider.

26.  Click the Connect button. Xcode creates an IBAction method like this:

```
@IBAction func ZChanged(_ sender: UISlider) {
    currentZ = GLKMathDegreesToRadians(sender.
    value)
    node.eulerAngles = SCNVector3(currentX,
    currentY, currentZ)
}
```

The entire ViewController.swift file should look like this:

```
import UIKit
import SceneKit
import ARKit
import GLKit

class ViewController: UIViewController, ARSCNViewDelegate  {

    @IBOutlet var sceneView: ARSCNView!

    let configuration = ARWorldTrackingConfiguration()
    let node = SCNNode()
```

```swift
var currentX : Float = 0
var currentY : Float = 0
var currentZ : Float = 0

override func viewDidLoad() {
    super.viewDidLoad()
    // Do any additional setup after loading the view,
    typically from a nib.
    sceneView.delegate = self
    sceneView.showsStatistics = true
    sceneView.debugOptions = [ARSCNDebugOptions.
    showWorldOrigin, ARSCNDebugOptions.showFeaturePoints]
    showShape()
}

override func viewWillAppear(_ animated: Bool) {
    super.viewWillAppear(animated)

    sceneView.session.run(configuration)
}

func showShape() {
    let pyramid = SCNPyramid(width: 0.05, height: 0.1,
    length: 0.05)
    pyramid.firstMaterial?.diffuse.contents = UIColor.green

    node.geometry = pyramid
    node.position = SCNVector3(0.05, 0.05, -0.05)
    sceneView.scene.rootNode.addChildNode(node)
}

@IBAction func XChanged(_ sender: UISlider) {
    currentX = GLKMathDegreesToRadians(sender.value)
    node.eulerAngles = SCNVector3(currentX, currentY,
    currentZ)
}
```

```
@IBAction func YChanged(_ sender: UISlider) {
    currentY = GLKMathDegreesToRadians(sender.value)
    node.eulerAngles = SCNVector3(currentX, currentY,
    currentZ)
}

@IBAction func ZChanged(_ sender: UISlider) {
    currentZ = GLKMathDegreesToRadians(sender.value)
    node.eulerAngles = SCNVector3(currentX, currentY,
    currentZ)
}

}
```

This app places a green pyramid at (0.05, 0.05, -0.05). To run this app, follow these steps:

1.  Connect an iOS device to your Macintosh through its USB cable.

2.  Click the Run button or choose Product ➤ Run.

3.  When the app runs, a green pyramid appears.

4.  Slide the x-, y-, and z-axes sliders left and right. Notice that the green pyramid rotates around the x-, y-, or z-axis, depending on which slider you're moving at the time, as shown in Figure 7-2.

5.  Click the Stop button or choose Product ➤ Stop.

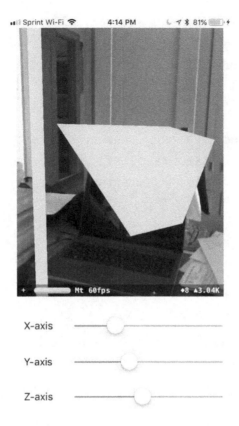

*Figure 7-2.* *The three sliders let you rotate the green pyramid around the x-, y-, and z-axes*

# Relational Object Rotation

By using Euler angles, it's easy to rotate a virtual object around its x-, y-, or z-axis. If you rotate an object, you may wonder what happens to any neighboring objects that are positioned relative to the rotating object. If you use relative positioning to place one virtual object next to another one, then rotating an object also causes any nearby objects to change their position too.

So if you have a green pyramid and use relative positioning to place an orange box next to the green pyramid, then rotating the green pyramid also moves the orange box. That's because the orange box uses relative positioning to place it a specific distance from the green pyramid. When the green pyramid rotates, the orange box changes its position as well.

Let's add a second virtual object, such as an orange box, and use relative positioning to place it 0.15 meters to the left (the x-axis), 0 meters on the y-axis, and 0 meters on the z-axis.

Edit the showShape function so it looks like this:

```
func showShape() {
    let pyramid = SCNPyramid(width: 0.05, height: 0.1,
    length: 0.05)
    pyramid.firstMaterial?.diffuse.contents = UIColor.green

    node.geometry = pyramid
    node.position = SCNVector3(0.05, 0.05, -0.05)
    sceneView.scene.rootNode.addChildNode(node)

    let box = SCNBox (width: 0.05, height: 0.05, length:
    0.05, chamferRadius: 0)
    box.firstMaterial?.diffuse.contents = UIColor.orange
    let boxNode = SCNNode()
    boxNode.geometry = box
    boxNode.position = SCNVector3(-0.15, 0, 0)
    node.addChildNode(boxNode)
}
```

This code creates an orange box that appears 0.15 meters to the left of the green pyramid. Since the orange box uses relative positioning based on the green pyramid's location, rotating the green pyramid automatically forces the orange box to change its position to maintain its fixed position to the green pyramid, as shown in Figure 7-3.

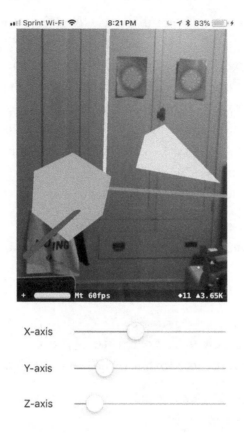

**Figure 7-3.** *Relative positioning automatically moves an object to maintain its fixed distance from another object*

Run this revised app and slide the x-axis, y-axis, and z-axis sliders left and right. Notice that the green pyramid rotates and forces the orange box to change its location based on the green pyramid's rotation.

Because the orange box is positioned relative to the green pyramid, rotating the green pyramid forces the orange box to move as well. What happens if we create a third virtual object that uses relative positioning with the orange box? Then rotating the pyramid will move the orange box, which in turn will move our third virtual object. Let's see how that works.

Rewrite the showShape function so it adds a red cylinder that uses relative positioning to orient itself according to the orange box's position. Now rotating the green pyramid moves the orange box, which maintains its position to the green pyramid, and also moves the red cylinder, which maintains its position to the orange box.

The showShape function should look like this:

```
func showShape() {
    let pyramid = SCNPyramid(width: 0.05, height: 0.1,
    length: 0.05)
    pyramid.firstMaterial?.diffuse.contents = UIColor.green

    node.geometry = pyramid
    node.position = SCNVector3(0.05, 0.05, -0.05)
    sceneView.scene.rootNode.addChildNode(node)

    let box = SCNBox (width: 0.05, height: 0.05, length:
    0.05, chamferRadius: 0)
    box.firstMaterial?.diffuse.contents = UIColor.orange
    let boxNode = SCNNode()
    boxNode.geometry = box
    boxNode.position = SCNVector3(-0.15, 0, 0)
    node.addChildNode(boxNode)

    let cylinder = SCNCylinder(radius: 0.04, height: 0.06)
    cylinder.firstMaterial?.diffuse.contents = UIColor.red
    let thirdNode = SCNNode()
    thirdNode.geometry = cylinder
    thirdNode.position = SCNVector3(0, -0.15, 0.1)
    boxNode.addChildNode(thirdNode)
}
```

This code creates a red cylinder with a radius of 0.04 meters and a height of 0.06 meters. Then it places it 0.15 meters below the orange box and 0.1 meters in front of the orange box. When you run this version of the app, move the x-, y-, and z-axes sliders and you'll see the green pyramid rotate and affect the position of the orange box, which in turn affects the position of the red cylinder, as shown in Figure 7-4.

**Figure 7-4.** *Relative positioning moves all related virtual objects*

At this point we have three virtual objects—a green pyramid, an orange box, and a red cylinder. However, we're only rotating the green pyramid. The orange box moves to maintain its relative position to the green pyramid and the red cylinder moves to maintain its relative position to the orange box.

What happens if we add a fourth virtual object that's only positioned according to the rootnode? In that case, rotating the green pyramid will have no effect on this fourth virtual object because this fourth virtual object only depends on the rootnode (world origin). Let's see this work.

Edit the showShape function to add a fourth virtual object, this time make it a blue torus like this:

```
let torus = SCNTorus(ringRadius: 0.02, pipeRadius: 0.004)
  torus.firstMaterial?.diffuse.contents = UIColor.blue
  let fourthNode = SCNNode()
  fourthNode.geometry = torus
  fourthNode.position = SCNVector3(0, -0.02, 0.1)
  sceneView.scene.rootNode.addChildNode(fourthNode)
```

Modify the showShape function like this:

```
func showShape() {
    let pyramid = SCNPyramid(width: 0.05, height: 0.1,
    length: 0.05)
    pyramid.firstMaterial?.diffuse.contents = UIColor.green

    node.geometry = pyramid
    node.position = SCNVector3(0.05, 0.05, -0.05)
    sceneView.scene.rootNode.addChildNode(node)

    let box = SCNBox (width: 0.05, height: 0.05,
    length: 0.05, chamferRadius: 0)
    box.firstMaterial?.diffuse.contents = UIColor.orange
    let boxNode = SCNNode()
    boxNode.geometry = box
    boxNode.position = SCNVector3(-0.15, 0, 0)
    node.addChildNode(boxNode)

    let cylinder = SCNCylinder(radius: 0.04, height: 0.06)
    cylinder.firstMaterial?.diffuse.contents = UIColor.red
    let thirdNode = SCNNode()
```

```
thirdNode.geometry = cylinder
thirdNode.position = SCNVector3(0, -0.15, 0.1)
boxNode.addChildNode(thirdNode)

let torus = SCNTorus(ringRadius: 0.02,
pipeRadius: 0.004)
torus.firstMaterial?.diffuse.contents = UIColor.blue
let fourthNode = SCNNode()
fourthNode.geometry = torus
fourthNode.position = SCNVector3(0, -0.02, 0.1)
sceneView.scene.rootNode.addChildNode(fourthNode)
}
```

Because the torus is positioned to the rootnode and not relative to any of the other virtual objects, rotating the green pyramid does not affect the position of the torus. This shows the difference between relative positioning and positioning to the rootnode when moving virtual objects in an augmented reality view.

# Summary

There are two ways to define a location of a virtual object in an augmented reality view. One, you can define the object's position in relation to the rootnode, which appears at the world origin (0, 0, 0). Two, you can define the object's position relative to another object's position.

To rotate an object, you need to define its Euler angles around the x-, y-, and z-axes. Euler angles use radians so you'll need to convert degrees to radians using a function stored in the GLKit framework. By using the GLKMathDegreesToRadians function, you can easily convert degrees to radians.

Rotating an object also changes the position of any nearby objects that are defined relative to the rotated object. Only objects positioned relative to the rootnode won't change when other objects are rotated.

# CHAPTER 8

# Drawing on the Screen

You've already seen how you can draw common geometric shapes in augmented reality such as cylinders, boxes, pyramids, and spheres. You've also seen how you can draw custom geometric shapes by defining starting and end points. Creating and displaying virtual objects on the screen typically occurs in code.

However, what if you want to give the user the choice of drawing items on the screen? That's what you'll learn in this chapter: how to let the user draw lines directly on an augmented reality view.

First, let's explain another debugging feature that you've been using all this time:

```
sceneView.showsStatistics = true
```

© Wallace Wang 2018
W. Wang, *Beginning ARKit for iPhone and iPad*,
https://doi.org/10.1007/978-1-4842-4102-8_8

This line of code shows the number of frames per second that the camera displays, as shown in Figure 8-1.

**Frames per second**

***Figure 8-1.*** *Viewing frames per second in an augmented reality app*

Frames per second defines how often the camera updates or renders its view. Each time the camera updates or renders its view (usually 60 frames per second), it runs a willRenderScene function like this:

```
func renderer(_ renderer: SCNSceneRenderer, willRenderScene
scene: SCNScene, atTime time: TimeInterval) {

}
```

So to draw something in an augmented reality view, we need to use this willRenderScene function to update or render an image on the screen.

To draw an item in an augmented reality, we need to create a new Xcode project by following these steps:

1.  Start Xcode. (Make sure you're using Xcode 10 or greater.)

2.  Choose File ➤ New ➤ Project. Xcode asks you to choose a template.

3.  Click the iOS category.

4.  Click the Single View App icon and click the Next button. Xcode asks for a product name, organization name, organization identifiers, and content technology.

5.  Click in the Product Name text field and type a descriptive name for your project, such as Drawing. (The exact name does not matter.)

6.  Click the Next button. Xcode asks where you want to store your project.

7.  Choose a folder and click the Create button. Xcode creates an iOS project.

Now modify the Info.plist file to allow access to the camera and to use ARKit by following these steps:

1.  Click the Info.plist file in the Navigator pane. Xcode displays a list of keys, types, and values.

2.  Click the disclosure triangle to expand the Required Device Capabilities category to display Item 0.

3.  Move the mouse pointer over Item 0 to display a plus (+) icon.

4.  Click this plus (+) icon to display a blank Item 1.

183

5.  Type arkit under the Value category in the Item
    1 row.

6.  Move the mouse pointer over the last row to display
    a plus (+) icon.

7.  Click on the plus (+) icon to create a new row.
    A popup menu appears.

8.  Choose Privacy – Camera Usage Description.

9.  Type AR needs to use the camera under the Value
    category in the Privacy – Camera Usage Description
    row.

Now it's time to modify the ViewController.swift file to use ARKit
and SceneKit by following these steps:

1.  Click on the ViewController.swift file in the
    Navigator pane.

2.  Edit the ViewController.swift file so it looks like this:

```swift
import UIKit
import SceneKit
import ARKit

class ViewController: UIViewController,
ARSCNViewDelegate {

let configuration = ARWorldTrackingConfiguration()

    override func viewDidLoad() {
        super.viewDidLoad()
        // Do any additional setup after loading the
        view, typically from a nib.

    }

}
```

To view augmented reality in our app, add a single ARKit SceneKit View (ARSCNView) and a UISwitch so the user interface looks similar to Figure 8-2.

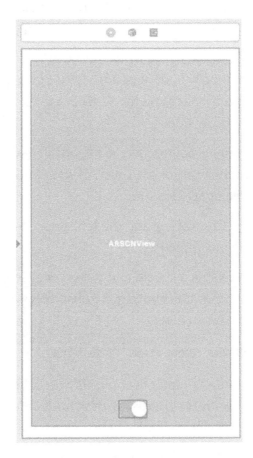

***Figure 8-2.*** *The user interface includes a single UISwitch on an ARSCNView*

After you've designed your user interface, you need to add constraints. To add constraints, choose Editor ➤ Resolve Auto Layout Issues ➤ Reset to Suggested Constraints at the bottom half of the menu under the All Views in Container category.

After designing the user interface, the next step is to connect the user interface items to the Swift code in the `ViewController.swift` file. To do this, follow these steps:

1. Click the `Main.storyboard` file in the Navigator pane.

2. Click the Assistant Editor icon or choose View ➤ Assistant Editor ➤ Show Assistant Editor to display the `Main.storyboard` and the `ViewController. swift` file side by side.

3. Move the mouse pointer over the ARSCNView, hold down the Control key, and Ctrl-drag under the `class ViewController` line.

4. Release the Control key and the left mouse button. A popup menu appears.

5. Click in the Name text field and type `sceneView`, then click the Connect button. Xcode creates an IBOutlet as shown here:

   **@IBOutlet var** `sceneView: ARSCNView!`

6. Move the mouse pointer over the UISwitch, hold down the Control key, and Ctrl-drag under the `IBOutlet sceneView` line.

7. Release the Control key and the left mouse button. A popup menu appears.

8. Click in the Name text field and type `switchDraw`, then click the Connect button. Xcode creates an IBOutlet as shown here:

   **@IBOutlet var** `switchDraw: UISwitch!`

9.  Edit the viewDidLoad function so it looks like this:

```
override func viewDidLoad() {
    super.viewDidLoad()
    // Do any additional setup after loading the
    view, typically from a nib.
    sceneView.delegate = self
    sceneView.showsStatistics = true
    sceneView.debugOptions = [ARSCNDebugOptions.
    showWorldOrigin, ARSCNDebugOptions.
    showFeaturePoints]
}
```

10. Edit the viewWillAppear function so it looks like this:

```
override func viewWillAppear(_ animated: Bool) {
    super.viewWillAppear(animated)
    sceneView.session.run(configuration)
}
```

11. Type the following underneath the viewWillAppear function:

```
func renderer(_ renderer: SCNSceneRenderer,
willRenderScene scene: SCNScene, atTime time:
TimeInterval) {

}
```

The renderer willRenderScene function runs every time the app updates the augmented reality view, which is usually 60 frames per second.

To draw on the augmented reality view, we must first retrieve the iOS device camera's location within the willRenderScene function. To do this, we can use the following, which retrieves the camera's position and direction:

```
guard let pov = sceneView.pointOfView else {return}
```

The guard statement just makes sure we get camera information from the iOS device. If for some reason we do not, then the guard statement immediately exits the willRenderScene function.

Assuming we get camera information from the iOS device, the next step is to transform this information into a 4 by 4 matrix that contains various information about the camera:

```
let transform = pov.transform
```

The third row of this 4 by 4 matrix contains the x, y, and z rotation of the camera. To retrieve this information, we need to use this code:

```
let rotation = SCNVector3(-transform.m31, -transform.m32,
-transform.m33)
```

Notice that there's a negative sign in front of each item retrieved from the third row of the matrix. This negative sign reverses the rotation information because without it, moving right on the x-axis would be negative (instead of positive), moving up on the y-axis would be negative (instead of positive), and moving back on the z-axis would be negative (instead of positive).

The rotation defines the camera's direction that it's facing. Next we need to retrieve the location of the camera from the fourth row of the 4 by 4 matrix like this:

```
let location = SCNVector3(transform.m41, transform.m42,
transform.m43)
```

Once we have the rotation and location of the camera, we need to add their x, y, and z coordinates to get the position of the camera like this:

```
let currentPosition = SCNVector3(rotation.x + location.x,
rotation.y + location.y, rotation.z + location.z)
```

The purpose of this app is to display a red pointer in the center of the screen. When the user turns the UISwitch to the On position, then the app will draw a green line wherever the user points the camera. To keep the app from drawing right away, let's turn the UISwitch to the Off position by following these steps:

1.  Click the `Main.storyboard` file in the Navigator pane. The user interface appears.

2.  Click on the UISwitch to select it.

3.  Click on the Show the Attributes Inspector icon or choose View ➤ Inspectors ➤ Show Attributes Inspector.

4.  Click on the State popup menu and choose Off (see Figure 8-3).

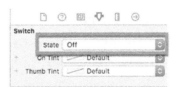

***Figure 8-3.*** *Changing the UISwitch State value to Off*

Now we need to write additional code inside the `renderer` function, which should currently look like this:

```
func renderer(_ renderer: SCNSceneRenderer, willRenderScene
scene: SCNScene, atTime time: TimeInterval) {
    guard let pov = sceneView.pointOfView else {return}
    let transform = pov.transform
```

189

```
let rotation = SCNVector3(-transform.m31, -transform.
m32, -transform.m33)
let location = SCNVector3(transform.m41, transform.m42,
transform.m43)
let currentPosition = SCNVector3(rotation.x +
location.x, rotation.y + location.y, rotation.z +
location.z)
```

    }

We need additional code inside this renderer function to determine whether to show the pointer or draw a line. Since this additional code will need to run at the same time that the app displays the augmented reality view from the camera, we need to use the DispatchQueue. This allows the app to show the camera and draw a line at the same time. A DispatchQueue simply defines code to run separately from the main code and looks like this:

```
DispatchQueue.main.async {


}
```

Inside this DispatchQueue, we need an if-else statement. If the UISwitch is turned on, then draw a line. Otherwise, display a pointer to show where the line will start to appear when the switch is turned on. This makes the DispatchQueue code look like this:

```
DispatchQueue.main.async {
    if self.switchDraw.isOn {
                // Draw a line
    } else {
                // Display a pointer
    }
}
```

First, let's add code to draw a green line in the augmented reality view. The first step is to create a node and define it as a sphere like this:

```
let drawNode = SCNNode()
drawNode.geometry = SCNSphere(radius: 0.01)
```

Next, we'll color the sphere green and place it at the current position that of the camera's location and rotation so it appears in the center of the augmented reality view:

```
drawNode.geometry?.firstMaterial?.diffuse.contents =
UIColor.green
drawNode.position = currentPosition
```

Then we'll need to add this green sphere to the rootnode (world origin) like this:

```
self.sceneView.scene.rootNode.addChildNode(drawNode)
```

The if portion of the DispatchQueue should look like this:

```
if self.switchDraw.isOn {
    let drawNode = SCNNode()
        drawNode.geometry = SCNSphere(radius: 0.01)
        drawNode.geometry?.firstMaterial?.diffuse.contents =
        UIColor.green
        drawNode.position = currentPosition
        self.sceneView.scene.rootNode.addChildNode(drawNode)
}
```

This code draws successive green spheres on the screen, creating the illusion of a line. Of course, the app only draws this green line if the UISwitch is set to On. If the user sets the UISwitch to Off, then the else portion of the if-else statement must run, which displays a pointer.

Let's create the pointer as a red sphere like this:

```
let point = SCNNode()
point.geometry = SCNSphere(radius: 0.005)
point.position = currentPosition
point.geometry?.firstMaterial?.diffuse.contents = UIColor.
red
```

Now we need to add it to the rootnode like this:

```
self.sceneView.scene.rootNode.addChildNode(point)
```

Just like creating a green sphere to draw a line, this code will display a red sphere and draw a line, which is not what we want. The problem is as the user moves the camera around, the app keeps drawing red spheres that creates the illusion of a line.

What we need is to draw a red sphere and then delete the previous red sphere so it does not create a line on the screen. To do that, we need the following code:

```
self.sceneView.scene.rootNode.enumerateChildNodes({ (node, _) in
    if node.name == "aiming point" {
        node.removeFromParentNode()
    }
})
```

The enumerateChildNodes creates a loop that examines every node connected to the rootnode. Then inside this loop we use the removeFromParentNode command to remove the node. This will delete all nodes connected to the rootnode, including our green line, so we need an if statement that checks if the node is called "aiming point". If so, then delete just that node.

That means we need to name the pointer node as "aiming point" like this:

```
point.name = "aiming point"
```

So the full DispatchQueue code should look like this:

```
DispatchQueue.main.async {
        if self.switchDraw.isOn {
    let drawNode = SCNNode()
    drawNode.geometry = SCNSphere(radius: 0.01)
    drawNode.geometry?.firstMaterial?.diffuse.contents =
    UIColor.green
    drawNode.position = currentPosition
    self.sceneView.scene.rootNode.addChildNode(drawNode)
    } else {
                let point = SCNNode()
        point.name = "aiming point"
        point.geometry = SCNSphere(radius: 0.005)
        point.position = currentPosition
        point.geometry?.firstMaterial?.diffuse.contents =
        UIColor.red
        self.sceneView.scene.rootNode.enumerateChildNodes
        ({ (node, _) in
                    if node.name == "aiming point" {
                        node.removeFromParentNode()
                    }
            })

        self.sceneView.scene.rootNode.addChildNode(point)
        }
    }
```

The entire `ViewController.swift` file should now look like this:

```swift
import UIKit
import SceneKit
import ARKit

class ViewController: UIViewController, ARSCNViewDelegate {

    @IBOutlet var sceneView: ARSCNView!
    @IBOutlet var switchDraw: UISwitch!

    let configuration = ARWorldTrackingConfiguration()

    override func viewDidLoad() {
        super.viewDidLoad()
        // Do any additional setup after loading the view,
        typically from a nib.
        sceneView.delegate = self
        sceneView.showsStatistics = true
        sceneView.debugOptions = [ARSCNDebugOptions.
        showWorldOrigin, ARSCNDebugOptions.showFeaturePoints]
    }

    override func viewWillAppear(_ animated: Bool) {
        super.viewWillAppear(animated)

        sceneView.session.run(configuration)
    }

    func renderer(_ renderer: SCNSceneRenderer, willRenderScene
    scene: SCNScene, atTime time: TimeInterval) {
        guard let pov = sceneView.pointOfView else {return}
        let transform = pov.transform
```

```
let rotation = SCNVector3(-transform.m31, -transform.
m32, -transform.m33)
let location = SCNVector3(transform.m41, transform.m42,
transform.m43)
let currentPosition = SCNVector3(rotation.x + location.x,
rotation.y + location.y, rotation.z + location.z)

DispatchQueue.main.async {
    if self.switchDraw.isOn {
        let drawNode = SCNNode()
        drawNode.geometry = SCNSphere(radius: 0.01)
        drawNode.geometry?.firstMaterial?.diffuse.
        contents = UIColor.green
        drawNode.position = currentPosition
        self.sceneView.scene.rootNode.
        addChildNode(drawNode)

    } else {
        let point = SCNNode()
        point.name = "aiming point"
        point.geometry = SCNSphere(radius: 0.005)
        point.position = currentPosition
        point.geometry?.firstMaterial?.diffuse.contents
        = UIColor.red

        self.sceneView.scene.rootNode.
        enumerateChildNodes({ (node, _) in
            if node.name == "aiming point" {
                node.removeFromParentNode()
            }
        })
```

```
            self.sceneView.scene.rootNode.
            addChildNode(point)
        }
      }
   }
}
```

Modify the code in your `ViewController.swift` file to match the code. Then, to see the app run, do the following:

1. Connect an iOS device to your Macintosh through its USB cable.

2. Click the Run button or choose Product ➤ Run.

3. When the app runs, move the iOS device around to see the red pointer in the middle of the screen.

4. Tap the UISwitch to turn it On.

5. Move the iOS device around and notice that it now draws a green line.

6. Tap the UISwitch to turn it Off.

7. Move the iOS device to a new location.

8. Tap the UISwitch to turn it On.

9. Move the iOS device to draw a separate green line (see Figure 8-4).

10. Click the Stop button or choose Product ➤ Stop.

**Figure 8-4.** *Drawing a line in augmented reality*

To polish this app, we need one more feature. You may notice that you can turn the UISwitch on to draw a green line, then turn the UISwitch off again to move the camera to a new location. Now if you turn the UISwitch back on again, you can draw a green line somewhere else in the augmented reality view.

However, if we keep adding green lines, eventually the screen gets filled with green lines. So let's add a simple feature to let us clear the entire screen by following these steps:

1. Click the Main.storyboard file in the Navigator pane.

2. Add a UIButton to the user interface.

197

3. Change the title of the UIButton to Clear. You may also want to resize the button to make it wider.

4. Click the Show the Attributes Inspector icon or choose View ➤ Inspectors ➤ Show Attributes Inspector.

5. Change the background color of the UIButton to white (see Figure 8-5).

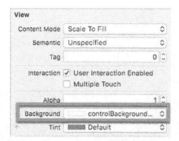

***Figure 8-5.*** *Changing the background color of a UIButton*

6. Choose Editor ➤ Resolve AutoLayout Issues ➤ Reset to Suggested Constraints.

7. Click the Show Assistant Editor icon or choose View ➤ Assistant Editor ➤ Show Assistant Editor. Xcode displays your Main.storyboard file and ViewController.swift file side by side.

8. Move the mouse pointer over the UIButton, hold down the Control key, and Ctrl-drag underneath the IBOutlet. A popup window appears.

9. Click in the Name text field and type clearButton.

10. Click the Connect button. Xcode creates an IBOutlet as follows:

    **@IBOutlet var** clearButton: UIButton!

198

11.  Click the Show Standard Editor icon or choose View
➤ Standard Editor ➤ Show Standard Editor.

12.  Click on the ViewController.swift file.

13.  Add the following code to the bottom of the
DispatchQueue code:

```
if self.clearButton.isHighlighted {
  self.sceneView.scene.rootNode.enumerateChildNodes
  ({ (node, _) in
    node.removeFromParentNode()
  })
}
```

The entire ViewController.swift file should look like this:

```
import UIKit
import SceneKit
import ARKit

class ViewController: UIViewController, ARSCNViewDelegate {

    @IBOutlet var sceneView: ARSCNView!
    @IBOutlet var switchDraw: UISwitch!
    @IBOutlet var clearButton: UIButton!

    let configuration = ARWorldTrackingConfiguration()

    override func viewDidLoad() {
        super.viewDidLoad()
        // Do any additional setup after loading the view,
        typically from a nib.
        sceneView.delegate = self
        sceneView.showsStatistics = true
```

```
    sceneView.debugOptions = [ARSCNDebugOptions.
    showWorldOrigin, ARSCNDebugOptions.showFeaturePoints]
}

override func viewWillAppear(_ animated: Bool) {
    super.viewWillAppear(animated)

    sceneView.session.run(configuration)
}

func renderer(_ renderer: SCNSceneRenderer, willRenderScene
scene: SCNScene, atTime time: TimeInterval) {
    guard let pov = sceneView.pointOfView else {return}
    let transform = pov.transform

    let rotation = SCNVector3(-transform.m31, -transform.
    m32, -transform.m33)
    let location = SCNVector3(transform.m41, transform.m42,
    transform.m43)
    let currentPosition = SCNVector3(rotation.x + location.x,
    rotation.y + location.y, rotation.z + location.z)

    DispatchQueue.main.async {
        if self.switchDraw.isOn {
            let drawNode = SCNNode()
            drawNode.geometry = SCNSphere(radius: 0.01)
            drawNode.geometry?.firstMaterial?.diffuse.
            contents = UIColor.green
            drawNode.position = currentPosition
            self.sceneView.scene.rootNode.
            addChildNode(drawNode)
```

```
        } else {
            let point = SCNNode()
            point.name = "aiming point"
            point.geometry = SCNSphere(radius: 0.005)
            point.position = currentPosition
            point.geometry?.firstMaterial?.diffuse.contents
            = UIColor.red

            self.sceneView.scene.rootNode.
            enumerateChildNodes({ (node, _) in
                if node.name == "aiming point" {
                    node.removeFromParentNode()
                }
            })

            self.sceneView.scene.rootNode.
            addChildNode(point)
        }
        if self.clearButton.isHighlighted {
            self.sceneView.scene.rootNode.
            enumerateChildNodes({ (node, _) in
                node.removeFromParentNode()
            })
        }

    }
  }
}
```

To see the app run, do the following:

1. Connect an iOS device to your Macintosh through its USB cable.

2. Click the Run button or choose Product ➤ Run.

3.  When the app runs, move the iOS device around to see the red pointer in the middle of the screen.

4.  Tap the UISwitch to turn it On.

5.  Move the iOS device around and notice that it now draws a green line.

6.  Tap the UISwitch to turn it Off.

7.  Move the iOS device to a new location.

8.  Tap the UISwitch to turn it On.

9.  Move the iOS device to draw a separate green line.

10. Tap the Clear button. Notice that the app now clears all the green lines you've drawn.

11. Click the Stop button or choose Product ➤ Stop.

# Summary

An augmented reality app relies on the camera in an iOS device. This camera typically refreshes images at the rate of 60 frames per second (fps). You can view the number of frames per second that your app displays by adding this line of code:

```
sceneView.showsStatistics = true)
```

The `renderer` function runs each time the app updates the image displayed, which is 60 frames per second. By drawing objects inside the `renderer` function, your app can constantly draw an image. In our example app, we drew a sphere but since the `renderer` function constantly drew a sphere, it drew multiple spheres. When the user moves the camera, this draws multiple green spheres that create the illusion of drawing a line.

To clear virtual objects, we can use the `enumerateChildNodes` loop that examines each node:

```
self.sceneView.scene.rootNode.enumerateChildNodes({ (node, _) in

})
```

To avoid removing all nodes, we can name a node and then use an `if` statement to remove only certain named nodes. Drawing in an augmented reality view requires getting the camera's current rotation and location so that the app can draw virtual objects wherever the user points the camera.

# CHAPTER 9

# Adding Touch Gestures to Augmented Reality

Up until now, we've created augmented reality apps that display virtual objects on the screen. What gives augmented reality a greater sense of existing in front of your eyes is when you can interact with virtual objects.

Naturally, you won't be able to touch or manipulate any virtual objects with your hand, but you can touch and manipulate virtual objects through the augmented reality view on your iOS screen. This means you can tap, drag, and manipulate items on the screen with your fingertips. Interacting with augmented reality can create a greater sense of realism.

Some of the different kinds of gestures available include:

- Tap—A brief touch on the screen before lifting the finger up

- Long press—Press a finger on the screen and hold it there for a period of time

- Swipe—Slide a finger left or right across an area

- Pan—Press a finger on the screen and then slide it across the screen

© Wallace Wang 2018
W. Wang, *Beginning ARKit for iPhone and iPad*,
https://doi.org/10.1007/978-1-4842-4102-8_9

- Pinch—A two-finger gesture that moves the two fingertips closer or farther apart

- Rotation—A two-finger gesture that moves the two fingertips in a circular motion

To interact with virtual objects in augmented reality, we must first detect a touch gesture such as a tap or a swipe. Once we can detect a touch gesture, our next step is to identify if the touch gesture touched a virtual object or not.

To detect a touch gesture in an augmented reality view, we need to create a new Xcode project by following these steps:

1. Start Xcode. (Make sure you're using Xcode 10 or greater.)

2. Choose File ➤ New ➤ Project. Xcode asks you to choose a template.

3. Click the iOS category.

4. Click the Single View App icon and click the Next button. Xcode asks for a product name, organization name, organization identifiers, and content technology.

5. Click in the Product Name text field and type a descriptive name for your project such as TouchGesture. (The exact name does not matter.)

6. Click the Next button. Xcode asks where you want to store your project.

7. Choose a folder and click the Create button. Xcode creates an iOS project.

Now modify the Info.plist file to allow access to the camera and to use ARKit by following these steps:

1.  Click the Info.plist file in the Navigator pane. Xcode displays a list of keys, types, and values.

2.  Click the disclosure triangle to expand the Required device capabilities category to display Item 0.

3.  Move the mouse pointer over Item 0 to display a plus (+) icon.

4.  Click this plus (+) icon to display a blank Item 1.

5.  Type arkit under the Value category in the Item 1 row.

6.  Move the mouse pointer over the last row to display a plus (+) icon.

7.  Click on the plus (+) icon to create a new row. A popup menu appears.

8.  Choose Privacy – Camera Usage Description.

9.  Type AR needs to use the camera under the Value category in the Privacy – Camera Usage Description row.

Now it's time to modify the ViewController.swift file to use ARKit and SceneKit by following these steps:

1.  Click on the ViewController.swift file in the Navigator pane.

2.  Edit the ViewController.swift file so it looks like this:

    ```swift
    import UIKit
    import SceneKit
    import ARKit

    class ViewController: UIViewController, ARSCNViewDelegate {

    let configuration = ARWorldTrackingConfiguration()
    ```

```
override func viewDidLoad() {
    super.viewDidLoad()
    // Do any additional setup after loading the
    view, typically from a nib.

}

}
```

To view augmented reality in our app, add a single ARKit SceneKit View (ARSCNView) so the user interface looks similar to Figure 9-1.

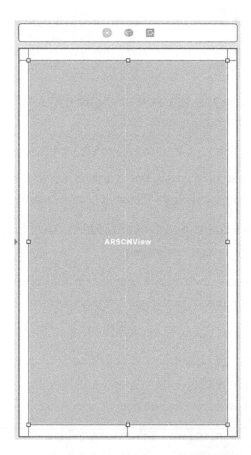

***Figure 9-1.*** *The user interface includes a single ARSCNView*

After you've designed your user interface, you need to add constraints. To add constraints, choose Editor ➤ Resolve Auto Layout Issues ➤ Reset to Suggested Constraints at the bottom half of the menu under the All Views in Container category.

The next step is to connect the user interface items to the Swift code in the `ViewController.swift` file. To do this, follow these steps:

1. Click the `Main.storyboard` file in the Navigator pane.

2. Click the Assistant Editor icon or choose View ➤ Assistant Editor ➤ Show Assistant Editor to display the `Main.storyboard` and the `ViewController.swift` file side by side.

3. Move the mouse pointer over the ARSCNView, hold down the Control key, and Ctrl-drag under the `class ViewController` line.

4. Release the Control key and the left mouse button. A popup menu appears.

5. Click in the Name text field and type `sceneView`, then click the Connect button. Xcode creates an IBOutlet as shown here:

   ```
   @IBOutlet var sceneView: ARSCNView!
   ```

6. Edit the `viewDidLoad` function so it looks like this:

   ```
   override func viewDidLoad() {
       super.viewDidLoad()
       // Do any additional setup after loading the
       view, typically from a nib.
       sceneView.delegate = self
       sceneView.showsStatistics = true
   ```

```
            sceneView.debugOptions = [ARSCNDebugOptions.
            showWorldOrigin, ARSCNDebugOptions.
            showFeaturePoints]
        }
```

7.  Edit the viewWillAppear function so it looks like this:

```
        override func viewWillAppear(_ animated: Bool) {
            super.viewWillAppear(animated)
            sceneView.session.run(configuration)
        }
```

# Recognizing Touch Gestures

There's a three-step process to recognizing touch gestures in an app:

- Create a function to handle the touch gesture when it's recognized

- Define a UIGestureRecognizer class that identifies the function to handle touch gestures

- Add the Touch Gesture Recognizer to the ARKit Scene View

First, you need to create a function that will run when your app recognizes a touch gesture. Unlike other functions, this touch gesture function needs the @objc keyword in front of it. This allows the function to access Objective-C code used to create Apple's frameworks, some of which still use Objective-C. The basic structure of a function to handle touch gestures looks like this, where handleTap is any arbitrary function name you choose:

```
@objc func handleTap() {

}
```

Second, you need to use the UITapGestureRecognizer class to define the function that will handle the tap gesture like this:

```
let tapGesture = UITapGestureRecognizer(target: self, action: #selector(handleTap))
```

If you want to detect other types of gestures such as rotation or pan, then you would need to use a different class such as UIRotationGestureRecognizer or UIPanGestureRecognizer.

The #selector keyword identifies the function name that will handle the touch gesture. The actual name, such as tapGesture, is arbitrary.

Finally, the third step is to add the gesture recognizer to the augmented reality scene like this:

```
sceneView.addGestureRecognizer(tapGesture)
```

This code adds the touch gesture (such as tapGesture) to the scene (sceneView), but both are arbitrary names that you can replace with anything else. This line then makes the scene (sceneView) able to recognize touch gestures and handle them through the @obj function you defined.

Detecting touch gestures can be fairly simple, so let's see how that works by following these steps:

1.  Click the Main.storyboard file in the Navigator pane. The user interface appears.

2.  Click the Assistant Editor icon or choose View ➤ Assistant Editor ➤ Show Assistant Editor to show the Main.storyboard and ViewController.swift file side by side.

3.  Move the mouse pointer over the ARSCNView, hold down the Control key, and Ctrl-drag under the class ViewController line in the ViewController. swift file.

4.  Release the Control key and the left mouse button.
    A window pops up.

5.  Click in the Name text field and type sceneView.

6.  Click the Connect button. Xcode creates an IBOutlet
    as follows:

    ```
    @IBOutlet var sceneView: ARSCNView!
    ```

7.  Edit the viewDidLoad function so it looks like this:

    ```
    override func viewDidLoad() {
        super.viewDidLoad()
        // Do any additional setup after loading the
        view, typically from a nib.
        sceneView.delegate = self
        sceneView.showsStatistics = true
        sceneView.debugOptions = [ARSCNDebugOptions.
        showWorldOrigin, ARSCNDebugOptions.
        showFeaturePoints]

        let tapGesture = UITapGestureRecognizer
        (target: self, action: #selector(handleTap))
        sceneView.addGestureRecognizer(tapGesture)
    }
    ```

8.  Underneath this viewDidLoad function, add the
    following two functions:

    ```
    override func viewWillAppear(_ animated: Bool) {
        super.viewWillAppear(animated)
        sceneView.session.run(configuration)
    }
    ```

```
@objc func handleTap() {
    print ("tap detected")
}
```

9. Connect an iOS device to your Macintosh through its USB cable.

10. Click the Run button or choose Product ➤ Run.

11. Tap anywhere on the screen when the camera view appears. Notice that each time you tap the screen, Xcode prints "tap detected" in the bottom pane of the Xcode window.

12. Click the Stop button or choose Product ➤ Stop.

Once we have the app to recognize taps anywhere on augmented reality view, the next step is to detect when those tap gestures occur over a virtual object such as a sphere or a box.

# Identifying Touch Gestures on Virtual Objects

Once you can identify touch gestures on an augmented reality view, the next step is to identify when those touch gestures occur on a virtual object. To do this, we need to modify our function that handles touch gestures. Currently, it looks like this:

```
@objc func handleTap() {

}
```

We need to modify this slightly so the function receives information about what the user actually tapped on the screen:

```
@objc func handleTap(sender: UITapGestureRecognizer) {

}
```

213

This information from the UITapGestureRecognizer can tell us whether the user tapped on a virtual object or not. First, we need to get the area or view of the tapped portion of the screen like this:

```
let areaTapped = sender.view as! SCNView
```

Once we know the area tapped, we need to get the actual coordinates of that area like this:

```
let tappedCoordinates = sender.location(in: areaTapped)
```

Now we need to determine if there is any virtual objects in the tapped area using a function called hitTest. This hitTest function does the hard work of identifying virtual objects within a specific set of coordinates:

```
let hitTest = areaTapped.hitTest(tappedCoordinates)
```

We need an if-else statement to respond depending if the hitTest identified a virtual object or not:

```
    if hitTest.isEmpty {

    } else {

    }
```

If the hitTest function fails to identify a virtual object, isEmpty should be true, so let's put a simple print statement inside to verify this:

```
    if hitTest.isEmpty {
        print ("Nothing")
    } else {

    }
```

If the `hitTest` function identifies a virtual object, it stores this information in an array, so we need to retrieve the first item from this array:

```
let results = hitTest.first!
```

Now we'll retrieve the name of the virtual object identified by the `hitTest` function and print it:

```
let name = results.node.name
print(name ?? "background")
```

The `print` statement on the second line either prints the name of the virtual object found or if a name hasn't been assigned to the virtual object, it defaults to printing "background" instead. That's because the `hitTest` function isn't always accurate so if you tap away from a virtual object like the pyramid or box, it might detect a background image as a virtual object.

The entire `handleTap` function should look like this:

```
@objc func handleTap(sender: UITapGestureRecognizer) {
    let areaTapped = sender.view as! SCNView
    let tappedCoordinates = sender.location(in: areaTapped)
    let hitTest = areaTapped.hitTest(tappedCoordinates)
    if hitTest.isEmpty {
        print ("Nothing")
    } else {
        let results = hitTest.first!
        let name = results.node.name
        print(name ?? "background")
    }
}
```

To see how the hitTest function works, we need to create one or more virtual objects, give each virtual object a name, and place it in the augmented reality view. This means creating an addShapes function like this:

```
func addShapes() {
    let node = SCNNode(geometry: SCNBox(width: 0.05,
    height: 0.05, length: 0.05, chamferRadius: 0))
    node.position = SCNVector3(0.1,0,-0.1)
    node.geometry?.firstMaterial?.diffuse.contents =
    UIColor.blue
    node.name = "box"
    sceneView.scene.rootNode.addChildNode(node)

    let node2 = SCNNode(geometry: SCNPyramid(width: 0.05,
    height: 0.06, length: 0.05))
    node2.position = SCNVector3(0.1,0.1,-0.1)
    node2.geometry?.firstMaterial?.diffuse.contents =
    UIColor.red
    node2.name = "pyramid"
    sceneView.scene.rootNode.addChildNode(node2)
}
```

Modify the entire ViewController.swift file so it looks like this:

```
import UIKit
import SceneKit
import ARKit

class ViewController: UIViewController, ARSCNViewDelegate {

    @IBOutlet var sceneView: ARSCNView!
    let configuration = ARWorldTrackingConfiguration()
```

```swift
override func viewDidLoad() {
    super.viewDidLoad()
    // Do any additional setup after loading the view,
    typically from a nib.
    sceneView.delegate = self
    sceneView.showsStatistics = true
    sceneView.debugOptions = [ARSCNDebugOptions.
    showWorldOrigin, ARSCNDebugOptions.showFeaturePoints]

    let tapGesture = UITapGestureRecognizer(target: self,
    action: #selector(handleTap))
    sceneView.addGestureRecognizer(tapGesture)

    addShapes()
}

override func viewWillAppear(_ animated: Bool) {
    super.viewWillAppear(animated)
    sceneView.session.run(configuration)
}

func addShapes() {
    let node = SCNNode(geometry: SCNBox(width: 0.05,
    height: 0.05, length: 0.05, chamferRadius: 0))
    node.position = SCNVector3(0.1,0,-0.1)
    node.geometry?.firstMaterial?.diffuse.contents =
    UIColor.blue
    node.name = "box"
    sceneView.scene.rootNode.addChildNode(node)

    let node2 = SCNNode(geometry: SCNPyramid(width: 0.05,
    height: 0.06, length: 0.05))
    node2.position = SCNVector3(0.1,0.1,-0.1)
```

```
        node2.geometry?.firstMaterial?.diffuse.contents =
        UIColor.red
        node2.name = "pyramid"
        sceneView.scene.rootNode.addChildNode(node2)
    }

    @objc func handleTap(sender: UITapGestureRecognizer) {
        let areaTapped = sender.view as! SCNView
        let tappedCoordinates = sender.location(in: areaTapped)
        let hitTest = areaTapped.hitTest(tappedCoordinates)
        if hitTest.isEmpty {
            print ("Nothing")
        } else {
            let results = hitTest.first!
            let name = results.node.name
            print(name ?? "background")
        }
    }

}
```

To test this app, follow these steps:

1.  Connect an iOS device to your Macintosh through its USB cable.

2.  Click the Run button or choose Product ➤ Run.

3.  Tap anywhere on the screen. The bottom debug pane of Xcode should display "Nothing" or "background".

4.  Tap on the pyramid. The bottom debug pane of Xcode should display "pyramid".

5.   Tap on the box. The bottom debug pane of Xcode
     should display "box". Notice each time you tap on
     the pyramid or box, your app identifies it by name.
     Each time you tap away from the pyramid and box,
     the app identifies is as "Nothing" or "background".

6.   Click the Stop button or choose Product ➤ Stop.

# Identifying Swipe Gestures on Virtual Objects

Besides detecting taps on a virtual object, you may also want to allow the
user to swipe across a virtual object. Swiping can involve one or more
fingertips that move up, down, left, or right. For each swipe gesture you
want to detect (up, down, left, or right), you have to define a separate
UISwipeGestureRecognizer like this:

```
let swipeRightGesture = UISwipeGestureRecognizer
(target: self, action: #selector(handleSwipe))

let swipeLeftGesture = UISwipeGestureRecognizer(target:
self, action: #selector(handleSwipe))

let swipeUpGesture = UISwipeGestureRecognizer(target:
self, action: #selector(handleSwipe))

let swipeDownGesture = UISwipeGestureRecognizer(target:
self, action: #selector(handleSwipe))
```

Each Swipe Gesture Recognizer can define the same function to
handle the swipe. In these examples, all four gestures are handled by a
function called handleSwipe.

By default, each swipe gesture only requires a single fingertip. If you want, you can require two or more fingertips by defining a numberOfTouchesRequired property, such as:

```swift
let swipeRightGesture = UISwipeGestureRecognizer
(target: self, action: #selector(handleSwipe))
swipeRightGesture.direction = .right
swipeRightGesture.numberOfTouchesRequired = 2
```

If you don't define the numberofTouchesRequired, Xcode defaults to 1 for a single fingertip to swipe. Most importantly, you must define a direction for the swipe gesture and add it to the scene. So if you want to detect all four swipe gestures, you need to define each swipe gestures separately like this:

```swift
let swipeRightGesture = UISwipeGestureRecognizer(target:
self, action: #selector(handleSwipe))
   swipeRightGesture.direction = .right
   sceneView.addGestureRecognizer(swipeRightGesture)

let swipeLeftGesture = UISwipeGestureRecognizer(target:
self, action: #selector(handleSwipe))
   swipeLeftGesture.direction = .left
   sceneView.addGestureRecognizer(swipeLeftGesture)

let swipeUpGesture = UISwipeGestureRecognizer(target:
self, action: #selector(handleSwipe))
   swipeUpGesture.direction = .up
   sceneView.addGestureRecognizer(swipeUpGesture)

let swipeDownGesture = UISwipeGestureRecognizer(target:
self, action: #selector(handleSwipe))
   swipeDownGesture.direction = .down
   sceneView.addGestureRecognizer(swipeDownGesture)
```

Once we've defined the four swipe gestures, the next step is to write the handleSwipe function to respond to the swipe. For this example, we'll detect both the swipe gesture and the object that the swipe gesture occurred on, such as on a virtual object.

The handleSwipe function needs to receive the UISwipeGestureRecognizer data like this:

```
@objc func handleSwipe(sender: UISwipeGestureRecognizer) {

}
```

Now we need to identify the swiped area by receiving the view, getting the coordinates of the touched area, and then using the hitTest method to identify where in the view the user swiped:

```
@objc func handleSwipe(sender: UISwipeGestureRecognizer) {
    let areaSwiped = sender.view as! SCNView
    let tappedCoordinates = sender.location(in: areaSwiped)
    let hitTest = areaSwiped.hitTest(tappedCoordinates)
}
```

Once we get the area swiped, we can respond by determining what the user may have swiped on and the direction the user swiped like this:

```
@objc func handleSwipe(sender: UISwipeGestureRecognizer) {
    let areaSwiped = sender.view as! SCNView
    let tappedCoordinates = sender.location(in: areaSwiped)
    let hitTest = areaSwiped.hitTest(tappedCoordinates)

    if hitTest.isEmpty {
        print ("Nothing")
    } else {
        let results = hitTest.first!
        let name = results.node.name
        print(name ?? "background")
    }
```

```
switch sender.direction {
case.up:
    print("Up")
case .down:
    print("Down")
case .right:
    print("Right")
case .left:
    print("Left")
default:
    break
}
}
```

To test this app, follow these steps:

1. Connect an iOS device to your Macintosh through its USB cable.

2. Click the Run button or choose Product ➤ Run.

3. Swipe anywhere on the screen. The bottom debug pane of Xcode should display the direction of your swipe. If you swiped over the box or pyramid, then you should also see the name of the virtual object as well.

4. Swipe on the pyramid. The bottom debug pane of Xcode should display "pyramid".

5. Swipe on the box. The bottom debug pane of Xcode should display "box". Notice each time you swipe across the pyramid or box, your app identifies it by name. Each time you swipe away from the pyramid and box, the app identifies it as "Nothing" or "background".

6. Click the Stop button or choose Product ➤ Stop.

# Identifying Virtual Objects with Pan Gestures

Another touch gesture that iOS can recognize is the pan, which essentially means placing one or more fingertips on the screen and sliding them around. A pan gesture is similar to a swipe except a swipe gesture slides up/down or right/left. A pan gesture can also move in a straight line but could also move in a squiggly line instead.

Creating a Pan Gesture Recognizer involves defining a function to handle pan gestures and then assigning the pan gesture to the scene like this:

```
let panGesture = UIPanGestureRecognizer(target: self,
action: #selector(handlePan))
sceneView.addGestureRecognizer(panGesture)
```

To further customize the pan gesture, we can define the minimum number of fingertips to start panning along with a maximum number. So if we wanted to detect one, two, or three fingers in a pan gesture, we could define a minimumNumberOfTouches as 1 and a maximumNumberOfTouches as 3 like this:

```
panGesture.maximumNumberOfTouches = 3
panGesture.minimumNumberOfTouches = 1
```

If we don't define either property, Xcode simply allows any number of fingertips to initiate a pan gesture with a minimum of at least one fingertip.

The function to handle the pan gesture can respond to three parts of a pan gesture:

- Location—Where the pan gesture started on the iOS device screen, where the upper-left corner is the origin (0, 0)

- Velocity—How fast the pan gesture moves in the x- and y-axes, measured in points per second

- Translation—How far the pan gesture moves in the x- and y-axes

223

We can retrieve the location, velocity, and translation information in a function that handles pan gestures like this:

```
@objc func handlePan(sender: UIPanGestureRecognizer) {
let location = sender.location(in: view)
let velocity = sender.velocity(in: view)
let translation = sender.translation(in: view)
 }
```

Then we can retrieve the x and y values of each item like this:

```
print(location.x, location.y)
print(velocity.x, velocity.y)
print(translation.x, translation.y)
```

For our app, we'll only use the translation property to identify how far the pan gesture moves. We need to identify whether the pan gesture occurs over a virtual object or not, so we need to get the coordinates panned over like this:

```
let areaPanned = sender.view as! SCNView
let tappedCoordinates = sender.location(in: areaPanned)
let hitTest = areaPanned.hitTest(tappedCoordinates)
```

Then we need to check if the pan gesture occurred over the box or pyramid like this:

```
if hitTest.isEmpty {
    print ("Nothing")
} else {
    let results = hitTest.first!
    let name = results.node.name
    print(name ?? "background")
```

```
    if sender.state == .began {
        print("Gesture began")
    } else if sender.state == .changed {
        print("Gesture is changing")
        print(translation.x, translation.y)
    } else if sender.state == .ended {
        print("Gesture ended")
    }
}
```

The entire ViewController.swift code should look like this:

```
import UIKit
import SceneKit
import ARKit

class ViewController: UIViewController, ARSCNViewDelegate {

    @IBOutlet var sceneView: ARSCNView!
    let configuration = ARWorldTrackingConfiguration()

    override func viewDidLoad() {
        super.viewDidLoad()
        // Do any additional setup after loading the view,
        typically from a nib.
        sceneView.delegate = self
        sceneView.showsStatistics = true
        sceneView.debugOptions = [ARSCNDebugOptions.
        showWorldOrigin, ARSCNDebugOptions.showFeaturePoints]

        let tapGesture = UITapGestureRecognizer(target: self,
        action: #selector(handleTap))
        sceneView.addGestureRecognizer(tapGesture)
```

```swift
    let swipeRightGesture = UISwipeGestureRecognizer
    (target: self, action: #selector(handleSwipe))
    swipeRightGesture.direction = .right
    sceneView.addGestureRecognizer(swipeRightGesture)

    let swipeLeftGesture = UISwipeGestureRecognizer
    (target: self, action: #selector(handleSwipe))
    swipeLeftGesture.direction = .left
    sceneView.addGestureRecognizer(swipeLeftGesture)

    let swipeUpGesture = UISwipeGestureRecognizer(target:
    self, action: #selector(handleSwipe))
    swipeUpGesture.direction = .up
    sceneView.addGestureRecognizer(swipeUpGesture)

    let swipeDownGesture = UISwipeGestureRecognizer(target:
    self, action: #selector(handleSwipe))
    swipeDownGesture.direction = .down
    sceneView.addGestureRecognizer(swipeDownGesture)

    let panGesture = UIPanGestureRecognizer(target: self,
    action: #selector(handlePan))
    sceneView.addGestureRecognizer(panGesture)

    addShapes()
}

override func viewWillAppear(_ animated: Bool) {
    super.viewWillAppear(animated)
    sceneView.session.run(configuration)
}

func addShapes() {
    let node = SCNNode(geometry: SCNBox(width: 0.05,
    height: 0.05, length: 0.05, chamferRadius: 0))
```

```
node.position = SCNVector3(0.1,0,-0.1)
node.geometry?.firstMaterial?.diffuse.contents =
UIColor.blue
node.name = "box"
sceneView.scene.rootNode.addChildNode(node)

let node2 = SCNNode(geometry: SCNPyramid(width: 0.05,
height: 0.06, length: 0.05))
node2.position = SCNVector3(0.1,0.1,-0.1)
node2.geometry?.firstMaterial?.diffuse.contents =
UIColor.red
node2.name = "pyramid"
sceneView.scene.rootNode.addChildNode(node2)
}

@objc func handleTap(sender: UITapGestureRecognizer) {
    let areaTapped = sender.view as! SCNView
    let tappedCoordinates = sender.location(in: areaTapped)
    let hitTest = areaTapped.hitTest(tappedCoordinates)

    if hitTest.isEmpty {
        print ("Nothing")
    } else {
        let results = hitTest.first!
        let name = results.node.name
        print(name ?? "background")
    }
}

@objc func handleSwipe(sender: UISwipeGestureRecognizer) {
    let areaSwiped = sender.view as! SCNView
    let tappedCoordinates = sender.location(in: areaSwiped)
    let hitTest = areaSwiped.hitTest(tappedCoordinates)
```

```
        if hitTest.isEmpty {
            print ("Nothing")
        } else {
            let results = hitTest.first!
            let name = results.node.name
            print(name ?? "background")
        }

        switch sender.direction {
        case.up:
            print("Up")
        case .down:
            print("Down")
        case .right:
            print("Right")
        case .left:
            print("Left")
        default:
            break
        }
    }

    @objc func handlePan(sender: UIPanGestureRecognizer) {
//        let location = sender.location(in: view)
//        print(location.x, location.y)
//        let velocity = sender.velocity(in: view)
//        print(velocity.x, velocity.y)

        let translation = sender.translation(in: view)

        let areaPanned = sender.view as! SCNView
        let tappedCoordinates = sender.location(in: areaPanned)
        let hitTest = areaPanned.hitTest(tappedCoordinates)
```

```swift
    if hitTest.isEmpty {
        print ("Nothing")
    } else {
        let results = hitTest.first!
        let name = results.node.name
        print(name ?? "background")

        if sender.state == .began {
            print("Gesture began")
        } else if sender.state == .changed {
            print("Gesture is changing")
            print(translation.x, translation.y)
        } else if sender.state == .ended {
            print("Gesture ended")
        }
    }
}

}
```

Modify the code in your `ViewController.swift` file to match this code. Then to see the app run, do the following:

1. Connect an iOS device to your Macintosh through its USB cable.

2. Click the Run button or choose Product ➤ Run.

3. Place one finger over the box or pyramid on the screen and slide it around. Notice that the debug area in Xcode identifies the area panned over, when the pan gesture starts, stops, and changes, and what the translation values are.

4. Click the Stop button or choose Product ➤ Stop.

# Identifying Long Press Gestures on Virtual Objects

A tap gesture occurs when the user presses a fingertip on the screen and releases it. A long press gesture is similar except that it allows the user to press and hold one or more fingertips on the screen, then release. You can modify four properties of a long press gesture:

- `minimumPressDuration`—Defines how long the user must press on the screen. The default is 0.5 seconds.

- `numberOfTouchesRequired`—Defines how many fingertips the user must press on the screen. The default is 1.

- `numberOfTapsRequired`—Defines how many times the user must press and lift one or more fingertips to initiate a long press gesture. The default is 0.

- `allowableMovement`—Defines how far the user can slide one or more fingertips to initiate a long press gesture. The default is 10 points.

To define a long press gesture and any four properties, you just need to define a function to handle the long press gesture and then add the long press gesture to a scene like this:

```
let longPressGesture = UILongPressGestureRecognizer
(target: self, action: #selector(handleLongPress))
longPressGesture.minimumPressDuration = 1
sceneView.addGestureRecognizer(longPressGesture)
```

This code defines the minimum press duration to 1 second but if you omit this line, then it will use the default minimum press duration of 0.5 seconds instead. This code also defines a function called handleLongPress to respond to the long press gesture, so we need to create this function like this:

```
@objc func handleLongPress(sender:
UILongPressGestureRecognizer) {

}
```

To determine where the user pressed, we need to identify the area like this:

```
let areaPressed = sender.view as! SCNView
let tappedCoordinates = sender.location(in: areaPressed)
let hitTest = areaPressed.hitTest(tappedCoordinates)
```

Then we need to use the hitTest function to identify if the user pressed on the box or pyramid like this:

```
if hitTest.isEmpty {
    print ("Nothing")
} else {
    let results = hitTest.first!
    let name = results.node.name ?? "background"
    print("Long press on \(name)")
}
```

The entire handleLongPress function should look like this:

```
@objc func handleLongPress(sender:
UILongPressGestureRecognizer) {
    let areaPressed = sender.view as! SCNView
    let tappedCoordinates = sender.location(in:
    areaPressed)
    let hitTest = areaPressed.hitTest(tappedCoordinates)

    if hitTest.isEmpty {
        print ("Nothing")
    } else {
```

```
            let results = hitTest.first!
            let name = results.node.name ?? "background"
            print("Long press on \(name)")
        }
    }
```

Add the handleLongPress function to your ViewController.swift file and define the long press recognizer like this:

```
let longPressGesture = UILongPressGestureRecognizer
(target: self, action: #selector(handleLongPress))
sceneView.addGestureRecognizer(longPressGesture)
```

Then to see the app run, do the following:

1.  Connect an iOS device to your Macintosh through its USB cable.

2.  Click the Run button or choose Product ➤ Run.

3.  Press one finger over the box or pyramid on the screen. Notice that the debug area in displays "Long press on box" or "Long press on pyramid".

4.  Click the Stop button or choose Product ➤ Stop.

# Adding Pinch and Rotation Gestures

Up until now, we've added gesture recognizers programmatically by writing at least two lines of code. First, we've created a constant to represent the gesture recognizer along with defining a function to handle the gesture like this:

```
let tapGesture = UITapGestureRecognizer(target: self, action:
#selector(handleTap))
```

Second, we added the gesture recognizer to the view like this:

```
sceneView.addGestureRecognizer(tapGesture)
```

A second way to add gesture recognizers to an app is to use the Object Library and drag a gesture recognizer directly on a scene. If you click on the Object Library and search for "gesture recognizer," Xcode displays a list of all available gesture recognizers, as shown in Figure 9-2.

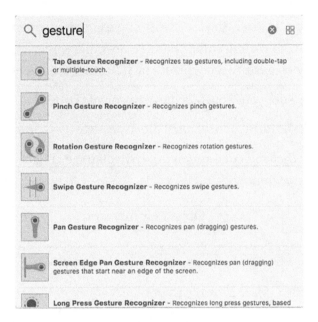

***Figure 9-2.*** *Viewing a list of gesture recognizers in the Object Library window*

Dragging and dropping a gesture recognizer on to a view is equivalent to writing code to add a gesture recognizer to a view:

```
sceneView.addGestureRecognizer(tapGesture)
```

233

Now if you open the Assistant Editor, you can Ctrl-drag from the gesture recognizer to the ViewController.swift file. If you Ctrl-drag to create an IBOutlet, this is equivalent to declaring a gesture recognizer like this:

```
let tapGesture = UITapGestureRecognizer(target: self, action:
#selector(handleTap))
```

Of course, every gesture recognizer needs a function that contains code to handle the gesture, so you also need to Ctrl-drag to create an IBAction method. By dragging and dropping a gesture recognizer on a view, you can avoid writing code. Let's see how this works with both the rotation and pinch gesture recognizers by following these steps:

1.   Make sure your TouchGestures project is open.

2.   Click the Main.storyboard file in the Navigator pane.

3.   Click the Object Library icon to display the Object Library window.

Object Library icon

*Figure 9-3.* *The Object Library icon*

4.   Type Rotation in the Object Library window. The Object Library window displays the Rotation Gesture Recognizer.

***Figure 9-4.*** *The Rotation Gesture Recognizer in the Object Library window*

5.  Drag the Rotation Gesture Recognizer and drop it over the ARSCNView. Xcode displays the Rotation Gesture Recognizer in the Document Outline, as shown in Figure 9-5. (You can toggle between hiding or showing the Document Outline by choosing Editor ➤ Show/Hide Document Outline.)

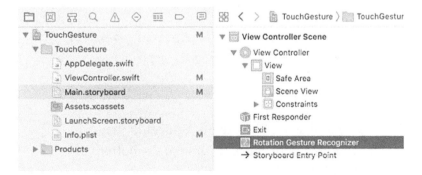

***Figure 9-5.*** *The Document Outline pane displays all user interface items*

6.  Repeat Steps 3-5, except drag and drop the Pinch Gesture Recognizer on to the ARSCNView so the Pinch Gesture Recognizer also appears in the Document Outline window.

7.  Click the Assistant Editor icon or choose View ➤ Assistant Editor ➤ Show Assistant Editor. Xcode displays the Document Outline, `Main.storyboard` file, and the `ViewController.swift` file side by side.

8.  Click on the Rotation Gesture Recognizer in the Document Outline and Ctrl-drag to the bottom of the `ViewController.swift` file.

9.  Release the Control key and the left mouse button. A popup window appears.

10. Make sure the Connection popup menu displays Action.

11. Click in the Name text field and type `handleRotation`.

12. Click in the Type popup menu and choose UIRotationGestureRecognizer.

13. Click the Connect button. Xcode creates an empty IBAction method like this:

```
@IBAction func handleRotation(_ sender:
UIRotationGestureRecognizer) {

}
```

14. Click on the Pinch Gesture Recognizer in the Document Outline and Ctrl-drag to the bottom of the `ViewController.swift` file.

15. Release the Control key and the left mouse button.
A popup window appears.

16. Make sure the Connection popup menu displays
Action.

17. Click in the Name text field and type `handlePinch`.

18. Click in the Type popup menu and choose
UIPinchGestureRecognizer.

19. Click the Connect button. Xcode creates an empty
IBAction method like this:

```
@IBAction func handlePinch(_ sender:
UIPinchGestureRecognizer) {

}
```

20. Edit both functions to include a `print` statement like this:

```
@IBAction func handleRotation(_ sender:
UIRotationGestureRecognizer) {
    print("Rotation detected")
}

@IBAction func handlePinch(_ sender:
UIPinchGestureRecognizer) {
    print("Pinch detected")
}
```

21. Connect an iOS device to your Macintosh through
its USB cable.

22. Click the Run button or choose Product ➤ Run.

23.    Press two fingers on the screen and rotate them in a circular motion. The Xcode debug area should display "Rotation detected".

24.    Press two fingers on the screen and pinch them closer together. The Xcode debug area should display "Pinch detected".

25.    Click the Stop button or choose Product ➤ Stop.

Notice that by dragging and dropping gesture recognizers on to the ARSCNView, we've saved ourselves writing code. You can use either method or a combination of both methods.

# Summary

The touch screen of an iOS device can recognize multiple types of touch gestures, from simple taps to rotation, swipes, and pans. To recognize gestures, you have two methods. First, you can add a gesture recognizer to your app by writing code such as:

```
let panGesture = UIPanGestureRecognizer(target: self,
action: #selector(handlePan))
sceneView.addGestureRecognizer(panGesture)
```

Then you'll need to write a function to handle the touch gesture such as:

```
@objc func handlePan(sender: UIPanGestureRecognizer) {

}
```

As an alternative, we can simply drag and drop a gesture recognizer from the Object Library on to the ARSCNView. Then we can Ctrl-drag to create an IBOutlet for the gesture recognizer and an IBAction method to handle the gesture when it's detected.

# CHAPTER 10

# Interacting with Augmented Reality

Touch gestures let the user control an augmented reality app through finger gestures alone such as taps, swipes, rotations, and pinches. Once you've added touch gestures to an augmented reality app, the next step is to use those touch gestures to manipulate virtual objects displayed in the augmented reality view.

In the previous chapter, we learned how to recognize when simple touch gestures occur on a virtual object such as a tap, long press, or swipe. In this chapter, we learn how to scale, rotate, and move a virtual object using a pinch, rotation, and pan touch gesture.

For this chapter's example, we'll create the different gesture recognizers through the Object Library. Let's create a new Xcode project by following these steps:

1. Start Xcode. (Make sure you're using Xcode 10 or greater.)

2. Choose File ➤ New ➤ Project. Xcode asks you to choose a template.

3. Click the iOS category.

© Wallace Wang 2018
W. Wang, *Beginning ARKit for iPhone and iPad,*
https://doi.org/10.1007/978-1-4842-4102-8_10

4.  Click the Augmented Reality App icon and click the Next button. Xcode asks for a product name, organization name, organization identifiers, and content technology.

5.  Click in the Product Name text field and type a descriptive name for your project, such as RotatePinch. (The exact name does not matter.)

6.  Make sure the Content Technology popup menu displays SceneKit.

7.  Click the Next button. Xcode asks where you want to store your project.

8.  Choose a folder and click the Create button. Xcode creates an iOS project.

This creates a simple augmented reality app that displays a cartoon airplane. Now that we have the airplane displayed for us automatically, let's start by learning to scale or resize the airplane virtual object in the augmented reality view using the pinch gesture.

The pinch gesture consists of placing two fingertips on the screen and then drawing them apart or together in a pinching motion. To place a pinch gesture recognizer in our app, follow these steps:

1.  Click the Main.storyboard file in the Navigator pane.

2.  Click the Object Library icon to display the Object Library window.

3.  Type pinch in the Object Library. The Object Library
    displays the pinch gesture recognizer, as shown in
    Figure 10-1.

***Figure 10-1.*** *Finding the pinch gesture recognizer in the Object
Library window*

4.  Drag the Pinch Gesture Recognizer from the Object
    Library window and drop it on the ARSCNView
    on the user interface. Although you dragged and
    dropped the Pinch Gesture Recognizer on to the
    user interface, you won't see any sign of it anywhere
    except in the Document Outline, as shown in
    Figure 10-2. If the Document Outline is not visible,
    click the Show Document Outline icon or choose
    Editor ➤ Show Document Outline.

*Figure 10-2.* *The Document Outline displays any gesture recognizers you place on the user interface*

5.  Click the Assistant Editor icon or choose View ➤ Assistant Editor ➤ Show Assistant Editor to display the `Main.storyboard` and the `ViewController.swift` file side by side.

6.  Move the mouse pointer over the Pinch Gesture Recognizer in the Document Outline, hold down the Control key, and Ctrl-drag above the last curly bracket at the bottom of the `ViewController.swift` file.

7.  Release the Control key and the left mouse button.
    A popup menu appears.

8.  Make sure the Connection popup menu displays
    Action.

9.  Click in the Name text field and type pinchGesture.

10. Click in the Type popup menu and choose
    UIPinchGestureRecognizer. Then click the Connect
    button. Xcode creates an IBAction method as shown
    here:

    ```
    @IBAction func pinchGesture(_ sender:
    UIPinchGestureRecognizer) {

    }
    ```

11. Edit this IBAction method pinchGesture as follows:

    ```
    @IBAction func pinchGesture(_ sender:
    UIPinchGestureRecognizer) {
            print ("Pinch gesture")
    }
    ```

12. Connect an iOS device to your Macintosh through
    its USB cable.

13. Click the Run button or choose Product ➤ Run. The
    first time you run this app, it will ask permission to
    access the camera so give it permission.

14. Place two fingertips on the screen and pinch in or
    out. The Xcode debug area should display Pinch
    Gesture to let you know that it successfully detected
    the pinch gesture.

15. Click the Stop button or choose Product ➤ Stop.

# Scaling with the Pinch Touch Gesture

The pinch gesture is a common touch gesture for zooming in or out of an image displayed on the screen, such as while looking at a digital photograph. Likewise, this same pinch gesture can be used to scale the virtual plane that appears in the augmented reality view.

Touch gestures consist of three states:

- .began—Occurs when the app first detects a specific touch gesture

- .changed—Occurs while the touch gesture is still going on

- .ended—Occurs when the app detects that the touch gesture has stopped

For the pinch gesture, we just care about when it's changing because as the user pinches in or out, we want to scale the size of the virtual plane in the augmented reality view. Edit the pinchGesture function like this:

```
@IBAction func pinchGesture(_ sender:
UIPinchGestureRecognizer) {
    if sender.state == .changed {
            print ("Pinch gesture")
    }
}
```

If you run this code and pinch on the screen, you should still see "Pinch gesture" appear in the debug area of Xcode. This verifies that the app still recognizes the pinch gesture.

We only want the pinch gesture to resize the virtual plane when the user pinches directly on the virtual plane and not on any other part of the augmented reality view. To detect what part of the screen the user pinched on, we first need to retrieve the entire augmented reality view like this:

```
let areaPinched = sender.view as? SCNView
```

Now we need to get the specific location that the user pinched on the screen:

```
let location = sender.location(in: areaPinched)
```

Finally, we need to use the `hitTest` method to determine if the user touched the virtual plane:

```
        let hitTestResults = sceneView.hitTest(location,
                               options: nil)

        if let hitTest = hitTestResults.first {

        }
```

If the user touched the first node in the augmented reality view (the plane is the only node), then we can identify the `hitTest` node with an arbitrary name such as:

```
        if let hitTest = hitTestResults.first {
            let plane = hitTest.node
        }
```

Now based on how far the user moves the pinch gesture, we can multiply this value by the virtual plane's current scale. If the user pinches out, the scale will be larger and the virtual plane should increase in size. If the user pinches in, the scale will be smaller and the virtual plane should decrease in size. The following three lines of code measure how the virtual plane should change in size in the x, y, and z direction:

```
let scaleX = Float(sender.scale) * plane.scale.x
let scaleY = Float(sender.scale) * plane.scale.y
let scaleZ = Float(sender.scale) * plane.scale.z
```

Once we know how much to scale the virtual plane in the x, y, and z direction, we can apply these values to the virtual plane itself like this:

```
plane.scale = SCNVector3(scaleX, scaleY, scaleZ)
```

Finally, we need to reset the virtual plane's new size to a scale of 1:

```
sender.scale = 1
```

The entire pinchGesture IBAction method should look like this:

```
@IBAction func pinchGesture(_ sender:
UIPinchGestureRecognizer) {
    if sender.state == .changed {
        let areaPinched = sender.view as? SCNView
        let location = sender.location(in: areaPinched)
        let hitTestResults = sceneView.hitTest(location,
                             options: nil)

        if let hitTest = hitTestResults.first {
            let plane = hitTest.node

            let scaleX = Float(sender.scale) * plane.
                         scale.x
            let scaleY = Float(sender.scale) * plane.
                         scale.y
            let scaleZ = Float(sender.scale) * plane.
                         scale.z
```

```
            plane.scale = SCNVector3(scaleX, scaleY, scaleZ)

            sender.scale = 1
        }
    }
}
```

Run this app through a connected iOS device and pinch directly on the virtual plane (not on the area around the virtual plane). You should be able to scale the virtual plane larger and smaller depending on which direction you pinch, as shown in Figure 10-3.

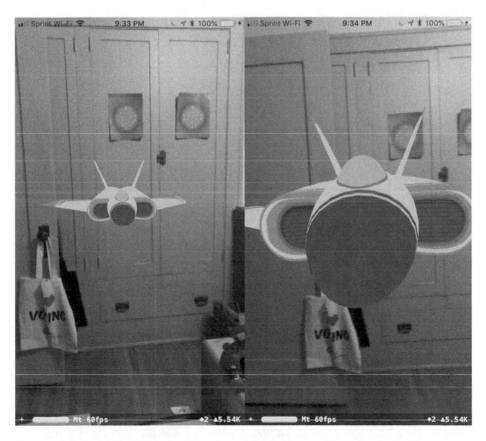

*Figure 10-3.* *Pinching scales the virtual plane bigger or smaller*

# Rotating with the Rotation Touch Gesture

The rotation gesture uses two fingertips much like the pinch gesture. The big difference is that while the pinch gesture involves moving the two fingertips closer or farther apart, the rotation touch gesture involves placing two fingertips on the screen and rotating clockwise or counter-clockwise while keeping the distance between the two fingertips unchanged.

To place a rotation gesture recognizer in our app, follow these steps:

1.  Click the Main.storyboard file in the Navigator pane.

2.  Click the Object Library icon to display the Object Library window.

3.  Type rotation in the Object Library. The Object Library displays the rotation gesture recognizer, as shown in Figure 10-4.

***Figure 10-4.*** *Finding the rotation gesture recognizer in the Object Library window*

4.  Drag the Rotation Gesture Recognizer from the Object Library window and drop it on the ARSCNView on the user interface. Although you dragged and dropped the Rotation Gesture Recognizer on to the user interface, you won't see any sign of it anywhere except in the Document Outline.

5.  Click the Assistant Editor icon or choose View ➤ Assistant Editor ➤ Show Assistant Editor to display the Main.storyboard and the ViewController. swift file side by side.

6.  Move the mouse pointer over the Rotation Gesture Recognizer in the Document Outline, hold down the Control key, and Ctrl-drag above the last curly bracket at the bottom of the ViewController. swift file.

7.  Release the Control key and the left mouse button. A popup menu appears.

8.  Make sure the Connection popup menu displays Action.

9.  Click in the Name text field and type rotationGesture.

10. Click in the Type popup menu and choose UIRotationGestureRecognizer. Then click the Connect button. Xcode creates an IBAction method as shown here:

```
@IBAction func rotationGesture(_ sender:
UIRotationGestureRecognizer) {

}
```

11.  Edit this IBAction method `rotationGesture` as
     follows:

```
@IBAction func rotationGesture(_ sender:
UIRotationGestureRecognizer) {
        print ("Rotation gesture")
}
```

12.  Connect an iOS device to your Macintosh through
     its USB cable.

13.  Click the Run button or choose Product ➤ Run.

14.  Place two fingertips on the screen and rotate them
     clockwise or counter-clockwise. The Xcode debug
     area should display "Rotation Gesture" to let you
     know that it successfully detected the rotation
     gesture.

15.  Click the Stop button or choose Product ➤ Stop.

With the rotation gesture, we need to identify when the rotation is
actually taking place and when the rotation finally stops. While the rotation
gesture is occurring, we'll need to rotate the virtual plane. As soon as the
rotation ends, we'll need to store the rotated angle as the virtual plane's
current angle.

First, we'll need to create two variables underneath the IBOutlet for the
`ARSCNView` like this:

```
var newAngleZ : Float = 0.0
var currentAngleZ : Float = 0.0
```

In this example, we'll be rotating the virtual plane around its z-axis
so the `currentAngleZ` stores the virtual plane's current angle. Then we'll
calculate a new angle, based on the rotation gesture, and store this new
angle in the `newAngleZ` variable.

250

Once these two variables are available, we can write code that detects when the rotation is happening (`.changed`) and when the rotation has stopped (`.ended`):

```
@IBAction func rotationGesture(_ sender:
UIRotationGestureRecognizer) {
    if sender.state == .changed {

    } else if sender.state == .ended {
            currentAngleZ = newAngleZ
    }
}
```

As soon as the rotation gesture ends, we want to store the new angle of rotation (newAngleZ) into the `currentAngleZ` variable.

Now as soon as we detect a rotation gesture, we need to verify that this rotation gesture occurs on the virtual plane. To do this, we need to retrieve the view touched, get the location of the user's fingertips, and use the `hitTest` method to determine if it touched any virtual object in the augmented reality view:

```
let areaTouched = sender.view as? SCNView
let location = sender.location(in: areaTouched)
let hitTestResults = sceneView.hitTest(location, options: nil)
```

Next, we'll need to check if the rotation gesture occurs over the first (and only virtual object) in the augmented reality view:

```
if let hitTest = hitTestResults.first {

}
```

Then we'll create a "plane" constant to represent the node that the user touched (the virtual plane) and store the rotation angle of the gesture in the newAngleZ variable.

```
let plane = hitTest.node
newAngleZ = Float(-sender.rotation)
```

The negative sign is necessary to coordinate the rotation gesture on the screen with the rotation of the virtual plane in the augmented reality view. Without this negative sign, the virtual plane would rotate in the opposite direction as the rotation gesture.

We'll add this new rotation angle to the virtual plane's current angle and then assign this new angle to rotate the virtual plane around the z-axis. To do this, we need to use the eulerAngles property that defines a virtual object's rotation around the x-, y-, and z-axes. Since we're only rotating the virtual plane around the z-axis, we only need to assign the new angle of rotation to the z-axis like this:

```
newAngleZ += currentAngleZ
plane.eulerAngles.z = newAngleZ
```

The complete rotation gesture IBAction method should look like this:

```
@IBAction func rotationGesture(_ sender:
UIRotationGestureRecognizer) {
    if sender.state == .changed {
        let areaTouched = sender.view as? SCNView
        let location = sender.location(in: areaTouched)

        let hitTestResults = sceneView.hitTest(location,
                            options: nil)

        if let hitTest = hitTestResults.first {
            let plane = hitTest.node
            newAngleZ = Float(-sender.rotation)
            newAngleZ += currentAngleZ
            plane.eulerAngles.z = newAngleZ
        }
```

```
    } else if sender.state == .ended {
            currentAngleZ = newAngleZ
    }
}
```

Remember, you must also add the two variables (newAngleZ and currentAngleZ) as Float variables by declaring them near the top of the ViewController.swift class like this:

```
var newAngleZ : Float = 0.0
var currentAngleZ : Float = 0.0
```

If you run this app, you can place two fingertips on the virtual plane and rotate. Then the virtual plane will rotate in the same direction, as shown in Figure 10-5.

***Figure 10-5.*** *Rotating the virtual plane with the rotation gesture*

# Moving Virtual Objects with the Pan Gesture

The pan gesture occurs when the user slides one fingertip across the screen in any direction. You can define both the minimum and maximum number of fingertips for a pan gesture such as at least two fingers but not more than four. By default, the minimum number of fingertips to detect a pan gesture is 1.

Xcode offers two types of pan gesture recognizers. The one we'll be using is simply called Pan Gesture Recognizer, which detects fingertip movement anywhere on the screen. The other pan gesture recognizer is called Screen Edge Pan Gesture Recognizer. If you've ever swiped up from the bottom of an iPhone screen to display options such as turning your iPhone into a flashlight, then you've used the Screen Edge Pan Gesture Recognizer that detects pans that start at the edge of a screen.

To place a regular pan gesture recognizer in our app, follow these steps:

1.   Click the Main.storyboard file in the Navigator pane.

2.   Click the Object Library icon to display the Object Library window.

3.   Type pan in the Object Library. The Object Library displays the pan gesture recognizer, as shown in Figure 10-6.

***Figure 10-6.*** *Finding the pan gesture recognizer in the Object Library window*

4.  Drag the Pan Gesture Recognizer from the Object Library window and drop it on the ARSCNView on the user interface. Although you dragged and dropped the Pan Gesture Recognizer on to the user interface, you won't see any sign of it anywhere except in the Document Outline.

5.  Click the Assistant Editor icon or choose View ➤ Assistant Editor ➤ Show Assistant Editor to display the Main.storyboard and the ViewController. swift file side by side.

6.  Move the mouse pointer over the Pan Gesture Recognizer in the Document Outline, hold down the Control key, and Ctrl-drag above the last curly bracket at the bottom of the ViewController.swift file.

7.  Release the Control key and the left mouse button. A popup menu appears.

8.  Make sure the Connection popup menu displays Action.

9.  Click in the Name text field and type panGesture.

10. Click in the Type popup menu and choose UIPanGestureRecognizer. Then click the Connect button. Xcode creates an IBAction method as shown here:

```
@IBAction func panGesture(_ sender:
UIPanGestureRecognizer) {

    }
}
```

11. Edit this IBAction method panGesture as follows:

```
@IBAction func panGesture(_ sender:
UIPanGestureRecognizer) {
                print ("Pan gesture")
}
```

12. Connect an iOS device to your Macintosh through its USB cable.

13. Click the Run button or choose Product ➤ Run.

14. Place one fingertip on the screen and slide it around the screen. The Xcode debug area should display "Pan Gesture" to let you know that it successfully detected the rotation gesture.

15. Click the Stop button or choose Product ➤ Stop.

Once we verify that the pan gesture works, the first step is to identify if the user is panning across the virtual plane in the augmented reality view. We need to retrieve the location on the view that the user pans across and use the hitTest method to verify that the user's fingertip is on a virtual object:

```
let areaPanned = sender.view as? SCNView
let location = sender.location(in: areaPanned)
let hitTestResults = areaPanned?.hitTest(location, options: nil)
```

Next, we have to determine if the user touched the first node (the virtual plane):

```
if let hitTest = hitTestResults?.first {

}
```

Once we know that the user touched the virtual plane, we need to create a "plane" constant that represents the virtual plan's parent node. A virtual object can consist of multiple nodes daisy-chained together to create the illusion of a single item. To move a virtual object, we need to move the parent node because this will automatically move any attached nodes. So we need an additional if let statement like this:

```
if let hitTest = hitTestResults?.first {
    if let plane = hitTest.node.parent {

    }
}
```

Finally, we need to detect when the pan gesture is occurring. This happens when the pan gesture state is equal to `.changed`, so we need a final `if` statement inside like this:

```
if let hitTest = hitTestResults?.first {
    if let plane = hitTest.node.parent {
        if sender.state == .changed {

        }
    }
}
```

Inside all of these multiple `if` statements, we need to get the translation property from the pan gesture, which defines how far the user has moved a fingertip across the screen. Because a screen is a flat, two-dimensional surface, we can only track movement across the x-axis and y-axis.

```
let translate = sender.translation(in: areaPanned)
```

After getting the translation movement from the pan gesture, we can finally apply this translation movement to the virtual object itself:

```
plane.localTranslate(by: SCNVector3(translate.x/10000,
-translate.y/10000,0.0))
```

This code applies the translation from the pan gesture in the x and y directions to the virtual plane. Since we can't detect any pan gesture on the z-axis, we won't translate in any direction along the z-axis, so the z value of the `SCNVector3` is 0.0.

Both the translate.x and translate.y values are divided by 10000 as an arbitrary value. Without dividing the translate.x or translate.y values by a large number, the actual movement of the virtual plane will appear choppy. Large values such as 10000 force the movement to occur more smoothly. Experiment with lower values to see how they create a choppy movement of the virtual plane when the user slides a fingertip across the screen.

The entire panGesture IBAction method should look like this:

```swift
@IBAction func panGesture(_ sender: UIPanGestureRecognizer) {
    let areaPanned = sender.view as? SCNView
    let location = sender.location(in: areaPanned)
    let hitTestResults = areaPanned?.hitTest(location,
                           options: nil)

    if let hitTest = hitTestResults?.first {
        if let plane = hitTest.node.parent {
            if sender.state == .changed {
                let translate = sender.translation
                            (in: areaPanned)
                plane.localTranslate(by:
                SCNVector3(translate.x/10000,
                -translate.y/10000,0.0))
            }
        }
    }
}
```

When you run this app, press a fingertip on the virtual plane and slide it around the screen. The virtual plane can then move in the x and y directions, as shown in Figure 10-7.

***Figure 10-7.*** *Moving the virtual plane through the pan gesture*

# Summary

Touch gestures can interact with virtual objects and make them move, rotate, or scale. When using touch gestures to interact with virtual objects, you need to use the hitTest function to detect when the user's touch gestures occur over a virtual object. Then you can modify that virtual object physical position.

Touch gestures provide a way for users to manipulate virtual objects within an augmented reality view and turn a static augmented reality view into an interactive one.

# CHAPTER 11

# Plane Detection

Placing virtual objects in mid-air is fine, but augmented reality works best when it also interacts with the real world. One of the most basic ways augmented reality interacts with the real world is through detecting horizontal or vertical planes. When ARKit can detect a flat surface, it can later place a virtual object so that it appears to be resting on that real flat surface, such as a table or floor.

Each time ARKit detects a plane, it places an anchor in that augmented reality view. This anchor, one per plane, contains information about the plane's:

- Orientation

- Position

- Size

As you move the camera in an iOS device around, ARKit constantly updates its information about a plane. Typically this involves recognizing that a plane may be larger than it initially thought. For example, when you first point an iOS device's camera at a floor, ARKit can only recognize that portion of the floor that the camera sees. As you move the iOS device's camera around, ARKit can detect other parts of the floor, forcing it to update its information on how large the plane might really be.

© Wallace Wang 2018
W. Wang, *Beginning ARKit for iPhone and iPad*,
https://doi.org/10.1007/978-1-4842-4102-8_11

For this chapter, let's create a new Xcode project by following these steps:

1. Start Xcode. (Make sure you're using Xcode 10 or greater.)

2. Choose File ➤ New ➤ Project. Xcode asks you to choose a template.

3. Click the iOS category.

4. Click the Single View App icon and click the Next button. Xcode asks for a product name, organization name, organization identifiers, and content technology.

5. Click in the Product Name text field and type a descriptive name for your project, such as PlaneDetection. (The exact name does not matter.)

6. Click the Next button. Xcode asks where you want to store your project.

7. Choose a folder and click the Create button. Xcode creates an iOS project.

Now modify the Info.plist file to allow access to the camera and to use ARKit by following these steps:

1. Click the Info.plist file in the Navigator pane. Xcode displays a list of keys, types, and values.

2. Click the disclosure triangle to expand the Required Device Capabilities category to display Item 0.

3. Move the mouse pointer over Item 0 to display a plus (+) icon.

4. Click this plus (+) icon to display a blank Item 1.

5. Type arkit under the Value category in the Item 1 row.

6. Move the mouse pointer over the last row to display a plus (+) icon.

7. Click on the plus (+) icon to create a new row. A popup menu appears.

8. Choose Privacy – Camera Usage Description.

9. Type AR needs to use the camera under the Value category in the Privacy – Camera Usage Description row.

Now it's time to modify the ViewController.swift file to use ARKit and SceneKit by following these steps:

1. Click on the ViewController.swift file in the Navigator pane.

2. Edit the ViewController.swift file so it looks like this:

```swift
import UIKit
import SceneKit
import ARKit

class ViewController: UIViewController,
ARSCNViewDelegate {

let configuration = ARWorldTrackingConfiguration()

    override func viewDidLoad() {
        super.viewDidLoad()
        // Do any additional setup after loading the
        view, typically from a nib.

    }

}
```

To view augmented reality in our app, add a single ARKit SceneKit View (ARSCNView) so the user interface looks similar to Figure 11-1.

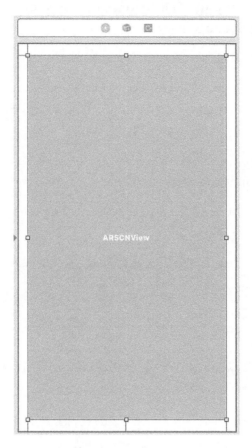

***Figure 11-1.***  *The user interface includes a single ARSCNView*

After you've designed your user interface, you need to add constraints. To add constraints, choose Editor ➤ Resolve Auto Layout Issues ➤ Reset to Suggested Constraints at the bottom half of the menu under the All Views in Container category.

The next step is to connect the user interface items to the Swift code in the ViewController.swift file. To do this, follow these steps:

1.  Click the Main.storyboard file in the Navigator pane.

2.  Click the Assistant Editor icon or choose View ➤ Assistant Editor ➤ Show Assistant Editor to display the Main.storyboard and the ViewController. swift file side by side.

3.  Move the mouse pointer over the ARSCNView, hold down the Control key, and Ctrl-drag under the class ViewController line.

4.  Release the Control key and the left mouse button. A popup menu appears.

5.  Click in the Name text field and type sceneView, then click the Connect button. Xcode creates an IBOutlet as shown here:

    **@IBOutlet var** sceneView: ARSCNView!

6.  Edit the viewDidLoad function so it looks like this:

```
override func viewDidLoad() {
    super.viewDidLoad()
    // Do any additional setup after loading the
    view, typically from a nib.
    sceneView.debugOptions = [ARSCNDebugOptions.
    showWorldOrigin, ARSCNDebugOptions.
    showFeaturePoints]
    sceneView.delegate = self

    configuration.planeDetection = .horizontal

    sceneView.session.run(configuration)
}
```

7.  Edit the `viewWillAppear` function so it looks like this:

```
override func viewWillAppear(_ animated: Bool) {
    super.viewWillAppear(animated)
    sceneView.session.run(configuration)
}
```

Notice that to detect a horizontal plane, we just need one line of code:

```
configuration.planeDetection = .horizontal
```

Detecting a horizontal plane requires ARKit identifying enough feature points (those tiny yellow dots) on a flat, horizontal surface. To increase the odds that ARKit will detect a horizontal plane, aim your iOS device's camera at a flat surface with plenty of texture or color variation such as a bed, a rug or carpet, or a table. In comparison, a solid white floor will be much harder to identify since there will be much less detail for ARKit to identify.

To detect if ARKit has identified a horizontal plane, we'll need a `didAdd renderer` function. This function runs each time ARKit identifies a horizontal plane and identifies it as a plane anchor called `ARPlaneAnchor`, which defines the position an orientation of the flat surface. Add the following `didAdd renderer` function in your `ViewController.swift` file:

```
func renderer(_ renderer: SCNSceneRenderer, didAdd node:
SCNNode, for anchor: ARAnchor) {
    guard anchor is ARPlaneAnchor else { return }
    print ("plane detected")
}
```

The first time ARKit identifies a horizontal plane, it assumes the horizontal plane is only as large as what it sees through the iOS device's camera. As you move the iOS device's camera around, ARKit will spot additional points of the horizontal plane. When that occurs, it updates its floor anchor information so it stores a larger dimension of the horizontal plane.

Each time ARKit updates its ARPlaneAnchor information by realizing a horizontal plane may be larger, it runs an didUpdate renderer function. Add the following didUpdate renderer function in the ViewController. swift file:

```
func renderer(_ renderer: SCNSceneRenderer, didUpdate node:
SCNNode, for anchor: ARAnchor) {
    guard anchor is ARPlaneAnchor else { return }
    print("updating floor anchor")
}
```

In both of these renderer functions, there's an initial guard statement that checks if the renderer function identifies a horizontal plane (ARPlaneAnchor). If not, then the renderer function exits. If the renderer function does identify a horizontal plane, then each renderer function prints a statement ("plane detected" or "updating floor anchor").

The entire ViewController.swift file should look like this:

```
import UIKit
import SceneKit
import ARKit

class ViewController: UIViewController, ARSCNViewDelegate {

    @IBOutlet var sceneView: ARSCNView!

    let configuration = ARWorldTrackingConfiguration()

    override func viewDidLoad() {
        super.viewDidLoad()
        // Do any additional setup after loading the view,
        typically from a nib.
        sceneView.debugOptions = [ARSCNDebugOptions.
        showWorldOrigin, ARSCNDebugOptions.showFeaturePoints]
        sceneView.delegate = self
```

```
        configuration.planeDetection = .horizontal

        sceneView.session.run(configuration)
    }

    func renderer(_ renderer: SCNSceneRenderer, didAdd node:
    SCNNode, for anchor: ARAnchor) {
        guard anchor is ARPlaneAnchor else { return }
        print ("plane detected")
    }

    func renderer(_ renderer: SCNSceneRenderer, didUpdate node:
    SCNNode, for anchor: ARAnchor) {
        guard anchor is ARPlaneAnchor else { return }
        print("updating plane anchor")
    }
}
```

To test this project, follow these steps:

1.  Connect an iOS device to your Macintosh through its USB cable.

2.  Click the Run button or choose Product ➤ Run. The first time you run this app, it will ask permission to access the camera so give it permission.

3.  Aim the iOS device's camera at a horizontal plane such as the seat of a chair or the floor. The first time ARKit identifies a horizontal plane, the Xcode debug area displays the message "plane detected".

4.  Move the iOS device around to capture more of the horizontal plane. Each time ARKit recognizes a new part of the horizontal plane, the Xcode debug area displays the message "updating plane anchor".

5.  Click the Stop button or choose Product ➤ Stop.

# Displaying Planes as Images

Once we can get ARKit to recognize horizontal surfaces, we can place an image on that horizontal surface. First, you need to get an image such as searching for "texture image public domain" in your favorite search engine. Now you can download any texture image you want, such as a brick sidewalk, wooden floor, or the rippling surface of water.

To add a .png or .jpg image to an Xcode project, simply drag and drop that image into the Navigator pane of your Xcode project, as shown in Figure 11-2.

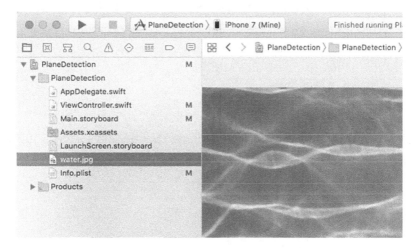

***Figure 11-2.*** *Drag and drop an image into the Navigator pane*

Once you've added a texture image for a plane, the next step is to create a plane, with a texture, and add it to the `sceneView` rootnode inside the `didAdd renderer` function like this:

```
let planeNode = displayTexture()
sceneView.scene.rootNode.addChildNode(planeNode)
```

269

To create the plane, we'll need to create a function called displayTexture, which creates a SCNNode, defines that node as an SCNPlane with a width and height of 0.5 meters, and appears at the position 0, 0, -0.5. Most importantly, the SCNPlane needs to use the texture image you dragged into the Navigator pane such as an image named water.jpg (change this name to the name of the image you dragged into your Xcode Navigator pane). The displayTexture function should look like this:

```
func displayTexture() -> SCNNode {
    let planeNode = SCNNode()
    planeNode.geometry = SCNPlane(width: 0.5, height: 0.5)
    planeNode.geometry?.firstMaterial?.diffuse.contents =
    UIImage(named: "water.jpg")
    planeNode.position = SCNVector3(0, 0, -0.5)

    return planeNode
}
```

If you run this code, it will create a plane that displays water.jpg as a vertical plane, as shown in Figure 11-3.

*Figure 11-3.  Displaying an image on a plane*

Besides rotating the plane 90 degrees along the x-axis so it appears flat, another problem is that if you look behind the plane, the image only appears on one side. To make the image appear on both sides of the plane, we need to define the plane as double-sided like this:

```
planeNode.geometry?.firstMaterial?.isDoubleSided = true
```

Then we need to rotate the plane around the x-axis by 90 degrees. Remember, Xcode measures everything in radians, so we'll first need to convert 90 degrees into radians like this:

```
let ninetyDegrees = GLKMathDegreesToRadians(90)
```

Then we can rotate the plane around its x-axis by defining its eulerAngles position like this:

```
planeNode.eulerAngles = SCNVector3(ninetyDegrees, 0, 0)
```

The entire displayTexture function should look like this:

```
func displayTexture() -> SCNNode {
    let planeNode = SCNNode()
    planeNode.geometry = SCNPlane(width: 0.5, height: 0.5)
    planeNode.geometry?.firstMaterial?.diffuse.contents =
    UIImage(named: "water.jpg")
    planeNode.position = SCNVector3(0, 0, -0.5)

    let ninetyDegrees = GLKMathDegreesToRadians(90)
    planeNode.eulerAngles = SCNVector3(ninetyDegrees, 0, 0)

    planeNode.geometry?.firstMaterial?.isDoubleSided = true

    return planeNode
}
```

The entire ViewController.swift file should look like this to display a horizontal plane with an image:

```
import UIKit
import SceneKit
import ARKit

class ViewController: UIViewController, ARSCNViewDelegate {

    @IBOutlet var sceneView: ARSCNView!

    let configuration = ARWorldTrackingConfiguration()

    override func viewDidLoad() {
        super.viewDidLoad()
```

```
    // Do any additional setup after loading the view,
    typically from a nib.
    sceneView.debugOptions = [ARSCNDebugOptions.
    showWorldOrigin, ARSCNDebugOptions.showFeaturePoints]
    sceneView.delegate = self

    configuration.planeDetection = .horizontal

    sceneView.session.run(configuration)

    let planeNode = displayTexture()
    sceneView.scene.rootNode.addChildNode(planeNode)
}


func displayTexture() -> SCNNode {
    let planeNode = SCNNode()
    planeNode.geometry = SCNPlane(width: 0.5, height: 0.5)
    planeNode.geometry?.firstMaterial?.diffuse.contents =
    UIImage(named: "water.jpg")
    planeNode.position = SCNVector3(0, 0, -0.5)

    let ninetyDegrees = GLKMathDegreesToRadians(90)
    planeNode.eulerAngles = SCNVector3(ninetyDegrees, 0, 0)

    planeNode.geometry?.firstMaterial?.isDoubleSided = true

    return planeNode
}

func renderer(_ renderer: SCNSceneRenderer, didAdd node:
SCNNode, for anchor: ARAnchor) {
    guard anchor is ARPlaneAnchor else { return }
    print ("plane detected")
}
```

```
func renderer(_ renderer: SCNSceneRenderer, didUpdate node:
SCNNode, for anchor: ARAnchor) {
    guard anchor is ARPlaneAnchor else { return }
    print("updating plane anchor")
  }
}
```

If you run this code, you'll see a horizontal plane displaying the texture image on both the top and bottom, as shown in Figure 11-4.

***Figure 11-4.*** *The plane appearing horizontally*

Right now the plane appears at an arbitrary size and position. What we want is to make that plane appear where ARKit detects a horizontal plane, such as a floor or table top.

First, delete these two lines from the viewDidLoad function:

```
let planeNode = displayTexture()
sceneView.scene.rootNode.addChildNode(planeNode)
```

Now, in the didAdd renderer function, add the following two lines:

```
let planeNode = displayTexture(anchor: anchor as!
ARPlaneAnchor)
node.addChildNode(planeNode)
```

The entire didAdd renderer function should look like this:

```
func renderer(_ renderer: SCNSceneRenderer, didAdd node:
SCNNode, for anchor: ARAnchor) {
    guard anchor is ARPlaneAnchor else { return }

    let planeNode = displayTexture(anchor: anchor as!
    ARPlaneAnchor)
    node.addChildNode(planeNode)
    print ("plane detected")
}
```

What this didAdd renderer function does now is that once it detects a horizontal plane, it stores the size and position of that horizontal plane as an ARPlaneAnchor. So we take this size and position information and pass it to the displayTexture function that creates the actual plane.

That means we need to change the displayTexture function so it can accept a parameter like this:

```
func displayTexture(anchor: ARPlaneAnchor) -> SCNNode {
```

Within the `displayTexture` function, we need to modify both the size of the plane and the position, both of which come from the `anchor` parameter that gets passed into the `displayTexture` function. First, we need to define the plane's size based on the anchor. To do that, we need to change the plane's size dimensions from an arbitrary fixed value to the size of the anchor like this:

```
planeNode.geometry = SCNPlane(width: CGFloat(anchor.
extent.x), height: CGFloat(anchor.extent.z))
```

Next, we need to define the horizontal plane's position based on the anchor like this:

```
planeNode.position = SCNVector3(anchor.center.x, anchor.
center.y, anchor.center.z)
```

The entire modified `ViewController.swift` file should now look like this:

```swift
import UIKit
import SceneKit
import ARKit

class ViewController: UIViewController, ARSCNViewDelegate {

    @IBOutlet var sceneView: ARSCNView!

    let configuration = ARWorldTrackingConfiguration()

    override func viewDidLoad() {
        super.viewDidLoad()
        // Do any additional setup after loading the view,
        typically from a nib.
        sceneView.debugOptions = [ARSCNDebugOptions.
        showWorldOrigin, ARSCNDebugOptions.showFeaturePoints]
        sceneView.delegate = self

        configuration.planeDetection = .horizontal
```

```swift
        sceneView.session.run(configuration)
    }

    func displayTexture(anchor: ARPlaneAnchor) -> SCNNode {
        let planeNode = SCNNode()
        planeNode.geometry = SCNPlane(width: CGFloat(anchor.
        extent.x), height: CGFloat(anchor.extent.z))
        planeNode.geometry?.firstMaterial?.diffuse.contents =
        UIImage(named: "water.jpg")
        planeNode.position = SCNVector3(anchor.center.x,
        anchor.center.y, anchor.center.z)

        let ninetyDegrees = GLKMathDegreesToRadians(90)
        planeNode.eulerAngles = SCNVector3(ninetyDegrees, 0, 0)

        planeNode.geometry?.firstMaterial?.isDoubleSided = true

        return planeNode
    }

    func renderer(_ renderer: SCNSceneRenderer, didAdd node:
    SCNNode, for anchor: ARAnchor) {
        guard anchor is ARPlaneAnchor else { return }

        let planeNode = displayTexture(anchor: anchor as!
        ARPlaneAnchor)
        node.addChildNode(planeNode)
        print ("plane detected")
    }

    func renderer(_ renderer: SCNSceneRenderer, didUpdate node:
    SCNNode, for anchor: ARAnchor) {
        guard anchor is ARPlaneAnchor else { return }
        print("updating plane anchor")
    }
}
```

If you run this code, you'll notice that when the app identifies a horizontal plane, it places a plane, displaying a texture image, in that location. However, one additional problem remains. The didUpdate renderer function constantly scans the real world and updates the ARPlaneAnchor for what it identifies as the horizontal plane.

That means we need to add code inside this didUpdate renderer function so when it recognizes that the horizontal plane is larger, it will display a larger virtual plane in that area.

The didUpdate renderer function runs every time ARKit detects that the horizontal plane is larger. Each time it needs to remove the currently displayed horizontal plane before adding an updated horizontal plane. To do this, we use the enumeratechildNodes loop to constantly remove the old horizontal plane like this:

```
node.enumerateChildNodes { (childNode, _) in
    childNode.removeFromParentNode()
}
```

After removing the old horizontal plane, we need to add a new one, so the entire didUpdate renderer function should look like this:

```
func renderer(_ renderer: SCNSceneRenderer, didUpdate node:
SCNNode, for anchor: ARAnchor) {
    guard anchor is ARPlaneAnchor else { return }

    node.enumerateChildNodes { (childNode, _) in
        childNode.removeFromParentNode()
    }
    let planeNode = displayTexture(anchor: anchor as!
    ARPlaneAnchor)
    node.addChildNode(planeNode)

    print("updating plane anchor")
}
```

The entire ViewController.swift file should now look like this:

```swift
import UIKit
import SceneKit
import ARKit

class ViewController: UIViewController, ARSCNViewDelegate {

    @IBOutlet var sceneView: ARSCNView!

    let configuration = ARWorldTrackingConfiguration()

    override func viewDidLoad() {
        super.viewDidLoad()
        // Do any additional setup after loading the view,
        typically from a nib.
        sceneView.debugOptions = [ARSCNDebugOptions.
        showWorldOrigin, ARSCNDebugOptions.showFeaturePoints]
        sceneView.delegate = self

        configuration.planeDetection = .horizontal

        sceneView.session.run(configuration)
    }

    func displayTexture(anchor: ARPlaneAnchor) -> SCNNode {
        let planeNode = SCNNode()
        planeNode.geometry = SCNPlane(width: CGFloat(anchor.
        extent.x), height: CGFloat(anchor.extent.z))
        planeNode.geometry?.firstMaterial?.diffuse.contents =
        UIImage(named: "water.jpg")
        planeNode.position = SCNVector3(anchor.center.x,
        anchor.center.y, anchor.center.z)
```

```
    let ninetyDegrees = GLKMathDegreesToRadians(90)
    planeNode.eulerAngles = SCNVector3(ninetyDegrees, 0, 0)

    planeNode.geometry?.firstMaterial?.isDoubleSided = true

    return planeNode
}

func renderer(_ renderer: SCNSceneRenderer, didAdd node:
SCNNode, for anchor: ARAnchor) {
    guard anchor is ARPlaneAnchor else { return }

    let planeNode = displayTexture(anchor: anchor as!
    ARPlaneAnchor)
    node.addChildNode(planeNode)
    print ("plane detected")
}

func renderer(_ renderer: SCNSceneRenderer, didUpdate node:
SCNNode, for anchor: ARAnchor) {
    guard anchor is ARPlaneAnchor else { return }

    node.enumerateChildNodes { (childNode, _) in
        childNode.removeFromParentNode()
    }
    let planeNode = displayTexture(anchor: anchor as!
    ARPlaneAnchor)
    node.addChildNode(planeNode)

    print("updating plane anchor")
}

}
```

To test this code, follow these steps:

1. Connect an iOS device to your Macintosh through its USB cable.

2. Click the Run button or choose Product ➤ Run. The first time you run this app, it will ask permission to access the camera so give it permission.

3. Aim the iOS device's camera at a horizontal plane such as the seat of a chair or the floor. The first time ARKit identifies a horizontal plane, the Xcode debug area displays the message "plane detected". That's when ARKit first displays the virtual plane that displays the texture image you dragged and dropped into the Navigator pane of Xcode.

4. Move the iOS device around to capture more of the horizontal plane. Each time ARKit recognizes a new part of the horizontal plane, the Xcode debug area displays the message "updating plane anchor". Notice that the horizontal virtual plane keeps expanding in size.

5. Click the Stop button or choose Product ➤ Stop.

# Placing Virtual Objects on a Horizontal Plane

One way users can interact with augmented reality is by placing virtual objects on horizontal planes identified in the real world, such as a floor or table top. This involves first detecting the horizontal plane, then placing a virtual object on that detected horizontal plane.

Let's create a new Xcode project by following these steps:

1. Start Xcode. (Make sure you're using Xcode 10 or greater.)

2. Choose File ➤ New ➤ Project. Xcode asks you to choose a template.

3. Click the iOS category.

4. Click the Single View App icon and click the Next button. Xcode asks for a product name, organization name, organization identifiers, and content technology.

5. Click in the Product Name text field and type a descriptive name for your project, such as PlacingObjects. (The exact name does not matter.)

6. Click the Next button. Xcode asks where you want to store your project.

7. Choose a folder and click the Create button. Xcode creates an iOS project.

Now modify the Info.plist file to allow access to the camera and to use ARKit by following these steps:

1. Click the Info.plist file in the Navigator pane. Xcode displays a list of keys, types, and values.

2. Click the disclosure triangle to expand the Required Device Capabilities category to display Item 0.

3. Move the mouse pointer over Item 0 to display a plus (+) icon.

4. Click this plus (+) icon to display a blank Item 1.

5. Type `arkit` under the Value category in the Item 1 row.

6. Move the mouse pointer over the last row to display a plus (+) icon.

7. Click on the plus (+) icon to create a new row. A popup menu appears.

8. Choose Privacy - Camera Usage Description.

9. Type `AR needs to use the camera` under the Value category in the Privacy - Camera Usage Description row.

Now it's time to modify the `ViewController.swift` file to use ARKit and SceneKit by following these steps:

1. Click on the `ViewController.swift` file in the Navigator pane.

2. Edit the `ViewController.swift` file so it looks like this:

```swift
import UIKit
import SceneKit
import ARKit

class ViewController: UIViewController,
ARSCNViewDelegate {

let configuration = ARWorldTrackingConfiguration()

    override func viewDidLoad() {
        super.viewDidLoad()
        // Do any additional setup after loading the
        view, typically from a nib.

    }

}
```

To view augmented reality in our app, add a single ARKit SceneKit View (ARSCNView) so it fills the entire user interface (see Figure 11-1).

After you've designed your user interface, you need to add constraints. To add constraints, choose Editor ➤ Resolve Auto Layout Issues ➤ Reset to Suggested Constraints at the bottom half of the menu under the All Views in Container category.

The next step is to connect the user interface items to the Swift code in the ViewController.swift file. To do this, follow these steps:

1. Click the Main.storyboard file in the Navigator pane.

2. Click the Assistant Editor icon or choose View ➤ Assistant Editor ➤ Show Assistant Editor to display the Main.storyboard and the ViewController. swift file side by side.

3. Move the mouse pointer over the ARSCNView, hold down the Control key, and Ctrl-drag under the class ViewController line.

4. Release the Control key and the left mouse button. A popup menu appears.

5. Click in the Name text field and type sceneView, then click the Connect button. Xcode creates an IBOutlet as shown here:

   **@IBOutlet var** sceneView: ARSCNView!

6. Edit the viewDidLoad function so it looks like this:

   ```
   override func viewDidLoad() {
       super.viewDidLoad()
       // Do any additional setup after loading the
       view, typically from a nib.
   ```

```
    sceneView.debugOptions = [ARSCNDebugOptions.
    showWorldOrigin, ARSCNDebugOptions.
    showFeaturePoints]
    sceneView.delegate = self

    configuration.planeDetection = .horizontal

    sceneView.session.run(configuration)
}
```

This app currently detects horizontal planes, but we also need it to accept tap gestures to place a virtual object on a detected horizontal plane. To place a tap gesture recognizer in our app, follow these steps:

1. Click the ViewController.swift file in the Navigator pane.

2. Add the following two lines to the end of the viewDidLoad function:

```
let tapGesture = UITapGestureRecognizer(target:
self, action: #selector(tapResponse))
sceneView.addGestureRecognizer(tapGesture)
```

3. Type the following underneath the viewDidLoad function:

```
@objc func tapResponse(sender:
UITapGestureRecognizer) {
    let scene = sender.view as! ARSCNView
    let tapLocation = sender.location(in: scene)
    let hitTest = scene.hitTest(tapLocation, types:
    .existingPlaneUsingExtent)
    if hitTest.isEmpty{
        print ("no plane detected")
    } else {
```

285

```
                 print("found a horizontal plane")
            }
        }
```

4. Connect an iOS device to your Macintosh through its USB cable.

5. Click the Run button or choose Product ➤ Run.

6. Point your iOS device's camera at a flat, horizontal surface until you see plenty of yellow feature points appearing. Then tap on the screen. The debug area of Xcode should display the "found a horizontal plane" message.

7. Point your iOS device's camera at a wall. Then tap on the screen. The debug area of Xcode should display the "no plane detected" message.

8. Click the Stop button or choose Product ➤ Stop.

This code shows that we can detect horizontal planes and recognize a tap gesture. This tap gesture will be used to place a virtual object when ARKit recognizes a horizontal plane. To do this, we must first modify the tapResponse function with two additional lines below the print("found a horizontal plane") line like this:

```
guard let hitResult = hitTest.first else { return }
addObject(hitResult: hitResult)
```

This first guard line checks to make sure that the user tapped on a horizontal plane. Then the second line calls an addObject function and sends the position of where the user tapped.

Next, we'll need to create an addObject function like this:

```
func addObject(hitResult: ARHitTestResult) {

}
```

This function receives the location of the horizontal plane send by the `tapResponse` function. What we'll add each time the user taps the screen on a horizontal plane will be an orange pyramid, so we can write the following code inside the `addObject` function:

```
func addObject(hitResult: ARHitTestResult) {
    let objectNode = SCNNode()
    objectNode.geometry = SCNPyramid(width: 0.1,
    height: 0.2, length: 0.1)
    objectNode.geometry?.firstMaterial?.diffuse.contents =
    UIColor.orange
}
```

Finally, we need to define the position of each pyramid. The x, y, and z positions where the user tapped is stored in a 4x4 matrix called `worldTransform`. The x, y, and z positions are stored in the third column of this `worldTransform` matrix so the last two lines in the `addObject` function look like this:

```
objectNode.position = SCNVector3(hitResult.worldTransform.
columns.3.x, hitResult.worldTransform.columns.3.y,
hitResult.worldTransform.columns.3.z)
sceneView.scene.rootNode.addChildNode(objectNode)
```

The first line retrieves the x, y, and z location of the tap on the screen, while the second line places the virtual object (the orange pyramid) where the user tapped. The entire `ViewController.swift` file should look like this:

```
import UIKit
import SceneKit
import ARKit
```

```
class ViewController: UIViewController, ARSCNViewDelegate {

    @IBOutlet var sceneView: ARSCNView!

    let configuration = ARWorldTrackingConfiguration()

    override func viewDidLoad() {
        super.viewDidLoad()
        // Do any additional setup after loading the view,
        typically from a nib.
        sceneView.debugOptions = [ARSCNDebugOptions.
        showWorldOrigin, ARSCNDebugOptions.showFeaturePoints]
        sceneView.delegate = self
        configuration.planeDetection = .horizontal

        sceneView.session.run(configuration)

        let tapGesture = UITapGestureRecognizer(target: self,
        action: #selector(tapResponse))
        sceneView.addGestureRecognizer(tapGesture)

    }

    @objc func tapResponse(sender: UITapGestureRecognizer) {
        let scene = sender.view as! ARSCNView
        let tapLocation = sender.location(in: scene)
        let hitTest = scene.hitTest(tapLocation, types:
        .existingPlaneUsingExtent)
        if hitTest.isEmpty{
            print ("no plane detected")
        } else {
            print("found a horizontal plane")
            guard let hitResult = hitTest.first else { return }
            addObject(hitResult: hitResult)
        }
    }
```

```
func addObject(hitResult: ARHitTestResult) {
    let objectNode = SCNNode()
    objectNode.geometry = SCNPyramid(width: 0.1, height:
    0.2, length: 0.1)
    objectNode.geometry?.firstMaterial?.diffuse.contents =
    UIColor.orange
    objectNode.position = SCNVector3(hitResult.
    worldTransform.columns.3.x, hitResult.worldTransform.
    columns.3.y, hitResult.worldTransform.columns.3.z)
    sceneView.scene.rootNode.addChildNode(objectNode)
}

}
```

To test this code, follow these steps:

1.  Connect an iOS device to your Macintosh through
    its USB cable.

2.  Click the Run button or choose Product ➤ Run. The
    first time you run this app, it will ask permission to
    access the camera, so give it permission.

3.  Aim the iOS device's camera at a horizontal plane,
    such as the seat of a chair or the floor. The first time
    ARKit identifies a horizontal plane, the Xcode debug
    area displays the message "plane detected".

4.  Tap the screen. An orange pyramid appears where
    you tapped, as shown in Figure 11-5. Repeat Steps
    3 and 4 to add orange pyramids to the detected
    horizontal plane.

*Figure 11-5.* *Adding orange pyramids to a horizontal plane*

5.    Click the Stop button or choose Product ➤ Stop.

# Detecting Vertical Planes

Detecting vertical planes is identical to detecting horizontal planes. Instead of defining planeDetection as .horizontal, you define it as .vertical like this:

```
configuration.planeDetection = .vertical
```

Now your app can detect vertical planes such as walls instead of only horizontal planes like floors. To see how detecting vertical planes can work, simply modify the PlacingObjects project by editing the viewDidLoad function so it detects vertical planes. The entire viewDidLoad function should look like this:

```
override func viewDidLoad() {
    super.viewDidLoad()
    // Do any additional setup after loading the view,
    typically from a nib.
    sceneView.debugOptions = [ARSCNDebugOptions.
    showWorldOrigin, ARSCNDebugOptions.showFeaturePoints]
    sceneView.delegate = self
    configuration.planeDetection = .vertical

    sceneView.session.run(configuration)

    let tapGesture = UITapGestureRecognizer(target: self,
    action: #selector(tapResponse))
    sceneView.addGestureRecognizer(tapGesture)

}
```

In the tapResponse function, simply replace horizontal with vertical in the print statement so the entire tapResponse function looks like this:

```
@objc func tapResponse(sender: UITapGestureRecognizer) {
    let scene = sender.view as! ARSCNView
    let tapLocation = sender.location(in: scene)
    let hitTest = scene.hitTest(tapLocation, types:
    .existingPlaneUsingExtent)
    if hitTest.isEmpty{
        print ("no plane detected")
```

```swift
    } else {
        print("found a vertical plane")
        guard let hitResult = hitTest.first else { return }
        addObject(hitResult: hitResult)
    }
}
```

Search the Internet for an image of your favorite painting and drag it into the Navigator pane, as shown in Figure 11-6.

*Figure 11-6.*  *Adding an image of a painting*

Most of the changes will need to occur in the addObject function. First, we need to create a plane to add, define the plane's size, and display the painting image on that plane like this:

```
let objectNode = SCNNode()
objectNode.geometry = SCNPlane(width: 0.3, height: 0.3)
    objectNode.geometry?.firstMaterial?.diffuse.contents =
    UIImage(named: "Mona_Lisa.jpg")
```

This code adds an image called Mona_Lisa.jpg to the plane, but you'll need to replace this image name with the name of the image you dragged and dropped into the Navigator pane.

The entire addObject function should look like this:

```
func addObject(hitResult: ARHitTestResult) {
    let objectNode = SCNNode()
    objectNode.geometry = SCNPlane(width: 0.3, height: 0.3)
    objectNode.geometry?.firstMaterial?.diffuse.contents =
    UIImage(named: "Mona_Lisa.jpg")

    objectNode.position = SCNVector3(hitResult.
    worldTransform.columns.3.x, hitResult.worldTransform.
    columns.3.y, hitResult.worldTransform.columns.3.z)
    sceneView.scene.rootNode.addChildNode(objectNode)
}
```

The entire ViewController.swift file should look like this:

```
import UIKit
import SceneKit
import ARKit

class ViewController: UIViewController, ARSCNViewDelegate {

    @IBOutlet var sceneView: ARSCNView!
```

```
let configuration = ARWorldTrackingConfiguration()

override func viewDidLoad() {
    super.viewDidLoad()
    // Do any additional setup after loading the view,
    typically from a nib.
    sceneView.debugOptions = [ARSCNDebugOptions.
    showWorldOrigin, ARSCNDebugOptions.showFeaturePoints]
    sceneView.delegate = self
    configuration.planeDetection = .vertical

    sceneView.session.run(configuration)

    let tapGesture = UITapGestureRecognizer(target: self,
    action: #selector(tapResponse))
    sceneView.addGestureRecognizer(tapGesture)

}

@objc func tapResponse(sender: UITapGestureRecognizer) {
    let scene = sender.view as! ARSCNView
    let tapLocation = sender.location(in: scene)
    let hitTest = scene.hitTest(tapLocation, types:
    .existingPlaneUsingExtent)
    if hitTest.isEmpty{
        print ("no plane detected")
    } else {
        print("found a vertical plane")
        guard let hitResult = hitTest.first else { return }
        addObject(hitResult: hitResult)
    }
}
```

```
func addObject(hitResult: ARHitTestResult) {
    let objectNode = SCNNode()
    objectNode.geometry = SCNPlane(width: 0.3, height: 0.3)
    objectNode.geometry?.firstMaterial?.diffuse.contents =
    UIImage(named: "Mona_Lisa.jpg")

    objectNode.position = SCNVector3(hitResult.
    worldTransform.columns.3.x, hitResult.worldTransform.
    columns.3.y, hitResult.worldTransform.columns.3.z)
    sceneView.scene.rootNode.addChildNode(objectNode)
}

}
```

To test this code, follow these steps:

1.  Connect an iOS device to your Macintosh through its USB cable.

2.  Click the Run button or choose Product ➤ Run. The first time you run this app, it will ask permission to access the camera so give it permission.

3.  Aim the iOS device's camera at a vertical plane such as a wall or a door. Pick a vertical surface that isn't smooth but has plenty of distinctive features for the app to identify as tiny yellow feature points on the screen. The more feature points the app can identify on a vertical plane, the more likely it will be able to identify that vertical plane. The first time ARKit identifies a vertical plane, the Xcode debug area displays the message "plane detected".

4.  Tap the screen. The image of your painting appears on the vertical plane, as shown in Figure 11-7.

**_Figure 11-7._**  _Adding a plane to a vertical surface_

    5.    Click the Stop button or choose Product ➤ Stop.

As you can see, detecting vertical planes is identical to detecting horizontal planes.

# Summary

Detecting horizontal or vertical planes can be crucial when you want to add virtual objects to the real world. You simply need to use one line of code to detect horizontal or vertical planes:

```
configuration.planeDetection = .horizontal
```

Or

```
configuration.planeDetection = .vertical
```

Once ARKit detects a horizontal or vertical plane, it can define that plane with a texture image, such as water, bricks, or sand. As you move an iOS device's camera around, the size of a detected plane will gradually grow.

# CHAPTER 12

# Physics on Virtual Objects

So far when we've added virtual objects to an augmented reality view, those virtual objects simply float in mid-air. While this might be suitable in some cases, in other cases you might want the virtual objects to behave more like real objects that can fall, bounce, and collide with one another.

To give virtual objects the same characteristics as real objects, you can define physical characteristics to any virtual object. That means you can define how a virtual object interacts with others (static, dynamic, or kinematic), the shape of a virtual object such as a box or sphere, and the force applied to a virtual object.

A virtual object can behave in one of three ways:

- Static—Cannot move and is unaffected by collisions or force.

- Dynamic—Affected by forces and collisions.

- Kinematic—Not affected by forces or collisions, but can affect dynamic virtual objects.

Static virtual objects are fine for scenery that simply exists. So far, all the virtual objects we've created so far have been static in that they don't move or affect any other virtual objects.

© Wallace Wang 2018
W. Wang, *Beginning ARKit for iPhone and iPad*,
https://doi.org/10.1007/978-1-4842-4102-8_12

Dynamic virtual objects are more interesting because they can move and be affected by gravity, which means they'll fall to the ground along the y-axis. A dynamic virtual object can move and bounce off other dynamic or kinematic virtual objects.

Kinematic virtual objects don't move but they can collide with dynamic virtual objects. In a video game, a stationary item like a road or an obstacle could be a kinematic virtual object.

To learn about applying physics to virtual objects, let's create a new Xcode project by following these steps:

1.  Start Xcode. (Make sure you're using Xcode 10 or greater.)

2.  Choose File ➤ New ➤ Project. Xcode asks you to choose a template.

3.  Click the iOS category.

4.  Click the Single View App icon and click the Next button. Xcode asks for a product name, organization name, organization identifiers, and content technology.

5.  Click in the Product Name text field and type a descriptive name for your project, such as Physics. (The exact name does not matter.)

6.  Click the Next button. Xcode asks where you want to store your project.

7.  Choose a folder and click the Create button. Xcode creates an iOS project.

Now modify the Info.plist file to allow access to the camera and to use ARKit by following these steps:

1.  Click the Info.plist file in the Navigator pane.
    Xcode displays a list of keys, types, and values.

2.  Click the disclosure triangle to expand the Required
    Device Capabilities category to display Item 0.

3.  Move the mouse pointer over Item 0 to display a
    plus (+) icon.

4.  Click this plus (+) icon to display a blank Item 1.

5.  Type arkit under the Value category in the Item 1
    row.

6.  Move the mouse pointer over the last row to display
    a plus (+) icon.

7.  Click on the plus (+) icon to create a new row.
    A popup menu appears.

8.  Choose Privacy – Camera Usage Description.

9.  Type AR needs to use the camera under the Value
    category in the Privacy – Camera Usage Description
    row.

Now it's time to modify the ViewController.swift file to use ARKit
and SceneKit by following these steps:

1.  Click on the ViewController.swift file in the
    Navigator pane.

2.  Edit the ViewController.swift file so it looks like this:

    ```
    import UIKit
    import SceneKit
    import ARKit
    ```

```
class ViewController: UIViewController,
ARSCNViewDelegate {

let configuration = ARWorldTrackingConfiguration()

    override func viewDidLoad() {
        super.viewDidLoad()
        // Do any additional setup after loading the
        view, typically from a nib.

    }

}
```

To view augmented reality in our app, add a single ARKit SceneKit View (ARSCNView) and expand it so it fills the entire user interface. Then add constraints by choosing Editor ➤ Resolve Auto Layout Issues ➤ Reset to Suggested Constraints at the bottom half of the menu under the All Views in Container category.

The next step is to connect the user interface items to the Swift code in the ViewController.swift file. To do this, follow these steps:

1. Click the Main.storyboard file in the Navigator pane.

2. Click the Assistant Editor icon or choose View ➤ Assistant Editor ➤ Show Assistant Editor to display the Main.storyboard and the ViewController. swift file side by side.

3. Move the mouse pointer over the ARSCNView, hold down the Control key, and Ctrl-drag under the class ViewController line.

4. Release the Control key and the left mouse button. A popup menu appears.

5.  Click in the Name text field and type sceneView,
    then click the Connect button. Xcode creates an
    IBOutlet as shown here:

    **@IBOutlet var** sceneView: ARSCNView!

6.  Edit the viewDidLoad function so it looks like this:

```
override func viewDidLoad() {
    super.viewDidLoad()
    // Do any additional setup after loading the
    view, typically from a nib.
    sceneView.debugOptions = [ARSCNDebugOptions.
    showWorldOrigin, ARSCNDebugOptions.
    showFeaturePoints]
    sceneView.delegate = self

    configuration.planeDetection = .horizontal

    sceneView.session.run(configuration)

    let tapGesture = UITapGestureRecognizer(target:
    self, action: #selector(tapResponse))
    sceneView.addGestureRecognizer(tapGesture)
}
```

The last two lines in the viewDidLoad function create
a tap gesture, which means we'll need a function to
handle the tap gesture, called tapGesture.

7.  Underneath the viewDidLoad function, write the
    following tapResponse function:

```
@objc func tapResponse(sender:
UITapGestureRecognizer) {
    let scene = sender.view as! ARSCNView
    let tapLocation = sender.location(in: scene)
```

```
let hitTest = scene.hitTest(tapLocation,
types: .existingPlaneUsingExtent)
if hitTest.isEmpty{
    print ("no plane detected")
} else {
    print("found a horizontal plane")
    guard let hitResult = hitTest.first
    else { return }
    addObject(hitResult: hitResult)
}
}
```

This tapResponse function identifies the location on the screen where the user tapped and then sends this information to an addObject function, which means we need to write the addObject function next.

8. Underneath the tapResponse function, write the following addObject function:

```
func addObject(hitResult: ARHitTestResult) {
    let objectNode = SCNNode()
    objectNode.geometry = SCNSphere(radius: 0.1)
    objectNode.geometry?.firstMaterial?.diffuse.
    contents = UIColor.orange
    objectNode.position = SCNVector3(hitResult.
    worldTransform.columns.3.x, hitResult.
    worldTransform.columns.3.y + 0.5, hitResult.
    worldTransform.columns.3.z)
    objectNode.physicsBody = SCNPhysicsBody(type:
    .dynamic, shape: nil)
    sceneView.scene.rootNode.addChildNode(objectNode)
}
```

The addObject function creates an orange sphere. Normally this orange sphere would float in mid-air but we've given it a physicsBody with this line:

```
objectNode.physicsBody = SCNPhysicsBody(type: .dynamic,
shape: nil)
```

This code defines the orange sphere as dynamic, which means it can be affected by forces and collisions with other virtual objects. Also its shape is defined as nil, which means ARKit will treat the sphere's boundaries as its body when calculating collisions with other virtual objects.

Now we need to detect a horizontal plane and draw a virtual plane in that spot. To do that, we need a didAdd renderer function like this:

```
func renderer(_ renderer: SCNSceneRenderer, didAdd node:
SCNNode, for anchor: ARAnchor) {
    guard anchor is ARPlaneAnchor else { return }

    let planeNode = displayPlane(anchor: anchor as!
    ARPlaneAnchor)
    node.addChildNode(planeNode)
}
```

Notice that this renderer function runs multiple times by constantly looking for a horizontal plane. When it identifies a horizontal plane, then it calls a displayPlane function to create that virtual plane. That means we need to write a displayPlane function like this:

```
func displayPlane(anchor: ARPlaneAnchor) -> SCNNode {
    let planeNode = SCNNode()
    planeNode.geometry = SCNPlane(width: CGFloat(anchor.
    extent.x), height: CGFloat(anchor.extent.z))
    planeNode.geometry?.firstMaterial?.diffuse.contents =
    UIColor.yellow
    planeNode.position = SCNVector3(anchor.center.x,
    anchor.center.y, anchor.center.z)
```

305

```
    let ninetyDegrees = GLKMathDegreesToRadians(90)
    planeNode.eulerAngles = SCNVector3(ninetyDegrees, 0, 0)
    planeNode.physicsBody = SCNPhysicsBody(type:
    .kinematic, shape: nil)
    planeNode.geometry?.firstMaterial?.isDoubleSided = true

    return planeNode
}
```

This `displayPlane` function receives information about horizontal plane stored in `ARPlaneAnchor`, which defines a plane's size and position. So we need to create a plane node and give it a size based on the `ARPlaneAnchor` information:

```
planeNode.geometry = SCNPlane(width: CGFloat(anchor.extent.x),
height: CGFloat(anchor.extent.z))
```

Then we color the virtual plane yellow and position it in the center of the horizontal plane that ARKit recognized. Next, we need to rotate the plane 90 degrees around the x-axis, so instead of appearing vertically like a wall, it appears horizontally like a floor.

Most importantly, we need to give this virtual plane a physics body like this:

```
planeNode.physicsBody = SCNPhysicsBody(type: .kinematic,
shape: nil)
```

This code defines the virtual plane as kinematic, which means it won't move when colliding with virtual objects, but it will affect any virtual objects colliding with it. We define its shape as nil, which tells ARKit to define the entire virtual plane as its physical body when calculating collisions with other virtual objects.

Finally, we need a renderer didUpdate function to expand the size of the virtual plane if the user moves the iOS device's camera to capture more of the horizontal plane. This renderer didUpdate function looks like this:

```
func renderer(_ renderer: SCNSceneRenderer, didUpdate node:
SCNNode, for anchor: ARAnchor) {
    guard anchor is ARPlaneAnchor else { return }

    node.enumerateChildNodes { (childNode, _) in
        childNode.removeFromParentNode()
    }
    let planeNode = displayPlane(anchor: anchor as!
    ARPlaneAnchor)
    node.addChildNode(planeNode)

}
```

This didUpdate renderer function removes the virtual plane and redraws a new virtual plane each time it detects that the horizontal plane is larger than it initially calculated. Then it calls the displayPlane function to draw a virtual plane in the augmented reality view.

To test this project, follow these steps:

1.  Connect an iOS device to your Macintosh through its USB cable.

2.  Click the Run button or choose Product ➤ Run. The first time you run this app, it will ask permission to access the camera so give it permission.

3.  Aim the iOS device's camera at a horizontal plane such as a table or the floor. The first time ARKit identifies a horizontal plane, the Xcode debug area displays the message "found a horizontal plane".

4.  Move the iOS device around to capture more of the horizontal plane. Each time ARKit recognizes a new part of the horizontal plane, the yellow plane grows in size.

5.  Tap the screen. Each time you tap the screen, an orange sphere should appear, as shown in Figure 12-1. Because the orange sphere was defined as a `.dynamic` physics body, it's affected by forces such as gravity, which causes the orange sphere to drop. If the orange sphere hits the yellow plane, it either bounces off it or rests on top of it. If you keep tapping the screen to add more orange spheres, the orange spheres will bounce off each other and the yellow plane. That's because the yellow sphere is defined as a `.kinematic` physics body, which means forces such as gravity do not affect it, but it can collide with other virtual objects such as the orange spheres.

**Figure 12-1.** *The orange sphere can fall and hit the yellow plane*

6.   Click the Stop button or choose Product ➤ Stop.

Because the orange sphere is defined as a .dynamic physics body, it's affected by gravity. Because the yellow plane is defined as a .kinematic physics body, it is not affected by gravity but can interact with other virtual objects like the orange spheres.

If you ever create a virtual object defined as a .dynamic physics body and don't want it affected by gravity, you can set its isAffectedByGravity property to false like this:

```
objectNode.physicsBody?.isAffectedByGravity = false
```

If you add this line to the `addObject` function, each time you tap on the screen to add an orange sphere, the orange sphere will just hover in mid-air because it won't be affected by gravity, even though it's defined as a `.dynamic` physics body.

# Applying Force on Virtual Objects

So far, we've created virtual objects that either hover in mid-air or respond to gravity by falling. Another way to interact with virtual objects is by applying a force to them. To apply a force on a virtual object, you need to define the force's direction and whether you want it to be instantaneous or not.

Let's create a new Xcode project to display three targets and fire a projectile at those three targets by following these steps:

1. Start Xcode. (Make sure you're using Xcode 10 or greater.)

2. Choose File ➤ New ➤ Project. Xcode asks you to choose a template.

3. Click the iOS category.

4. Click the Single View App icon and click the Next button. Xcode asks for a product name, organization name, organization identifiers, and content technology.

5. Click in the Product Name text field and type a descriptive name for your project, such as `PhysicsForce`. (The exact name does not matter.)

6. Click the Next button. Xcode asks where you want to store your project.

7. Choose a folder and click the Create button. Xcode creates an iOS project.

Now modify the `Info.plist` file to allow access to the camera and to use ARKit by following these steps:

1. Click the `Info.plist` file in the Navigator pane. Xcode displays a list of keys, types, and values.

2. Click the disclosure triangle to expand the Required Device Capabilities category to display Item 0.

3. Move the mouse pointer over Item 0 to display a plus (+) icon.

4. Click this plus (+) icon to display a blank Item 1.

5. Type `arkit` under the Value category in the Item 1 row.

6. Move the mouse pointer over the last row to display a plus (+) icon.

7. Click on the plus (+) icon to create a new row. A popup menu appears.

8. Choose Privacy – Camera Usage Description.

9. Type `AR needs to use the camera` under the Value category in the Privacy – Camera Usage Description row.

Now it's time to modify the `ViewController.swift` file to use ARKit and SceneKit by following these steps:

1. Click on the `ViewController.swift` file in the Navigator pane.

2. Edit the `ViewController.swift` file so it looks like this:

```
import UIKit
import SceneKit
import ARKit
```

```
class ViewController: UIViewController,
ARSCNViewDelegate {

let configuration = ARWorldTrackingConfiguration()

    override func viewDidLoad() {
        super.viewDidLoad()
        // Do any additional setup after loading the
        view, typically from a nib.

    }

}
```

To view augmented reality in our app, add a single ARKit SceneKit View (ARSCNView) so it fills the entire user interface (see Figure 11-1 in Chapter 11).

After you've designed your user interface, you need to add constraints. To add constraints, choose Editor ➤ Resolve Auto Layout Issues ➤ Reset to Suggested Constraints at the bottom half of the menu under the All Views in Container category.

The next step is to connect the user interface items to the Swift code in the ViewController.swift file. To do this, follow these steps:

1. Click the Main.storyboard file in the Navigator pane.

2. Click the Assistant Editor icon or choose View ➤ Assistant Editor ➤ Show Assistant Editor to display the Main.storyboard and the ViewController. swift file side by side.

3. Move the mouse pointer over the ARSCNView, hold down the Control key, and Ctrl-drag under the class ViewController line.

4. Release the Control key and the left mouse button. A popup menu appears.

5. Click in the Name text field and type sceneView, then click the Connect button. Xcode creates an IBOutlet as shown here:

```
@IBOutlet var sceneView: ARSCNView!
```

6. Edit the viewDidLoad function so it looks like this:

```
override func viewDidLoad() {
    super.viewDidLoad()
    // Do any additional setup after loading the
    view, typically from a nib.
    sceneView.debugOptions = [ARSCNDebugOptions.
    showWorldOrigin, ARSCNDebugOptions.
    showFeaturePoints]
    sceneView.delegate = self

    sceneView.session.run(configuration)

    let tapGesture = UITapGestureRecognizer(target:
    self, action: #selector(tapResponse))
    sceneView.addGestureRecognizer(tapGesture)

}
```

At this point, we've added a tap gesture recognizer so we need to write a function to handle this tap gesture by following these steps:

1. Click the ViewController.swift file in the Navigator pane.

2. Type the following underneath the viewDidLoad function:

```
@objc func tapResponse(sender:
UITapGestureRecognizer) {

}
```

Each time the user taps the screen, we want a sphere to shoot out from the center of the screen and away from the user. To do this, we must first get the current orientation and location of the camera. That means making sure the user tapped on an augmented reality view and then retrieving information about the current camera's orientation and location in a matrix using these three lines of code:

```
guard let scene = sender.view as? ARSCNView else { return }
guard let pov = scene.pointOfView else { return }
let transform = pov.transform
```

The transform constant stores a 4 by 4 matrix that contains information about the camera's position and orientation. To retrieve the orientation information, we need to access the third column of this matrix:

```
let orientation = SCNVector3(-transform.m31, -transform.m32,
-transform.m33)
```

All of this information needs to be reversed (hence the negative signs) because the orientation faces toward us and we need it to face the opposite direction away from us.

The location of the camera can be retrieved in the fourth column of the matrix like this:

```
let location = SCNVector3(transform.m41, transform.m42,
transform.m43)
```

To get the final position of the camera, we need to combine the orientation with the location like this:

```
let position = SCNVector3(orientation.x + location.x,
orientation.y + location.y, orientation.z + location.z)
```

Once we know the position of the camera, we need to create a projectile, which will be a sphere that's colored purple and appears at the center of the screen, which is the position of the camera:

```
let projectile = SCNNode()
projectile.geometry = SCNSphere(radius: 0.35)
projectile.geometry?.firstMaterial?.diffuse.contents =
UIColor.purple
projectile.position = position
```

This creates a purple sphere that will float in mid-air in the center of the screen when the user taps the screen. We need to give the projectile a physics body that defines its type as .dynamic, which means it can collide with other virtual objects:

```
projectile.physicsBody = SCNPhysicsBody(type: .dynamic,
shape: SCNPhysicsShape(node: projectile, options: nil))
projectile.physicsBody?.isAffectedByGravity = false
```

The first line defines the purple sphere as a physics body capable of moving and colliding, and the second line turns off its gravity. Otherwise gravity would just make the purple sphere plummet to the ground.

Now it's time to apply a force to the purple sphere. First, declare a constant named force and set its value to an arbitrary value of 50. Then apply that force on the project using the applyForce method like this:

```
let force: Float = 50
projectile.physicsBody?.applyForce(SCNVector3
(orientation.x * force, orientation.y * force, orientation.z
* force), asImpulse: true)
```

This code applies a force to the projectile but this force is relatively weak, so we need to multiply it by the arbitrary force constant (50). The asImpulse value is true to create an instantaneous force on the projectile. If this asImpulse value were false, then the force would be applied continuously on the projectile.

The entire tapResponse function should look like this:

```
@objc func tapResponse(sender: UITapGestureRecognizer) {
    guard let scene = sender.view as? ARSCNView else { return }
    guard let pov = scene.pointOfView else { return }
    let transform = pov.transform
    let orientation = SCNVector3(-transform.m31,
    -transform.m32, -transform.m33)
    let location = SCNVector3(transform.m41, transform.m42,
    transform.m43)
    let position = SCNVector3(orientation.x + location.x,
    orientation.y + location.y, orientation.z + location.z)
    let projectile = SCNNode()
    projectile.geometry = SCNSphere(radius: 0.35)
    projectile.geometry?.firstMaterial?.diffuse.contents =
    UIColor.purple
    projectile.position = position
    projectile.physicsBody = SCNPhysicsBody(type: .dynamic,
    shape: SCNPhysicsShape(node: projectile, options: nil))
    projectile.physicsBody?.isAffectedByGravity = false
    let force: Float = 50
    projectile.physicsBody?.applyForce(SCNVector3
    (orientation.x * force, orientation.y * force,
    orientation.z * force), asImpulse: true)
    sceneView.scene.rootNode.addChildNode(projectile)
}
```

To test this code, follow these steps:

1. Connect an iOS device to your Macintosh through its USB cable.

2.  Click the Run button or choose Product ➤ Run. The
    first time you run this app, it will ask permission to
    access the camera so give it permission.

3.  Aim the iOS device's camera and tap the screen.
    Each time you tap the screen, a purple sphere
    should shoot out and gradually disappear.

4.  Click the Stop button or choose Product ➤ Stop.

Modify the force constant with different values such as 20 or 75 to see
the effect it has on the force applied to the purple sphere.

# Colliding with Virtual Objects

To make a virtual object collide with another one, the two colliding virtual
objects need to be either `.static` or `.dynamic` physics body types. At the
end of the `viewDidLoad` function, add this line to call a function called
`addTargets`:

```
addTargets()
```

The projectile purples sphere is defined as a `.dynamic` physics body,
which means that any other virtual objects that we want to collide with
the purple sphere must be `.dynamic` or `.static` physics bodies. First, let's
create an `addTargets` function:

```
func addTargets() {

}
```

Add a pyramid in the `addTargets` function that defines an orange color, specific dimensions, and a position based on the world origin. Then define the pyramid as a `.static` physics body and add it to the scene like this:

```
let pyramidNode = SCNNode()
pyramidNode.geometry = SCNPyramid(width: 4, height: 4.5,
length: 4)
pyramidNode.geometry?.firstMaterial?.diffuse.contents =
UIColor.orange
pyramidNode.position = SCNVector3(-3, 1, -15)
pyramidNode.physicsBody = SCNPhysicsBody(type: .static,
shape: nil)
sceneView.scene.rootNode.addChildNode(pyramidNode)
```

Create a green box with specific dimensions and position it nearby like this:

```
let boxNode = SCNNode()
boxNode.geometry = SCNBox(width: 3.5, height: 3.5, length:
3.5, chamferRadius: 0)
boxNode.geometry?.firstMaterial?.diffuse.contents = UIColor.
green
boxNode.position = SCNVector3(5, 1, -15)
boxNode.physicsBody = SCNPhysicsBody(type: .static, shape: nil)
sceneView.scene.rootNode.addChildNode(boxNode)
```

Notice that when defining the physics body of the pyramid and box, the shape is defined as nil, which means to use the shape of the virtual object as its boundaries like this:

```
pyramidNode.physicsBody = SCNPhysicsBody(type: .static,
shape: nil)
boxNode.physicsBody = SCNPhysicsBody(type: .static, shape: nil)
```

The final virtual object to create inside the `addTargets` function is a torus, which looks like a doughnut or a hoop. Creating a blue torus involves defining physical dimensions, a color, and a position:

```
let torusNode = SCNNode()
torusNode.geometry = SCNTorus(ringRadius: 2, pipeRadius: 0.5)
torusNode.geometry?.firstMaterial?.diffuse.contents =
UIColor.blue
torusNode.position = SCNVector3(0, -2, -15)
```

First, we'll need to rotate the torus 90 degrees around the x-axis or else it will appear as a flat disk. To rotate the torus, we need to first convert 90 degrees into radians and then apply the value in radians into rotating the torus around its x-axis like this:

```
let ninetyDegrees = GLKMathDegreesToRadians(90)
 torusNode.eulerAngles = SCNVector3(ninetyDegrees, 0, 0)
```

Now we need to define the physics body of the torus. If we simply define its shape as nil like this:

```
torusNode.physicsBody = SCNPhysicsBody(type: .static, shape: nil)
```

This will create torus that looks like it has a hole in the middle of it, but really doesn't. That's because the nil value for its shape simply uses the entire boundary of the torus as the boundaries for detecting collections, including the inner hole. To make the hole behave like empty air, we need to define the torus's physics body to use the boundaries of the actual shape itself, not just the outer boundaries. To do this, we can use this code:

```
torusNode.physicsBody = SCNPhysicsBody(type: .static, shape:
SCNPhysicsShape(node: torusNode, options: [SCNPhysicsShape.
Option.type: SCNPhysicsShape.ShapeType.concavePolyhedron]))
```

The entire ViewController.swift file should look like this:

```swift
import UIKit
import SceneKit
import ARKit

class ViewController: UIViewController, ARSCNViewDelegate  {

    @IBOutlet var sceneView: ARSCNView!

    let configuration = ARWorldTrackingConfiguration()

    override func viewDidLoad() {
        super.viewDidLoad()
        // Do any additional setup after loading the view,
        typically from a nib.
        sceneView.debugOptions = [ARSCNDebugOptions.
        showWorldOrigin, ARSCNDebugOptions.showFeaturePoints]
        sceneView.delegate = self

        sceneView.session.run(configuration)

        let tapGesture = UITapGestureRecognizer(target: self,
        action: #selector(tapResponse))
        sceneView.addGestureRecognizer(tapGesture)

        addTargets()
    }

    @objc func tapResponse(sender: UITapGestureRecognizer) {
        guard let scene = sender.view as? ARSCNView else { return }
        guard let pov = scene.pointOfView else { return }
        let transform = pov.transform
        let orientation = SCNVector3(-transform.m31,
        -transform.m32, -transform.m33)
```

```swift
    let location = SCNVector3(transform.m41, transform.m42,
    transform.m43)
    let position = SCNVector3(orientation.x + location.x,
    orientation.y + location.y, orientation.z + location.z)
    let projectile = SCNNode()
    projectile.geometry = SCNSphere(radius: 0.35)
    projectile.geometry?.firstMaterial?.diffuse.contents =
    UIColor.purple
    projectile.position = position
    projectile.physicsBody = SCNPhysicsBody(type: .dynamic,
    shape: SCNPhysicsShape(node: projectile, options: nil))
    projectile.physicsBody?.isAffectedByGravity = false
    let force: Float = 50
    projectile.physicsBody?.applyForce(SCNVector3
    (orientation.x * force, orientation.y * force,
    orientation.z * force), asImpulse: true)
    sceneView.scene.rootNode.addChildNode(projectile)
}

func addTargets() {
    let pyramidNode = SCNNode()
    pyramidNode.geometry = SCNPyramid(width: 4, height:
    4.5, length: 4)
    pyramidNode.geometry?.firstMaterial?.diffuse.contents =
    UIColor.orange
    pyramidNode.position = SCNVector3(-3, 1, -15)
    pyramidNode.physicsBody = SCNPhysicsBody(type: .static,
    shape: nil)
    sceneView.scene.rootNode.addChildNode(pyramidNode)
```

```
let torusNode = SCNNode()
torusNode.geometry = SCNTorus(ringRadius: 2, pipeRadius: 0.5)
torusNode.geometry?.firstMaterial?.diffuse.contents =
UIColor.blue
torusNode.position = SCNVector3(0, -2, -15)
torusNode.physicsBody = SCNPhysicsBody(type: .static,
shape: SCNPhysicsShape(node: torusNode, options:
[SCNPhysicsShape.Option.type: SCNPhysicsShape.
ShapeType.concavePolyhedron]))

let ninetyDegrees = GLKMathDegreesToRadians(90)
torusNode.eulerAngles = SCNVector3(ninetyDegrees, 0, 0)

sceneView.scene.rootNode.addChildNode(torusNode)

let boxNode = SCNNode()
boxNode.geometry = SCNBox(width: 3.5, height: 3.5,
length: 3.5, chamferRadius: 0)
boxNode.geometry?.firstMaterial?.diffuse.contents =
UIColor.green
boxNode.position = SCNVector3(5, 1, -15)
boxNode.physicsBody = SCNPhysicsBody(type: .static,
shape: nil)
sceneView.scene.rootNode.addChildNode(boxNode)
    }

}
```

To test this code, follow these steps:

1.  Connect an iOS device to your Macintosh through its USB cable.

2.  Click the Run button or choose Product ➤ Run.

3.  The world origin should appear along with an orange pyramid, a blue torus, and a green box. Aim the center of the screen and tap the screen to shoot a purple projectile out. Each time the purple projectile hits a virtual object, it should ricochet off it, as shown in Figure 12-2. Make sure you aim for all three virtual objects and aim for the center of the torus to see the purple sphere shoot through its center.

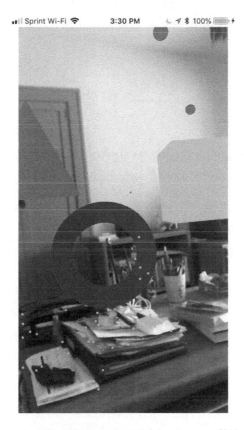

**Figure 12-2.** *The purple sphere should bounce off the other three virtual objects when they collide*

4.  Click the Stop button or choose Product ➤ Stop.

# Detecting Collisions

Turning virtual objects into .dynamic and .static physics bodies lets them collide against each other. However, in many cases you may want to identify when a virtual object collides with another one. To do that, you must first create an enumeration structure that assigns each virtual object to an arbitrary numeric value.

In our example, we have a purple sphere that acts as a projectile, an orange pyramid, a blue torus, and a green box. So we can define an enumeration structure underneath the IBOutlet like this:

```
enum contactType : Int {
    case projectile = 1
    case target = 2
}
```

Next we have to assign the enum value of each virtual object to its categoryBitMask property inside the addTargets function like this:

```
projectile.physicsBody?.categoryBitMask = contactType.
projectile.rawValue
pyramidNode.physicsBody?.categoryBitMask = contactType.target.
rawValue
torusNode.physicsBody?.categoryBitMask = contactType.target.
rawValue
boxNode.physicsBody?.categoryBitMask = contactType.target.
rawValue
```

Once we've identified all the virtual objects with an arbitrary value for its categoryBitMask property, we need to use the SCNPhysicsContactDelegate for our class like this:

```
class ViewController: UIViewController, ARSCNViewDelegate,
SCNPhysicsContactDelegate  {
```

This delegate allows us to get notifications when virtual objects collide. After defining the SCNPhysicsContactDelegate, we must also assign the class as the contact delegate like this:

```
sceneView.scene.physicsWorld.contactDelegate = self
```

We also need to define the contactTestBitMask for the projectile in the tapResponse function. This defines what type of collisions we want to track. Since we want to be notified when the projectile hits any of the three virtual objects (pyramid, torus, or box), we can use the following:

```
projectile.physicsBody?.contactTestBitMask = contactType.
target.rawValue
```

Since all of our targets (pyramid, torus, and box) are assigned the same contactType.target enumerated value, we need to identify when the projectile hits each different virtual object. That means we need to give each virtual object a unique name in the addTargets function like this:

```
projectile.name = "Projectile"
pyramidNode.name = "Pyramid"
torusNode.name = "Torus"
boxNode.name = "Box"
```

Now we need to use the didBegin physicsWorld function to detect collisions like this:

```
func physicsWorld(_ world: SCNPhysicsWorld, didBegin
contact: SCNPhysicsContact) {

}
```

This function runs every time two virtual objects collide. When two virtual objects collide, the didBegin physicsWorld identifies the two objects as nodeA and nodeB. Unfortunately, we don't know which node represents the projectile and which node represents the target. First, we need to declare a variable to hold the node containing the target:

```
var targetNode : SCNNode!
```

Now we need to determine if nodeA is the projectile or the target that was hit. To determine this information, we just need to look for the name of the node:

```
if contact.nodeA.name == "Projectile" {
    targetNode = contact.nodeB
} else {
    targetNode = contact.nodeA
}
```

If nodeA is named Projectile, then we know that nodeB contains the target. If nodeA is not named Projectile, then we know nodeA contains the target.

Now depending on the targetNode's name, we can change the color of the virtual object that the projectile hit using a switch statement. If the projectile hit the pyramid, the pyramid will change color to magenta. If the projectile hits the torus, then the torus will change color to yellow. If the projectile hits the box, the box will change color to red:

```
switch targetNode.name {
 case "Pyramid":
     targetNode.geometry?.firstMaterial?.diffuse.
     contents = UIColor.magenta
 case "Torus":
     targetNode.geometry?.firstMaterial?.diffuse.
     contents = UIColor.yellow
```

```
    case "Box":
        targetNode.geometry?.firstMaterial?.diffuse.
        contents = UIColor.red
    default:
        return
    }
```

The entire ViewController.swift file should look like this:

```
import UIKit
import SceneKit
import ARKit

class ViewController: UIViewController, ARSCNViewDelegate,
SCNPhysicsContactDelegate  {

    @IBOutlet var sceneView: ARSCNView!

    let configuration = ARWorldTrackingConfiguration()

    enum contactType : Int {
        case projectile = 1
        case target = 2
    }

    override func viewDidLoad() {
        super.viewDidLoad()
        // Do any additional setup after loading the view,
        typically from a nib.
        sceneView.debugOptions = [ARSCNDebugOptions.
        showWorldOrigin, ARSCNDebugOptions.showFeaturePoints]
        sceneView.delegate = self
        sceneView.scene.physicsWorld.contactDelegate = self

        sceneView.session.run(configuration)
```

```swift
    let tapGesture = UITapGestureRecognizer(target: self,
    action: #selector(tapResponse))
    sceneView.addGestureRecognizer(tapGesture)

    addTargets()
}

@objc func tapResponse(sender: UITapGestureRecognizer) {
    guard let scene = sender.view as? ARSCNView else {
    return }
    guard let pov = scene.pointOfView else { return }
    let transform = pov.transform
    let orientation = SCNVector3(-transform.m31,
    -transform.m32, -transform.m33)
    let location = SCNVector3(transform.m41, transform.m42,
    transform.m43)
    let position = SCNVector3(orientation.x + location.x,
    orientation.y + location.y, orientation.z + location.z)
    let projectile = SCNNode()
    projectile.geometry = SCNSphere(radius: 0.35)
    projectile.geometry?.firstMaterial?.diffuse.contents =
    UIColor.purple
    projectile.position = position
    projectile.physicsBody = SCNPhysicsBody(type: .dynamic,
    shape: SCNPhysicsShape(node: projectile, options: nil))
    projectile.physicsBody?.isAffectedByGravity = false
    projectile.physicsBody?.categoryBitMask = contactType.
    projectile.rawValue
    projectile.physicsBody?.contactTestBitMask =
    contactType.target.rawValue
    projectile.name = "Projectile"
    let force: Float = 50
```

```
    projectile.physicsBody?.applyForce(SCNVector3
    (orientation.x * force, orientation.y * force,
    orientation.z * force), asImpulse: true)
    sceneView.scene.rootNode.addChildNode(projectile)
}

func addTargets() {
    let pyramidNode = SCNNode()
    pyramidNode.geometry = SCNPyramid(width: 4, height:
    4.5, length: 4)
    pyramidNode.geometry?.firstMaterial?.diffuse.contents =
    UIColor.orange
    pyramidNode.position = SCNVector3(-3, 1, -15)
    pyramidNode.physicsBody = SCNPhysicsBody(type: .static,
    shape: nil)
    pyramidNode.physicsBody?.categoryBitMask = contactType.
    target.rawValue
    pyramidNode.name = "Pyramid"
    sceneView.scene.rootNode.addChildNode(pyramidNode)

    let torusNode = SCNNode()
    torusNode.geometry = SCNTorus(ringRadius: 2,
    pipeRadius: 0.5)
    torusNode.geometry?.firstMaterial?.diffuse.contents =
    UIColor.blue
    torusNode.position = SCNVector3(0, -2, -15)
    torusNode.physicsBody = SCNPhysicsBody(type: .static,
    shape: SCNPhysicsShape(node: torusNode, options:
    [SCNPhysicsShape.Option.type: SCNPhysicsShape.
    ShapeType.concavePolyhedron]))
    torusNode.physicsBody?.categoryBitMask = contactType.
    target.rawValue
    torusNode.name = "Torus"
```

```
let ninetyDegrees = GLKMathDegreesToRadians(90)
torusNode.eulerAngles = SCNVector3(ninetyDegrees, 0, 0)

sceneView.scene.rootNode.addChildNode(torusNode)

let boxNode = SCNNode()
boxNode.geometry = SCNBox(width: 3.5, height: 3.5,
length: 3.5, chamferRadius: 0)
boxNode.geometry?.firstMaterial?.diffuse.contents =
UIColor.green
boxNode.position = SCNVector3(5, 1, -15)
boxNode.physicsBody = SCNPhysicsBody(type: .static,
shape: nil)
boxNode.physicsBody?.categoryBitMask = contactType.
target.rawValue
boxNode.name = "Box"
sceneView.scene.rootNode.addChildNode(boxNode)
}

func physicsWorld(_ world: SCNPhysicsWorld, didBegin
contact: SCNPhysicsContact) {
    var targetNode : SCNNode!

    if contact.nodeA.name == "Projectile" {
        targetNode = contact.nodeB
    } else {
        targetNode = contact.nodeA
    }

    switch targetNode.name {
    case "Pyramid":
        targetNode.geometry?.firstMaterial?.diffuse.
        contents = UIColor.magenta
```

```
    case "Torus":
        targetNode.geometry?.firstMaterial?.diffuse.
        contents = UIColor.yellow
    case "Box":
        targetNode.geometry?.firstMaterial?.diffuse.
        contents = UIColor.red
    default:
        return
    }
  }
}
```

To test this code, follow these steps:

1. Connect an iOS device to your Macintosh through its USB cable.

2. Click the Run button or choose Product ➤ Run.

3. The world origin should appear along with an orange pyramid, a blue torus, and a green box. Aim the center of the screen and tap the screen to shoot a purple projectile out. Each time the purple projectile hits a virtual object, the virtual object should change to a different color to let you visually see that it was hit.

4. Click the Stop button or choose Product ➤ Stop.

# Summary

By default, virtual objects simply hover in mid-air within an augmented reality view. By applying a physics body to a virtual object, you can have it be affected by gravity so it falls down, or have it interact and collide with other virtual objects.

You can define a virtual object with different types of physics bodies that define how it reacts to collisions. To initiate a collision, you can apply a force to a virtual object along the x-, y-, and z-axes. To determine what a virtual object may have hit, you need to define an enumeration structure that identifies different virtual objects that might collide. Then you need to write a `didBegin physicsWorld` function to respond to that collision.

Adding physics, force, and collision detection gives your app a chance to make virtual objects respond like real-life items and notify you when they physically touch in a collision.

# CHAPTER 13

# Interacting with the Real World

When we've placed virtual objects in an augmented reality view, those virtual objects can interact with each other in different ways. The simplest way two virtual objects can interact is by placing one in front of another. Then the closest virtual object blocks your view of the second virtual object.

For greater realism within an augmented reality view, you can also have real-world objects appear to block virtual objects, which is called *occlusion*. We can mimic a real-world object blocking the view of a virtual object by creating an invisible virtual object that matches the position and size of a real-world object.

Another form of interaction occurs when virtual objects can interact with real-world objects. The simplest example is horizontal or vertical plane detection where ARKit can identify walls or floors. Of course, ARKit can also recognize points in the real world. It can, for example, compare the distance between two points that exist in the real world, such as the distance from one corner of a table to another corner.

To learn about occlusion with virtual objects, let's create a new Xcode project by following these steps:

1.  Start Xcode. (Make sure you're using Xcode 10 or greater.)

© Wallace Wang 2018
W. Wang, *Beginning ARKit for iPhone and iPad*,
https://doi.org/10.1007/978-1-4842-4102-8_13

2. Choose File ➤ New ➤ Project. Xcode asks you to choose a template.

3. Click the iOS category.

4. Click the Single View App icon and click the Next button. Xcode asks for a product name, organization name, organization identifiers, and content technology.

5. Click in the Product Name text field and type a descriptive name for your project, such as Occlusion. (The exact name does not matter.)

6. Click the Next button. Xcode asks where you want to store your project.

7. Choose a folder and click the Create button. Xcode creates an iOS project.

Now modify the Info.plist file to allow access to the camera and to use ARKit by following these steps:

1. Click the Info.plist file in the Navigator pane. Xcode displays a list of keys, types, and values.

2. Click the disclosure triangle to expand the Required Device Capabilities category to display Item 0.

3. Move the mouse pointer over Item 0 to display a plus (+) icon.

4. Click this plus (+) icon to display a blank Item 1.

5. Type arkit under the Value category in the Item 1 row.

6. Move the mouse pointer over the last row to display a plus (+) icon.

7. Click on the plus (+) icon to create a new row. A popup menu appears.

8. Choose Privacy – Camera Usage Description.

9. Type AR needs to use the camera under the Value category in the Privacy – Camera Usage Description row.

Now it's time to modify the ViewController.swift file to use ARKit and SceneKit by following these steps:

1. Click on the ViewController.swift file in the Navigator pane.

2. Edit the ViewController.swift file so it looks like this:

```
import UIKit
import SceneKit
import ARKit

class ViewController: UIViewController,
ARSCNViewDelegate {

let configuration = ARWorldTrackingConfiguration()

    var x : Float = 0
    var y : Float = 0
    var z : Float = 0

    override func viewDidLoad() {
        super.viewDidLoad()
        // Do any additional setup after loading the
        view, typically from a nib.

    }

}
```

This code declares three variables x, y, and z. These variables will be used to store the location of a horizontal plane. Once our app detects a horizontal plane, we'll draw a virtual object underneath the horizontal plane using these x, y, and z variables.

To view augmented reality in our app, add a single ARKit SceneKit View (ARSCNView) and expand it so it fills the entire user interface. Then add constraints by choosing Editor ➤ Resolve Auto Layout Issues ➤ Reset to Suggested Constraints at the bottom half of the menu under the All Views in Container category.

The next step is to connect the user interface items to the Swift code in the `ViewController.swift` file. To do this, follow these steps:

1.  Click the `Main.storyboard` file in the Navigator pane.

2.  Click the Assistant Editor icon or choose View ➤ Assistant Editor ➤ Show Assistant Editor to display the `Main.storyboard` and the `ViewController. swift` file side by side.

3.  Move the mouse pointer over the ARSCNView, hold down the Control key, and Ctrl-drag under the `class ViewController` line.

4.  Release the Control key and the left mouse button. A popup menu appears.

5.  Click in the Name text field and type `sceneView`, then click the Connect button. Xcode creates an IBOutlet as shown here:

    **@IBOutlet var** sceneView: ARSCNView!

6.  Edit the viewDidLoad function so it looks like this:

```
override func viewDidLoad() {
    super.viewDidLoad()
    // Do any additional setup after loading the
    view, typically from a nib.
    sceneView.debugOptions = [ARSCNDebugOptions.
    showWorldOrigin, ARSCNDebugOptions.
    showFeaturePoints]
    sceneView.delegate = self

    configuration.planeDetection = .horizontal

    sceneView.session.run(configuration)

    let tapGesture = UITapGestureRecognizer(target:
    self, action: #selector(tapResponse))
    sceneView.addGestureRecognizer(tapGesture)
}
```

The last two lines in the viewDidLoad function create
a tap gesture, which means we'll need a function to
handle the tap gesture, called tapGesture.

7.  Underneath the viewDidLoad function, write the
following tapResponse function:

```
@objc func tapResponse(sender: UITapGestureRecognizer) {
    let boxNode = SCNNode()
    boxNode.geometry = SCNBox(width: 0.08, height:
    0.08, length: 0.08, chamferRadius: 0)
    boxNode.geometry?.firstMaterial?.diffuse.
    contents = UIColor.green
    boxNode.position = SCNVector3(x, y, z)
    sceneView.scene.rootNode.addChildNode(boxNode)
}
```

This tapResponse function identifies the location on the screen where the user tapped and then displays a green box at the x, y, and z coordinates, which represent the center coordinates of as horizontal plane.

8. Underneath the tapResponse function, write the following didAdd renderer function:

```
func renderer(_ renderer: SCNSceneRenderer,
didAdd node: SCNNode, for anchor: ARAnchor) {
    guard anchor is ARPlaneAnchor else { return }

    let planeNode = detectPlane(anchor: anchor as!
    ARPlaneAnchor)
    node.addChildNode(planeNode)
}
```

This renderer function runs the first time ARKit detects a horizontal plane. Once it detects a horizontal plane, it runs the detectPlane function (which we'll need to write later).

9. Write the following didUpdate renderer function:

```
func renderer(_ renderer: SCNSceneRenderer,
didUpdate node: SCNNode, for anchor: ARAnchor) {
    guard anchor is ARPlaneAnchor else { return }

    node.enumerateChildNodes { (childNode, _) in
        childNode.removeFromParentNode()
    }
    let planeNode = detectPlane(anchor: anchor as!
    ARPlaneAnchor)
    node.addChildNode(planeNode)
```

```
    print("updating plane anchor")
}
```

This didUpdate renderer function constantly resizes the horizontal plane as the iOS camera detects more of the horizontal plane. Notice that this function also calls the detectPlane function while also printing "updating plane anchor" each time it detects the expands the size of the horizontal plane.

10. Finally, write the following detectPlane function:

```
func detectPlane(anchor: ARPlaneAnchor) -> SCNNode {
    let planeNode = SCNNode()
    planeNode.geometry = SCNPlane(width:
    CGFloat(anchor.extent.x), height:
    CGFloat(anchor.extent.z))
    planeNode.geometry?.firstMaterial?.diffuse.
    contents = UIColor.yellow
    planeNode.position = SCNVector3(anchor.
    center.x, anchor.center.y, anchor.center.z)

    x = anchor.center.x
    y = anchor.center.y - 0.4
    z = anchor.center.z

    let ninetyDegrees = GLKMathDegreesToRadians(90)
    planeNode.eulerAngles = SCNVector3
    (ninetyDegrees, 0, 0)

    planeNode.geometry?.firstMaterial?.
    isDoubleSided = true

    return planeNode
}
```

The first two lines in the detectPlane function create a node and then define the plane's size based on the width and height of the detected plane. The extent property contains the detected horizontal plane's width and height

The next two lines define a yellow color for the plane and position the plate at the center of the detected plane anchor.

The next three lines store the values of the plane's x, y, and z position, except it subtracts 0.4 meters from the plane's y position. This creates a y value below and underneath the horizontal plane.

The next two lines use the GLKMathDegreesToRadians to convert 90 degrees into radians. Then it rotates the plane 90 degrees around the x-axis because the plane will initially be drawn vertically. Rotating the plane 90 degrees around the x-axis makes the plane appear horizontally.

Finally, the last line defines the plate as double-sided so the color yellow appears on the top and bottom.

To test this project, follow these steps:

1.  Connect an iOS device to your Macintosh through its USB cable.

2.  Click the Run button or choose Product ➤ Run. The first time you run this app, it will ask permission to access the camera, so give it permission.

3.  Aim the iOS device's camera at a horizontal plane that has empty space underneath it, such as a table. When ARKit identifies enough feature points, it draws a yellow plane on top of the horizontal surface the iOS camera is aimed at.

4.   Tap the screen. This places a green box 0.4 meters underneath the yellow plane. You may need to move to the side to see the green box underneath the yellow plane. Notice that yellow plane blocks your view of the green box when the yellow plane appears over the green box, as shown in Figure 13-1.

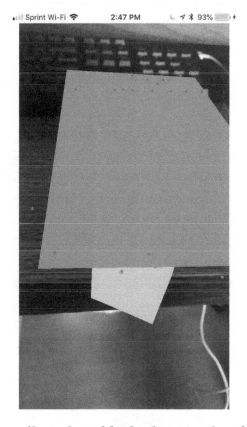

*Figure 13-1.*   *The yellow plane blocks the green box from view*

5.   Click the Stop button or choose Product ➤ Stop.

Occlusion works by displaying an invisible horizontal plane on a detected horizontal surface, such as a table top. Since the invisible horizontal plane can't be seen, it will look like it's not there. Yet it will block the green box from view unless you move to the side. This creates the illusion that the horizontal surface (such as a table top) is actually blocking the view of the green box.

To create an invisible horizontal plane, just comment out the line in the detectPlane function that displays the plane as yellow. Then replace it with two lines like this:

```
planeNode.geometry?.firstMaterial?.colorBufferWriteMask = []
planeNode.renderingOrder = -1
```

This creates a plane with no color and rendering order of -1. Most virtual objects have a default renderingOrder value of 0, but a higher renderingOrder value makes the virtual object appear drawn last. So a -1 renderingOrder value means that the virtual object always appears over other virtual objects. This helps create the illusion that the real horizontal plane will block the view of the green virtual box even though it's really an invisible horizontal plane that's doing it.

The entire detectPlane function should look like this:

```
func detectPlane(anchor: ARPlaneAnchor) -> SCNNode {
    let planeNode = SCNNode()
    //planeNode.geometry = SCNPlane(width: CGFloat(anchor.
    extent.x), height: CGFloat(anchor.extent.z))
    planeNode.geometry?.firstMaterial?.colorBufferWriteMask = []
    planeNode.renderingOrder = -1
    planeNode.geometry?.firstMaterial?.diffuse.contents =
    UIColor.yellow
    planeNode.position = SCNVector3(anchor.center.x,
    anchor.center.y, anchor.center.z)
```

```
x = anchor.center.x
y = anchor.center.y - 0.4
z = anchor.center.z

let ninetyDegrees = GLKMathDegreesToRadians(90)
planeNode.eulerAngles = SCNVector3(ninetyDegrees, 0, 0)

planeNode.geometry?.firstMaterial?.isDoubleSided = true

return planeNode
}
```

To test this project, follow these steps:

1. Connect an iOS device to your Macintosh through its USB cable.

2. Click the Run button or choose Product ➤ Run. The first time you run this app, it will ask permission to access the camera, so give it permission.

3. Aim the iOS device's camera at a horizontal plane that has empty space underneath it, such as a table. When you see a lot of feature points on the horizontal plane and see "updating plane anchor" in the Xcode debug area, you'll know that ARKit has detected a horizontal plane and placed an invisible virtual plane on top of it.

4. Tap the screen. This draws a green box 0.4 meters underneath the invisible horizontal plane, but you won't be able to see it unless you move to the side, as shown in Figure 13-2.

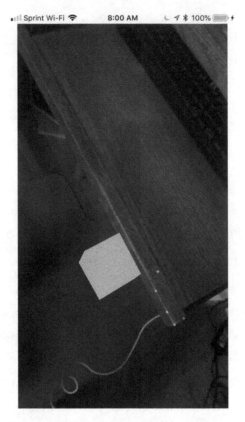

***Figure 13-2.*** *The green box appears underneath the real horizontal surface*

5.  Move directly over the green box. Notice that real horizontal surface appears to cut off your view of the green box, as shown in Figure 13-3.

**Figure 13-3.** *The green box appears cut from view by the real horizontal surface*

6.   Click the Stop button or choose Product ➤ Stop.

# Detecting Points in the Real World

ARKit can detect horizontal and vertical planes, but you can also make it detect individual points as well. For example, a measuring app would let you point the center of an iOS device's camera at an object to record that position. Then, as you move the iOS device's camera and tap to identify another position, such a measuring app could determine the distance between the two points.

Let's create an Xcode project to identify two points in the real world and calculate the distance between them by following these steps:

1.   Start Xcode. (Make sure you're using Xcode 10 or greater.)

2.   Choose File ➤ New ➤ Project. Xcode asks you to choose a template.

3.   Click the iOS category.

4.   Click the Single View App icon and click the Next button. Xcode asks for a product name, organization name, organization identifiers, and content technology.

5.   Click in the Product Name text field and type a descriptive name for your project, such as `Ruler`. (The exact name does not matter.)

6.   Click the Next button. Xcode asks where you want to store your project.

7.   Choose a folder and click the Create button. Xcode creates an iOS project.

Now modify the `Info.plist` file to allow access to the camera and to use ARKit by following these steps:

1.   Click the `Info.plist` file in the Navigator pane. Xcode displays a list of keys, types, and values.

2.   Click the disclosure triangle to expand the Required Device Capabilities category to display Item 0.

3.   Move the mouse pointer over Item 0 to display a plus (+) icon.

4.   Click this plus (+) icon to display a blank Item 1.

5.   Type `arkit` under the Value category in the Item 1 row.

6.  Move the mouse pointer over the last row to display a plus (+) icon.

7.  Click on the plus (+) icon to create a new row. A popup menu appears.

8.  Choose Privacy – Camera Usage Description.

9.  Type AR needs to use the camera under the Value category in the Privacy – Camera Usage Description row.

Now it's time to modify the ViewController.swift file to use ARKit and SceneKit by following these steps:

1.  Click on the ViewController.swift file in the Navigator pane.

2.  Edit the ViewController.swift file so it looks like this:

```
import UIKit
import SceneKit
import ARKit

class ViewController: UIViewController,
ARSCNViewDelegate {

let configuration = ARWorldTrackingConfiguration()

    override func viewDidLoad() {
        super.viewDidLoad()
        // Do any additional setup after loading the
        view, typically from a nib.

    }

}
```

3.  Click the Main.storyboard file in the Navigator pane.

4.  Drag and drop an ARSCNView and expand it to fill the entire view.

5.  Click the Add New Constraints icon near the bottom of the Xcode screen. A popup window appears.

6.  Make sure the values on the top, bottom, left, and right edges are all 0. Then click the constraint in each direction so they appear in red, as shown in Figure 13-4.

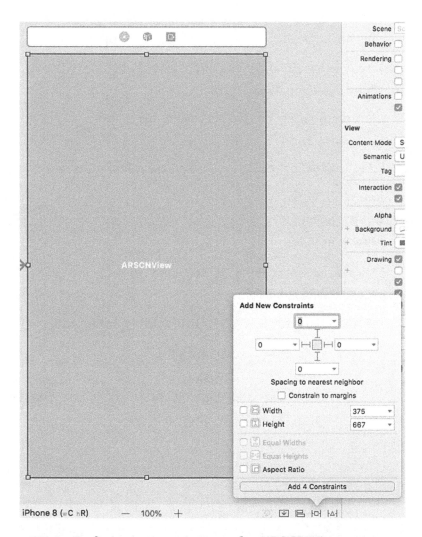

***Figure 13-4.*** *Defining constraints on the ARSCNView*

7. Click the Add 4 Constraints button to define constraints on the ARSCNView.

8. Drag and drop a UILabel on the ARSCNView.

9. Click on the UILabel and click the Attributes Inspector icon, or choose View ➤ Inspectors ➤ Show Attributes Inspector.

10. Click in the text field that displays Label and type a plus sign (+). Press Return.

11. Click on the T icon that appears on the far right of the Font popup menu. A popup window appears, as shown in Figure 13-5.

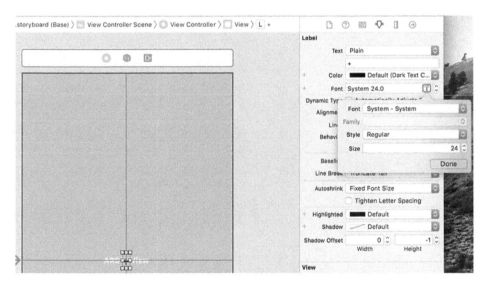

***Figure 13-5.*** *Defining a size for the text in the UILabel*

12. Click in the Size text field and type 24. Then click the Done button.

13. Click the Align icon near the bottom of the Xcode screen to display a popup window.

349

14.  Select the Horizontally in Container and Vertically
     in Container check boxes. Then click the Add 2
     Constraints button. Xcode centers your UILabel,
     displaying the plus sign, in the center of the screen,
     as shown in Figure 13-6.

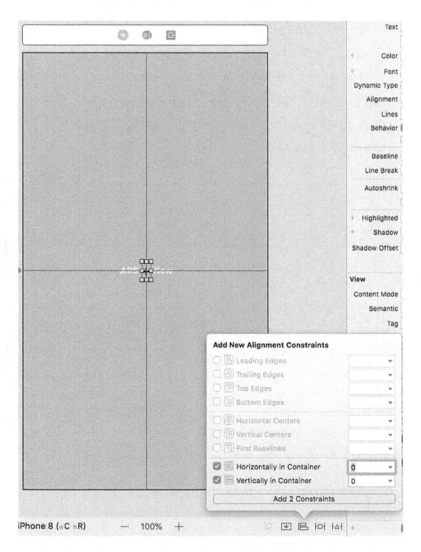

***Figure 13-6.***  *Aligning the UILabel horizontally and vertically*

The whole purpose of the plus sign in the label is to show us where the center of the camera is when viewed through an augmented reality view.

The next step is to connect the user interface items to the Swift code in the `ViewController.swift` file. To do this, follow these steps:

1. Click the `Main.storyboard` file in the Navigator pane.

2. Click the Assistant Editor icon or choose View ➤ Assistant Editor ➤ Show Assistant Editor to display the `Main.storyboard` and the `ViewController.swift` file side by side.

3. Move the mouse pointer over the ARSCNView, hold down the Control key, and Ctrl-drag under the `class ViewController` line.

4. Release the Control key and the left mouse button. A popup menu appears.

5. Click in the Name text field and type `sceneView`, then click the Connect button. Xcode creates an IBOutlet as shown here:

   **@IBOutlet var** sceneView: ARSCNView!

6. Edit the `viewDidLoad` function so it looks like this:

   ```
   override func viewDidLoad() {
       super.viewDidLoad()
       // Do any additional setup after loading the
       view, typically from a nib.
       sceneView.debugOptions = [ARSCNDebugOptions.
       showWorldOrigin, ARSCNDebugOptions.
       showFeaturePoints]
       sceneView.delegate = self
   ```

```
            sceneView.session.run(configuration)

            let tapGesture = UITapGestureRecognizer(target:
            self, action: #selector(tapResponse))
            sceneView.addGestureRecognizer(tapGesture)

        }
```

At this point, we've added a Tap Gesture Recognizer so we need to write a function to handle this tap gesture by following these steps:

1.  Click the ViewController.swift file in the Navigator pane.

2.  Type the following underneath the viewDidLoad function:

```
    @objc func tapResponse(sender: UITapGestureRecognizer) {
    print ("Tapped screen")

        }
```

If you test this app, you'll be able to see the plus sign as a tiny black crosshair that appears in the center of the screen. This center is where we want to use for defining our two points to measure in the real world. For now, tapping the screen just displays "Tapped screen" in the Xcode debug area.

# Defining a Point in the Real World

For our ruler app to work, we need to define two points in the real world and then measure the distance between them. That means placing two points in the real world and storing the location of those points.

Each time the user taps the screen, we want to display a small sphere that defines a point in the real world. Then the user will need to point and tap the iOS device at another point so the app can measure the distance between the two points.

Inside the `tapResponse` function, we need to get the center of the screen where the center of the camera is pointed at, which is where the plus sign appears on the screen. To do that, we need to retrieve the scene that the user tapped on and identify the center like this:

```
let scene = sender.view as! ARSCNView
let location = scene.center
```

Next, we need to use the `hitTest` method to identify a feature point where the camera is pointing. A feature point represents a real-world surface that ARKit can recognize so the code looks like this:

```
let hitTestResults = scene.hitTest(location, types: .featurePoint)
```

As long as ARKit can identify a feature point, we can proceed so we need an `if` statement like this:

```
if hitTestResults.isEmpty == false {

}
```

Inside this `if` statement, we need to retrieve the first item retrieved from the `hitTestResults` constant:

```
guard let hitTestResults = hitTestResults.first else { return }
```

Once we've identified a point that the camera is pointing at, we can create a green sphere to appear at that point:

```
let sphereNode = SCNNode()
sphereNode.geometry = SCNSphere(radius: 0.003)
sphereNode.geometry?.firstMaterial?.diffuse.contents = 
UIColor.green
```

To place the green sphere where the center of the camera is pointing, we need to retrieve the x, y, and z coordinates of the camera through its `worldTransform` property, which is a matrix. The third column of the matrix contains the position we need, so we can define the green sphere's position like this:

```
sphereNode.position = SCNVector3(hitTestResults.
worldTransform.columns.3.x, hitTestResults.worldTransform.
columns.3.y, hitTestResults.worldTransform.columns.3.z)
```

Finally we need to add the sphere to the scene like this:

```
sceneView.scene.rootNode.addChildNode(sphereNode)
```

The entire tapResponse function should look like this:

```
@objc func tapResponse(sender: UITapGestureRecognizer) {
    let scene = sender.view as! ARSCNView
    let location = scene.center

    let hitTestResults = scene.hitTest(location, types:
    .featurePoint)

    if hitTestResults.isEmpty == false {

        guard let hitTestResults = hitTestResults.first
        else { return }

        let sphereNode = SCNNode()
        sphereNode.geometry = SCNSphere(radius: 0.003)
        sphereNode.geometry?.firstMaterial?.diffuse.
        contents = UIColor.green
        sphereNode.position = SCNVector3(hitTestResults.
        worldTransform.columns.3.x, hitTestResults.
        worldTransform.columns.3.y, hitTestResults.
        worldTransform.columns.3.z)
        sceneView.scene.rootNode.addChildNode(sphereNode)
    }
```

If you test this app, you'll be able to point the plus sign in the center of the screen at any real item and tap the screen to place a green sphere.

# Measuring Distance Between Virtual Objects

Our ruler app will define two feature points detected in the real world, display green spheres to mark their locations, and then calculate the distance between the two virtual objects. Finally, it will display the result on the screen. First, we'll need to keep track of the two points using an array of SCNNodes:

```
var realPoints = [SCNNode]()
```

This array will store the location of the two feature points, identified by green spheres. After we place a green sphere in the augmented reality view, we need to store that sphere's location in the array by using the append method like this:

```
realPoints.append(sphereNode)
```

If the number of spheres added to the augmented reality view is exactly two, then we can calculate the distance between those two points. If the number of spheres added is only one or zero, then we don't need to do anything, so we need an if statement that counts the number of spheres in the array like this:

```
if realPoints.count == 2 {

}
```

Inside this if statement, we need to retrieve the two stored spheres:

```
if realPoints.count == 2 {
  let pointOne = realPoints.first!
  let pointTwo = realPoints.last!

}
```

This code retrieves the first and last elements stored in the `realPoints` array. Now we need to get the x, y, and z positions by subtracting the second sphere (`pointTwo`) from the position of the first sphere (`pointOne`):

```
if realPoints.count == 2 {
    let pointOne = realPoints.first!
    let pointTwo = realPoints.last!

    let x = pointTwo.position.x - pointOne.position.x
    let y = pointTwo.position.y - pointOne.position.y
    let z = pointTwo.position.z - pointOne.position.z
}
```

We can define the position using these x, y, and z values:

```
if realPoints.count == 2 {
    let pointOne = realPoints.first!
    let pointTwo = realPoints.last!

    let x = pointTwo.position.x - pointOne.position.x
    let y = pointTwo.position.y - pointOne.position.y
    let z = pointTwo.position.z - pointOne.position.z

    let position = SCNVector3(x, y, z)


}
```

Now we can calculate the distance using Pythagorean's theorem. Since we're working in three dimensions, we need to use the x, y, and z coordinates to define the distance like this:

$$distance = \sqrt{x^2 + y^2 + z^2}$$

In Swift, this equation looks like this:

```
let distance = sqrt(position.x * position.x +
position.y * position.y + position.z * position.z)
```

So the complete `if` statement looks like this:

```
if realPoints.count == 2 {
  let pointOne = realPoints.first!
  let pointTwo = realPoints.last!

  let x = pointTwo.position.x - pointOne.position.x
  let y = pointTwo.position.y - pointOne.position.y
  let z = pointTwo.position.z - pointOne.position.z

  let position = SCNVector3(x, y, z)

  let distance = sqrt(position.x * position.x + position.y *
  position.y + position.z * position.z)
}
```

Now that we can accurately calculate the distance between two points, defined by green spheres in the augmented reality view, the final step is to display the results on the screen. To do this, we can create SCNText, which displays text as a virtual object.

We want to display the distance in between the two green spheres. To do that, we need to calculate a halfway point in between the two green spheres for the distance result to appear. At the end of the `if` statement, we need to calculate a location like this:

```
let x1 = (pointOne.position.x + pointTwo.position.x) / 2
let y1 = pointOne.position.y + pointTwo.position.y
let z1 = pointOne.position.z + pointTwo.position.z

let centerPosition = SCNVector3(x1, y1, z1)
```

Then we need to call a `displayText` function that takes the distance between the two points and a position to display the actual answer as virtual text:

```
displayText(answer: distance, position: centerPosition)
```

This means we need to create a `displayText` function that defines SCNText and displays the distance as yellow text that floats in the augmented reality view:

```
func displayText(answer: Float, position: SCNVector3) {
    let textDisplay = SCNText(string: "\(answer) meters",
    extrusionDepth: 0.5)
    textDisplay.firstMaterial?.diffuse.contents = UIColor.
    yellow

    let textNode = SCNNode()
    textNode.geometry = textDisplay
    textNode.position = position
    textNode.scale = SCNVector3(0.003, 0.003, 0.003)

    sceneView.scene.rootNode.addChildNode(textNode)
}
```

The entire `ViewController.swift` file should look like this:

```
import UIKit
import SceneKit
import ARKit

class ViewController: UIViewController, ARSCNViewDelegate {

    @IBOutlet var sceneView: ARSCNView!

    var realPoints = [SCNNode]()

    let configuration = ARWorldTrackingConfiguration()
```

```swift
override func viewDidLoad() {
    super.viewDidLoad()
    // Do any additional setup after loading the view,
    typically from a nib.
    sceneView.debugOptions = [ARSCNDebugOptions.
    showWorldOrigin, ARSCNDebugOptions.showFeaturePoints]
    sceneView.delegate = self

    sceneView.session.run(configuration)

    let tapGesture = UITapGestureRecognizer(target: self,
    action: #selector(tapResponse))
    sceneView.addGestureRecognizer(tapGesture)
}

@objc func tapResponse(sender: UITapGestureRecognizer) {
    let scene = sender.view as! ARSCNView
    let location = scene.center

    let hitTestResults = scene.hitTest(location, types:
    .featurePoint)

    if hitTestResults.isEmpty == false {

        guard let hitTestResults = hitTestResults.first
        else { return }

        let sphereNode = SCNNode()
        sphereNode.geometry = SCNSphere(radius: 0.003)
        sphereNode.geometry?.firstMaterial?.diffuse.
        contents = UIColor.green
        sphereNode.position = SCNVector3(hitTestResults.
        worldTransform.columns.3.x, hitTestResults.
        worldTransform.columns.3.y, hitTestResults.
        worldTransform.columns.3.z)
```

```
        sceneView.scene.rootNode.addChildNode(sphereNode)

        realPoints.append(sphereNode)

        if realPoints.count == 2 {
            let pointOne = realPoints.first!
            let pointTwo = realPoints.last!

            let x = pointTwo.position.x - pointOne.position.x
            let y = pointTwo.position.y - pointOne.position.y
            let z = pointTwo.position.z - pointOne.position.z

            let position = SCNVector3(x, y, z)

            let distance = sqrt(position.x * position.x +
            position.y * position.y + position.z * position.z)

            let x1 = (pointOne.position.x + pointTwo.
            position.x) / 2
            let y1 = pointOne.position.y + pointTwo.position.y
            let z1 = pointOne.position.z + pointTwo.position.z

            let centerPosition = SCNVector3(x1, y1, z1)

            displayText(answer: distance, position:
            centerPosition)
        }
    }
}

func displayText(answer: Float, position: SCNVector3) {
    let textDisplay = SCNText(string: "\(answer) meters",
    extrusionDepth: 0.5)
    textDisplay.firstMaterial?.diffuse.contents = UIColor.
    yellow
```

```
let textNode = SCNNode()
textNode.geometry = textDisplay
textNode.position = position
textNode.scale = SCNVector3(0.003, 0.003, 0.003)

sceneView.scene.rootNode.addChildNode(textNode)
    }

}
```

To test this app, follow these steps:

1. Connect an iOS device to your Macintosh through its USB cable.

2. Click the Run button or choose Product ➤ Run.

3. Move the plus sign in the center of the screen to the corner or tip of the object you want to measure, such as a pencil, book, or table.

4. Tap the screen to place the first green sphere on the screen.

5. Move the plus sign in the center of the screen to another corner or tip of the object you want to measure.

6. Tap the screen to place the second green sphere on the screen. Your app now displays the distance result, as shown in Figure 13-7.

**Figure 13-7.** *Measuring a real-world object*

7.   Click the Stop button or choose Product ➤ Stop.

# Summary

Augmented reality combines reality with virtual objects. To create the illusion that virtual objects can interact with the real world, you can use occlusion. By displaying invisible planes that you place in the real world, occlusion can create the illusion that real objects like horizontal or vertical surfaces can actually cover and hide a virtual object. Without placing an invisible plane to block a user's view, virtual objects always appear floating in mid-air no matter what real-world objects may seem to get in the way.

Another way to interact with the real world is by using feature points to identify points in the real world. By placing virtual objects at these real points, you can mimic measuring the distance between two real points by using virtual objects.

By making virtual objects appear to interact with real-world items, you can create more realistic augmented reality experiences for the users of your app.

# CHAPTER 14

# Image Detection

Another way ARKit can interact with the real world is through image detection. Image detection involves storing images and then using the camera to recognize those exact same images when viewed through an augmented reality view.

Image detection is similar but different from machine learning image recognition. With image recognition, an app can recognize items it has never seen before such as different varieties of cars, pencils, or computers. Image detection simply recognizes a stored image. If you don't store an image ahead of time, image detection can never recognize it.

Image detection can be handy because it allows an app to recognize a fixed image and then respond in different ways, such as displaying more information about that image. For example, a museum might offer an augmented reality app that lets users point an iPhone at a painting. As soon as the app recognizes that painting, it can display additional information about that painting in the user's native language such as English, Spanish, Arabic, or Japanese.

To learn about image detection, let's create a new Xcode project by following these steps:

1. Start Xcode. (Make sure you're using Xcode 10 or greater.)

2. Choose File ➤ New ➤ Project. Xcode asks you to choose a template.

3. Click the iOS category.

© Wallace Wang 2018
W. Wang, *Beginning ARKit for iPhone and iPad*,
https://doi.org/10.1007/978-1-4842-4102-8_14

4. Click the Single View App icon and click the Next button. Xcode asks for a product name, organization name, organization identifiers, and content technology.

5. Click in the Product Name text field and type a descriptive name for your project, such as ImageDetection. (The exact name does not matter.)

6. Click the Next button. Xcode asks where you want to store your project.

7. Choose a folder and click the Create button. Xcode creates an iOS project.

Now modify the Info.plist file to allow access to the camera and to use ARKit by following these steps:

1. Click the Info.plist file in the Navigator pane. Xcode displays a list of keys, types, and values.

2. Click the disclosure triangle to expand the Required Device Capabilities category to display Item 0.

3. Move the mouse pointer over Item 0 to display a plus (+) icon.

4. Click this plus (+) icon to display a blank Item 1.

5. Type arkit under the Value category in the Item 1 row.

6. Move the mouse pointer over the last row to display a plus (+) icon.

7. Click on the plus (+) icon to create a new row. A popup menu appears.

8. Choose Privacy – Camera Usage Description.

9. Type AR needs to use the camera under the Value category in the Privacy – Camera usage Description row.

Now it's time to modify the `ViewController.swift` file to use ARKit and SceneKit by following these steps:

1. Click on the `ViewController.swift` file in the Navigator pane.

2. Edit the `ViewController.swift` file so it looks like this:

```swift
import UIKit
import SceneKit
import ARKit

class ViewController: UIViewController,
ARSCNViewDelegate {

let configuration = ARWorldTrackingConfiguration()

    override func viewDidLoad() {
        super.viewDidLoad()
        // Do any additional setup after loading the view,
        typically from a nib.

    }

}
```

To view augmented reality in our app, add a single ARKit SceneKit View (ARSCNView) and expand it so it fills the entire user interface. Then add constraints by choosing Editor ➤ Resolve Auto Layout Issues ➤ Reset to Suggested Constraints at the bottom half of the menu under the All Views in Container category.

The next step is to connect the user interface items to the Swift code in the `ViewController.swift` file. To do this, follow these steps:

1. Click the `Main.storyboard` file in the Navigator pane.

2.  Click the Assistant Editor icon or choose View ➤ Assistant Editor ➤ Show Assistant Editor to display the Main.storyboard and the ViewController. swift file side by side.

3.  Move the mouse pointer over the ARSCNView, hold down the Control key, and Ctrl-drag under the class ViewController line.

4.  Release the Control key and the left mouse button. A popup menu appears.

5.  Click in the Name text field and type sceneView, then click the Connect button. Xcode creates an IBOutlet as shown here:

    ```
    @IBOutlet var sceneView: ARSCNView!
    ```

6.  Edit the viewDidLoad function so it looks like this:

    ```
    override func viewDidLoad() {
        super.viewDidLoad()
        // Do any additional setup after loading the view,
          typically from a nib.
        sceneView.debugOptions = [ARSCNDebugOptions.
        showWorldOrigin, ARSCNDebugOptions.
        showFeaturePoints]
        sceneView.delegate = self

        sceneView.session.run(configuration)
    }
    ```

# Storing Images

Before ARKit can recognize physical objects in the real world, you need to store images of those items in your app. In addition to storing an image, you must also specify the width and height of that real-world object. That way when ARKit spots that actual item through the iOS device's camera, it can compare that image with its stored image. If they match in both appearance and size, then ARKit can recognize that real-world item.

First, you must capture an image of the item you want to detect. Since these images need to be high resolution, you can capture public domain images off the Internet such as at NASA (`www.nasa.gov`). Then you can display these images on your computer screen for your iOS device to recognize. Once you have an image on your Macintosh, you'll need to store it in your Xcode project.

To store one or more images that you want ARKit to recognize, follow these steps:

1. Click the `Assets.xcassets` folder in the Navigator pane.

2. Click + icon in the bottom of the pane. A popup menu appears.

3. Choose New AR Resource Group, as shown in Figure 14-1. Xcode creates an AR Resources folder.

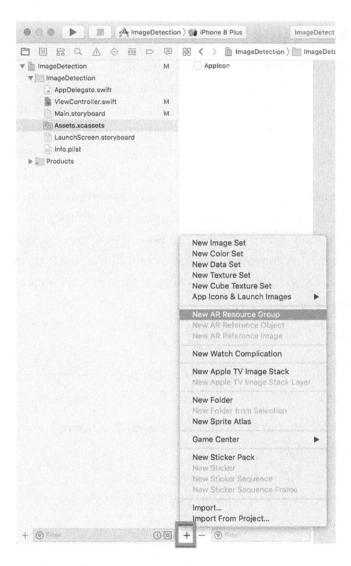

***Figure 14-1.*** *The yellow plane blocks the green box from view*

4. Drag and drop the images into your newly added AR Resource folder that you want ARKit to recognize in the real world. Xcode displays a yellow alert icon in the bottom-right corner of your images.

5. Click the Attributes Inspector icon or choose
   View ➤ Inspectors ➤ Show Attributes Inspector.
   An AR Reference Image pane appears, as shown
   in Figure 14-2.

***Figure 14-2.*** *Defining the width and height of the item to recognize*

6. Click in the Width and Height text fields and type
   the actual width and height of the real item. You
   can also click the Units popup menu to change the
   default measurement unit from meters to something
   else, such as inches or centimeters.

Once we've added one or more images of the real objects we want
ARKit to recognize, we need to write actual Swift code to recognize the
image when spotted through an iOS device's camera.

First, we need to access the folder containing the images of items to
recognize. This folder can be called anything such as "AR Resources". This
means using a guard statement to verify that the image folder even exists
like this:

```
guard let storedImages = ARReferenceImage.
referenceImages(inGroupNamed: "AR Resources", bundle: nil) else {
        fatalError("Missing AR Resources images")
}
```

This code looks for a folder named AR Resources. If it fails to find it, it ends the program and displays "Missing AR Resources Images." If it finds an AR Resources folder, then we can define where the detected images are stored like this:

```
configuration.detectionImages = storedImages
```

Finally, we need to use the didAdd renderer function, which runs every time the camera updates its view. If the camera detects a recognized image (ARImageAnchor) then we can verify this by printing "Item recognized" like this:

```
func renderer(_ renderer: SCNSceneRenderer, didAdd node:
SCNNode, for anchor: ARAnchor) {
    if anchor is ARImageAnchor {
        print("Item recognized")
    }
}
```

The entire ViewController.swift file should look like this:

```
import UIKit
import SceneKit
import ARKit

class ViewController: UIViewController, ARSCNViewDelegate {

    @IBOutlet var sceneView: ARSCNView!

    let configuration = ARWorldTrackingConfiguration()

    override func viewDidLoad() {
        super.viewDidLoad()
        // Do any additional setup after loading the view,
        typically from a nib.
```

```
sceneView.debugOptions = [ARSCNDebugOptions.
showWorldOrigin, ARSCNDebugOptions.showFeaturePoints]
sceneView.delegate = self

guard let storedImages =  ARReferenceImage.
referenceImages(inGroupNamed: "AR Resources",
bundle: nil) else {
    fatalError("Missing AR Resources images")
}

configuration.detectionImages = storedImages

sceneView.session.run(configuration)
}

func renderer(_ renderer: SCNSceneRenderer, didAdd node:
SCNNode, for anchor: ARAnchor) {
    if anchor is ARImageAnchor {
        print("Item recognized")
    }
}
}
```

To test this app, place the item that you took a picture of and stored in the AR Resources folder and put that item on a table or floor. Then follow these steps:

1. Connect an iOS device to your Macintosh through its USB cable.

2. Click the Run button or choose Product ➤ Run. The first time you run this app, it will ask permission to access the camera so give it permission.

3. Load the picture on your computer that you stored in your project's AR Resources folder.

4.  Aim the iOS device's camera at the screen that displays the picture you want ARKit to recognize. When ARKit recognizes the image, it displays "Item recognized" in the debug area of Xcode.

5.  Click the Stop button or choose Product ➤ Stop.

# Detecting Multiple Images

Just recognizing a single image would be limiting. That's why to recognize multiple images, an app just needs to store multiple images in its AR Resources folder. Now an app will be able to recognize different images and respond based on what image it recognizes.

To identify which particular image ARKit recognizes, you can give each image a unique name. Now each time the app recognizes an image, it can retrieve the name of that image to determine exactly which image is in front of the iOS device's camera.

When you store an image in the AR Resources folder, you must not only define its width and height, but also its name, which can be any arbitrary, descriptive name, as shown in Figure 14-3.

*Figure 14-3.*  *Every image needs a unique name*

Once you've added two or more images into the AR Resources folder, you can retrieve the name property of a recognized image to determine which image currently appears in front of the iOS device's camera.

To see how to identify a recognized image, let's modify the
ImageDetection project by following these steps:

1. Drag and drop a second image into the AR
   Resources folder. Make sure you give that second
   image a unique name so both stored images have
   different names.

2. Underneath the classViewController line, create a
   structure like this:

```swift
struct Images {
    var title: String
    var info: String
}
```

3. Next, create an empty array to hold this structure
   like this:

```swift
var imageArray: [Images] = []
```

4. In the viewDidLoad function, add the following
   function call:

```swift
getData()
```

5. At the bottom of the ViewController.swift file, write
   the following getData function. In this example, the
   project contains two pictures of rockets so the text in
   the getData function reflects this, but you can type
   any text you want that best corresponds with the two
   images stored in your project:

```swift
func getData() {
    let item1 = Images(title: "CRS-15 SpaceX rocket",
    info: "Commercial Resupply Service")
```

```
let item2 = Images(title: "Saturn V rocket", info:
"Apollo moon launch vehicle")

imageArray.append(item1)
imageArray.append(item2)
}
```

The getData function creates two structures and fills the elements of those structures with text for the title and info properties. Then it stores that structure into an array. Now we need to use the name property of each image to identify what image the app currently recognizes.

6.  Write the following nodeFor renderer function:

```
func renderer(_ renderer: SCNSceneRenderer, nodeFor
anchor: ARAnchor) -> SCNNode? {
    guard let imageAnchor = anchor as? ARImageAnchor
    else { return nil }

    switch imageAnchor.referenceImage.name {
    case "CRS-15":
        print(imageArray[0].title)
        print(imageArray[0].info)
    case "SaturnV":
        print(imageArray[1].title)
        print(imageArray[1].info)
    default:
        print("Nothing found")
    }
    return node
}
```

This function runs when it recognizes an image (ARImageAnchor). Then it uses the name property of the recognized image to determine which information to display. The entire ViewController.swift file should look like this:

```
import UIKit
import SceneKit
import ARKit

class ViewController: UIViewController, ARSCNViewDelegate  {

    @IBOutlet var sceneView: ARSCNView!

    let configuration = ARWorldTrackingConfiguration()

    struct Images {
        var title: String
        var info: String
    }

    var imageArray: [Images] = []

    override func viewDidLoad() {
        super.viewDidLoad()
        // Do any additional setup after loading the view,
        typically from a nib.
        sceneView.debugOptions = [ARSCNDebugOptions.
        showWorldOrigin, ARSCNDebugOptions.showFeaturePoints]
        sceneView.delegate = self

        guard let storedImages =  ARReferenceImage.referenceImages
        (inGroupNamed: "AR Resources", bundle: nil) else {
            fatalError("Missing AR Resources images")
        }
```

377

```
    configuration.detectionImages = storedImages

    getData()

    sceneView.session.run(configuration)
}

func renderer(_ renderer: SCNSceneRenderer, didAdd node:
SCNNode, for anchor: ARAnchor) {
    if anchor is ARImageAnchor {
        print("Item recognized")
    }
}

func renderer(_ renderer: SCNSceneRenderer, nodeFor anchor:
ARAnchor) -> SCNNode? {
    guard let imageAnchor = anchor as? ARImageAnchor else {
    return nil }

    switch imageAnchor.referenceImage.name {
    case "CRS-15":
        print(imageArray[0].title)
        print(imageArray[0].info)
    case "SaturnV":
        print(imageArray[1].title)
        print(imageArray[1].info)
    default:
        print("Nothing found")
    }

    let node = SCNNode()
    node.addChildNode(planeNode)

    return node
}
```

```
func getData() {
    let item1 = Images(title: "CRS-15 SpaceX rocket",
    info: "Commercial Resupply Service")
    let item2 = Images(title: "Saturn V rocket",
    info: "Apollo moon launch vehicle")

    imageArray.append(item1)
    imageArray.append(item2)
    }
}
```

To test this code, follow these steps:

1. Connect an iOS device to your Macintosh through its USB cable.

2. Click the Run button or choose Product ➤ Run.

3. Point the iOS device's camera at one of the images stored in the app's AR Resources folder.

4. The Xcode debug area displays text related to your image.

5. Click the Stop button or choose Product ➤ Stop.

# Displaying Information in Augmented Reality

Right now, our app only displays information about each image in the Xcode debug area, which users will never see. What we really need to do is take the information about each recognized image and display it within the augmented reality view.

First, we need to identify the boundaries of the image that the app recognizes. We can do that be creating a plane that's the exact width and height of the recognized image like this:

```
let plane = SCNPlane(width: imageAnchor.referenceImage.
physicalSize.width, height: imageAnchor.referenceImage.
physicalSize.height)
```

Now we need to give the plane a color so we can see it. Later we'll make this plane clear, but for now, we want to make sure that the plane completely covers any recognized image:

```
plane.firstMaterial?.diffuse.contents = UIColor.yellow
```

Next we need to create a node to hold the plane. Since the plane will appear flat, we also need to rotate it -90 degrees so it faces the camera:

```
let planeNode = SCNNode()
planeNode.geometry = plane

let ninetyDegrees = GLKMathDegreesToRadians(-90)
planeNode.eulerAngles = SCNVector3(ninetyDegrees, 0, 0)
```

Finally, we need to add this planeNode to the augmented reality view:

```
let node = SCNNode()
node.addChildNode(planeNode)
```

The entire nodeFor renderer function should look like this:

```
func renderer(_ renderer: SCNSceneRenderer, nodeFor anchor:
ARAnchor) -> SCNNode? {
    guard let imageAnchor = anchor as? ARImageAnchor else {
    return nil }
```

```swift
        let plane = SCNPlane(width: imageAnchor.referenceImage.
        physicalSize.width, height: imageAnchor.referenceImage.
        physicalSize.height)

        plane.firstMaterial?.diffuse.contents = UIColor.yellow

        let planeNode = SCNNode()
        planeNode.geometry = plane

        let ninetyDegrees = GLKMathDegreesToRadians(-90)
        planeNode.eulerAngles = SCNVector3(ninetyDegrees, 0, 0)

    switch imageAnchor.referenceImage.name {
        case "CRS-15":
            print(imageArray[0].title)
            print(imageArray[0].info)
        case "SaturnV":
            print(imageArray[1].title)
            print(imageArray[1].info)
        default:
            print("Nothing found")
        }

        return node
}

        let node = SCNNode()
        node.addChildNode(planeNode)

        return node
}
```

If you test this code, you'll see that as soon as you point an iOS device's camera at an image that the app can recognize, it immediately covers the entire image with a yellow plane, as shown in Figure 14-4. Try this with different size images to see that the yellow plane correctly recognizes the shape of every image stored in its AR Resources folder.

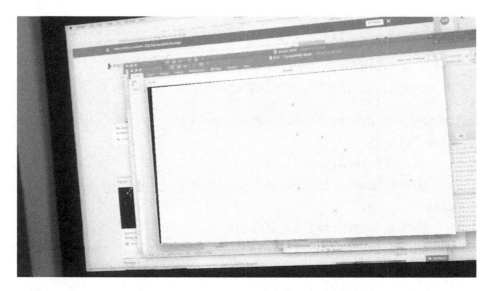

*Figure 14-4.* *A yellow plane completely masks a recognized image*

The reason for knowing the recognized image's size is so we can properly display text in the lower-left corner of that image. We'll be displaying both title and info of each image based on the structure we created earlier:

```
struct Images {
    var title: String
    var info: String
}
```

Before we write any more code and we know that the plane completely covers up any recognized images, we don't need to see the plane any more, so we can make it clear like this:

```
plane.firstMaterial?.diffuse.contents = UIColor.clear
```

Although the plane still exists, it's hidden from the user. We just need to use the plane as a reference so we know where to place text. First, we want to place the title text in the lower-right corner of each recognized image. This involves creating SCNText using the title text stored in our structure, defining a flatness value for our SCNText as 0.1, and a font size of 10 points like this:

```
let title = SCNText(string: imageArray[0].title, extrusionDepth: 0.0)
title.flatness = 0.1
title.font = UIFont.boldSystemFont(ofSize: 10)
```

Now we need to create an SCNNode, assign the SCNText to that node, and color it white while scaling its size smaller:

```
let titleNode = SCNNode()
titleNode.geometry = title
titleNode.geometry?.firstMaterial?.diffuse.contents = UIColor.white
titleNode.scale = SCNVector3(0.0015, 0.0015, 0.0015)
```

Feel free to experiment with other scaling values besides 0.0015 until you achieve the text appearance you like best. Finally, we need to place this title text relative to the plane and add it to the planeNode like this:

```
titleNode.position.x = -Float(plane.width) / 2.2
titleNode.position.y = -Float(plane.height) / 2.2
planeNode.addChildNode(titleNode)
```

The x and y positions are defined by the plane's width and height divided by 2.2. Experiment with different values so you can see how higher or lower values affect the location of text.

Displaying the info text for each image is similar like this

```
let info = SCNText(string: imageArray[0].info,
extrusionDepth: 0.0)
info.flatness = 0.1
info.font = UIFont.boldSystemFont(ofSize: 8)
let infoNode = SCNNode()
infoNode.geometry = info
infoNode.geometry?.firstMaterial?.diffuse.contents =
UIColor.gray
infoNode.scale = SCNVector3(0.0015, 0.0015, 0.0015)
infoNode.position.x = -Float(plane.width) / 2.2
infoNode.position.y = -Float(plane.height) / 1.8
planeNode.addChildNode(infoNode)
```

The entire ViewController.swift file should look similar to the following except you may choose different text to match the specific images you stored in your AR Resources folder:

```
import UIKit
import SceneKit
import ARKit

class ViewController: UIViewController, ARSCNViewDelegate  {

    @IBOutlet var sceneView: ARSCNView!

    let configuration = ARWorldTrackingConfiguration()

    struct Images {
        var title: String
        var info: String
    }
```

```swift
var imageArray: [Images] = []

override func viewDidLoad() {
    super.viewDidLoad()
    // Do any additional setup after loading the view,
    typically from a nib.
    sceneView.debugOptions = [ARSCNDebugOptions.
    showWorldOrigin, ARSCNDebugOptions.showFeaturePoints]
    sceneView.delegate = self

    guard let storedImages = ARReferenceImage.referenceImages
    (inGroupNamed: "AR Resources", bundle: nil) else {
        fatalError("Missing AR Resources images")
    }

    configuration.detectionImages = storedImages

    getData()

    sceneView.session.run(configuration)
}

func renderer(_ renderer: SCNSceneRenderer, didAdd node:
SCNNode, for anchor: ARAnchor) {
    if anchor is ARImageAnchor {
        print("Item recognized")
    }
}

func renderer(_ renderer: SCNSceneRenderer, nodeFor anchor:
ARAnchor) -> SCNNode? {
    guard let imageAnchor = anchor as? ARImageAnchor else {
    return nil }
```

```
let plane = SCNPlane(width: imageAnchor.referenceImage.
physicalSize.width, height: imageAnchor.referenceImage.
physicalSize.height)

plane.firstMaterial?.diffuse.contents = UIColor.clear

let planeNode = SCNNode()
planeNode.geometry = plane

let ninetyDegrees = GLKMathDegreesToRadians(-90)
planeNode.eulerAngles = SCNVector3(ninetyDegrees, 0, 0)

switch imageAnchor.referenceImage.name {
case "CRS-15":
    let title = SCNText(string: imageArray[0].title,
    extrusionDepth: 0.0)
    title.flatness = 0.1
    title.font = UIFont.boldSystemFont(ofSize: 10)
    let titleNode = SCNNode()
    titleNode.geometry = title
    titleNode.geometry?.firstMaterial?.diffuse.contents =
    UIColor.white
    titleNode.scale = SCNVector3(0.0015, 0.0015, 0.0015)
    titleNode.position.x = -Float(plane.width) / 2.2
    titleNode.position.y = -Float(plane.height) / 2.2
    planeNode.addChildNode(titleNode)

    let info = SCNText(string: imageArray[0].info,
    extrusionDepth: 0.0)
    info.flatness = 0.1
    info.font = UIFont.boldSystemFont(ofSize: 8)
    let infoNode = SCNNode()
    infoNode.geometry = info
```

```
    infoNode.geometry?.firstMaterial?.diffuse.contents
    = UIColor.gray
    infoNode.scale = SCNVector3(0.0015, 0.0015, 0.0015)
    infoNode.position.x = -Float(plane.width) / 2.2
    infoNode.position.y = -Float(plane.height) / 1.8
    planeNode.addChildNode(infoNode)

case "SaturnV":
    let title = SCNText(string: imageArray[1].title,
    extrusionDepth: 0.0)
    title.flatness = 0.1
    title.font = UIFont.boldSystemFont(ofSize: 10)
    let titleNode = SCNNode()
    titleNode.geometry = title
    titleNode.geometry?.firstMaterial?.diffuse.contents =
    UIColor.white
    titleNode.scale = SCNVector3(0.0015, 0.0015, 0.0015)
    titleNode.position.x = -Float(plane.width) / 2.2
    titleNode.position.y = -Float(plane.height) / 2.2
    planeNode.addChildNode(titleNode)

    let info = SCNText(string: imageArray[1].info,
    extrusionDepth: 0.0)
    info.flatness = 0.1
    info.font = UIFont.boldSystemFont(ofSize: 8)
    let infoNode = SCNNode()
    infoNode.geometry = info
    infoNode.geometry?.firstMaterial?.diffuse.contents
    = UIColor.gray
```

```
            infoNode.scale = SCNVector3(0.0015, 0.0015, 0.0015)
            infoNode.position.x = -Float(plane.width) / 2.2
            infoNode.position.y = -Float(plane.height) / 1.8
            planeNode.addChildNode(infoNode)

        default:
            print("Nothing found")
        }

        let node = SCNNode()
        node.addChildNode(planeNode)

        return node
    }

    func getData() {
        let item1 = Images(title: "CRS-15 SpaceX rocket",
        info: "Commercial Resupply Service")
        let item2 = Images(title: "Saturn V rocket",
        info: "Apollo moon launch vehicle")

        imageArray.append(item1)
        imageArray.append(item2)
    }

}
```

If you run this app, you'll see the title text appear in the lower-right corner of the image while the info text appears below, as shown in Figure 14-5.

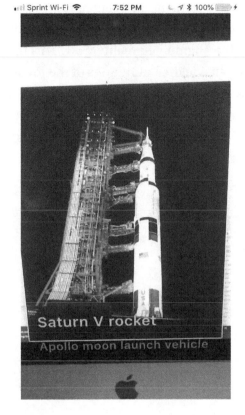

*Figure 14-5.  Displaying text in an augmented reality view*

# Summary

Image detection works by storing one or more images in a special AR
Resources folder and then using the iOS device's camera to run multiple
renderer functions when ARKit recognizes one of its many stored images.
When you drag and drop an image into the AR Resources folder, you must
define that image's physical width and height. In addition, you also need to
give each image a distinct name so you can use that name later to identify
which recognized image the iOS device's camera currently has found.

Once you're able to use the name of each recognized image to specify which particular image has been recognized, you can display text related to that image within the augmented reality view. This text can appear positioned within or outside the boundaries of the recognized image.

Image detection works best with high-resolution pictures. By using image detection, your augmented reality apps can respond to real-world objects and provide information about that object as virtual text that's only visible when seen through the camera of an iOS device.

# CHAPTER 15

# Displaying Video and Virtual Models

In Chapter 14, we learned how to use image detection to detect specific items and then respond by displaying text related to that particular image. In this chapter, we'll continue using image detection but instead of displaying text as virtual objects, we're going to learn how to display videos or virtual models.

When using videos with image detection, users will be able to aim an iOS device's camera at a still image and the augmented reality view will display a video over that image.

When using virtual models with image detection, users will be able to aim an iOS device's camera at a still image and see a three-dimension virtual model float in mid-air in front of the image.

To learn about using video and virtual models with image detection, we're going to modify the image detection project created in Chapter 14. You can make a copy of that project or just modify the existing code.

First, let's edit the code in the project to make room for adding code to display video and virtual models. Delete all the code inside the `switch` statement in the `nodeFor renderer` function so it looks like this:

```
switch imageAnchor.referenceImage.name {
case "CRS-15":
    print("1st image")
```

```
    case "SaturnV":
        print("2nd image")

    default:
        print("Nothing found")
    }
```

Now we need to drag and drop an .scn file into our Xcode project. The simplest way to do that is to create an Augmented Reality App by choosing File ➤ New ➤ Project. This creates a sample augmented reality app that includes the ship.scn SceneKit file inside an art.scnassets folder.

With two Xcode windows open side by side, drag and drop ship.scn and its accompanying texture.png file from the sample augmented reality project Xcode window into the Navigator pane of your current project's Xcode window.

Now you'll need to drag and drop a .mov video file into the Navigator pane as well. This video can be anything you want, such as a video captured off your iPhone or a video file downloaded from the Internet.

When you have both the ship.scn and a .mov file in the Navigator pane of your current project, click on each file and make sure the check box is selected under the Target Membership category, as shown in Figure 15-1. If the Target Membership check box is not selected, Xcode won't include the file in your current project even though it appears in the Navigator pane.

*Figure 15-1.* *The Target Membership check box must be selected for your .scn and .mp4 files*

# Displaying Virtual Objects in Mid-Air

The goal is to have ARKit use image detection to recognize an image in the real world. As soon as it recognizes an image, it displays a virtual object in front of that image. All code will be written inside the `switch` statement in the `nodeFor renderer` function. To display a virtual object after recognizing an image, follow these steps:

1.  Click on the `ship.scn` file in the Navigator pane. Xcode displays both the image and a list of the nodes that make up that image, as shown in Figure 15-2. The rootnode name for the `ship.scn` file is "ship".

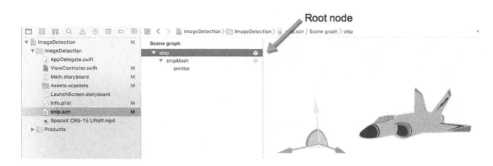

***Figure 15-2.*** *Identifying the rootnode name of an image*

2. Write the following inside the first case statement inside the switch statement to create a variable that represents the ship.scn virtual object like this:

```
let item = SCNScene(named: "ship.scn")
```

3. Now we need to identify the parent or rootnode of the virtual object by writing the following line:

```
let itemNode = item?.rootNode.childNode
(withName: "ship", recursively: true)
```

4. Now we need to position the virtual object node in the augmented reality view by retrieving the position from the ARImageAnchor:

```
itemNode?.position = SCNVector3(anchor.
transform.columns.3.x, anchor.transform.
columns.3.y,anchor.transform.columns.3.z)
sceneView.scene.rootNode.addChildNode(itemNode!)
```

At this point, the code will recognize the first image and then display ship.scn in mid-air. However, to create a more interesting visual effect, we can also rotate the virtual object around.

5.  Add the following two lines above the code from
    Step 4. The following code defines rotation around
    the x-, y-, and z-axes and keeps this rotation
    animation going forever:

```
let rotateMe = SCNAction.rotateBy(x: 0.5,
y: 0.1, z: 0.2, duration: 1)
let repeatMe = SCNAction.repeatForever(rotateMe)
itemNode?.runAction(repeatMe)
```

The rotation values for the x-, y-, and z-axes are arbitrary, so feel free
to experiment with different values so you can see how they change the
rotation of the virtual object.

The entire ViewController.swift file should look like this:

```
import UIKit
import SceneKit
import ARKit

class ViewController: UIViewController, ARSCNViewDelegate  {

    @IBOutlet var sceneView: ARSCNView!

    let configuration = ARWorldTrackingConfiguration()

    struct Images {
        var title: String
        var info: String
    }

    var imageArray: [Images] = []

    override func viewDidLoad() {
        super.viewDidLoad()
        // Do any additional setup after loading the view,
        typically from a nib.
```

```swift
    sceneView.debugOptions = [ARSCNDebugOptions.
    showWorldOrigin, ARSCNDebugOptions.showFeaturePoints]
    sceneView.delegate = self

    guard let storedImages =  ARReferenceImage.
    referenceImages(inGroupNamed: "AR Resources",
    bundle: nil) else {
        fatalError("Missing AR Resources images")
    }

    configuration.detectionImages = storedImages

    getData()

    sceneView.session.run(configuration)
}

func renderer(_ renderer: SCNSceneRenderer, nodeFor anchor:
ARAnchor) -> SCNNode? {
    guard let imageAnchor = anchor as? ARImageAnchor else {
    return nil }

    let plane = SCNPlane(width: imageAnchor.referenceImage.
    physicalSize.width, height: imageAnchor.referenceImage.
    physicalSize.height)

    plane.firstMaterial?.diffuse.contents = UIColor.clear

    let planeNode = SCNNode()
    planeNode.geometry = plane

    let ninetyDegrees = GLKMathDegreesToRadians(-90)
    planeNode.eulerAngles = SCNVector3(ninetyDegrees, 0, 0)

    switch imageAnchor.referenceImage.name {
    case "CRS-15":
        print("1st image")
```

```
        let item = SCNScene(named: "ship.scn")
        let itemNode = item?.rootNode.childNode
        (withName: "ship", recursively: true)

        let rotateMe = SCNAction.rotateBy(x: 0.5, y:
        0.1, z: 0.2, duration: 1)
        let repeatMe = SCNAction.repeatForever(rotateMe)
        itemNode?.runAction(repeatMe)

        itemNode?.position = SCNVector3(anchor.transform.
        columns.3.x, anchor.transform.columns.3.y,anchor.
        transform.columns.3.z)
        sceneView.scene.rootNode.addChildNode(itemNode!)
    case "SaturnV":
        print("2nd image")

    default:
        print("Nothing found")
    }

    let node = SCNNode()
    node.addChildNode(planeNode)

    return node
}

func getData() {
    let item1 = Images(title: "CRS-15 SpaceX rocket",
    info: "Commercial Resupply Service")
    let item2 = Images(title: "Saturn V rocket",
    info: "Apollo moon launch vehicle")

    imageArray.append(item1)
    imageArray.append(item2)
}

}
```

To test this app, follow these steps:

1.  Connect an iOS device to your Macintosh through its USB cable.

2.  Click the Run button or choose Product ➤ Run.

3.  Load the first picture on your computer that you stored in your project's AR Resources folder.

4.  Aim the iOS device's camera at the screen that displays the picture you want ARKit to recognize. When ARKit recognizes the image, it displays the ship.scn virtual object that rotates slowly in the air, as shown in Figure 15-3.

***Figure 15-3.*** *The ship.scn virtual object appears and rotates when the app recognizes the first image*

5.  Click the Stop button or choose Product ➤ Stop.

Repeat these steps except point the iOS device's camera at the second image stored in the AR Resources folder. Notice that the virtual object does not appear for this second virtual object.

# Displaying Video on a Plane

After detecting an image, an app can present additional information through text or by displaying a virtual object. Yet another way an app can respond is by displaying a video where the video appears over the detected image so the image appears to come to life.

The first step is to convert any video file into a QuickTime .mov file format. To do that, simply load the QuickTime Player program and load the video file that you currently have stored in a different file format, such as .mp4. Now choose File ➤ Export. Choose a video resolution such as 480p or 720p, as shown in Figure 15-4. Keep in mind that higher resolution means a larger video file size. After choosing a video resolution, QuickTime Player will save your video as a QuickTime movie.

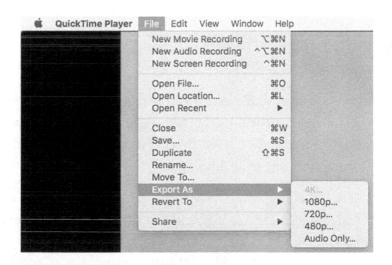

***Figure 15-4.***  *The QuickTime Player program can export QuickTime .mov files*

Before we even attempt to display video, we need to make sure we can view the augmented reality view through the iOS device's camera:

```
guard let currentFrame = sceneView.session.currentFrame else
{ return nil }
```

To play video, we can use a SceneKit class called SKVideoNode that allows us to load a QuickTime .mov file and play it immediately, like this:

```
let videoNode = SKVideoNode(fileNamed: "SaturnV.mov")
videoNode.play()
```

Next, we need to define this videoNode in a SKScene class where we define the video size, its scale such as aspectFill to maintain the aspect ratio of the original video regardless of the size of the plane it appears on, and then add that videoNode to the SKScene. Finally, we need to position the videoNode in the middle like this:

```
let videoScene = SKScene(size: CGSize(width: 640,
height: 480))
videoScene.scaleMode = .aspectFit
videoScene.addChild(videoNode)
videoNode.position = CGPoint(x: videoScene.size.width/2,
y: videoScene.size.height/2)
```

Now we need to create a plane that will appear over the detected image. This plane needs to be the exact same size as the detected image and then display the video. The video also needs to play on both sides of the plane since we're going to be flipping the plane:

```
let videoPlane = SCNPlane(width: imageAnchor.
referenceImage.physicalSize.width, height: imageAnchor.
referenceImage.physicalSize.height)
videoPlane.firstMaterial?.diffuse.contents = videoScene
videoPlane.firstMaterial?.isDoubleSided = true
```

Now we need to create an SCNNode to contain the plane (which displays the video). This SCNNode will hold the plane and then we need to flip the plane and position it over the plane that covers the detected image. Finally, we need to add the plane to the planeNode:

```
let tvPlaneNode = SCNNode(geometry: videoPlane)

var translation = matrix_identity_float4x4
translation.columns.3.z = -1.0

tvPlaneNode.simdTransform = matrix_multiply(currentFrame.
camera.transform, translation)
tvPlaneNode.eulerAngles = SCNVector3(Double.pi, 0, 0)

tvPlaneNode.position = SCNVector3(0,0,0)
planeNode.addChildNode(tvPlaneNode)
```

The complete ViewController.swift file should look like this:

```
import UIKit
import SceneKit
import ARKit

class ViewController: UIViewController, ARSCNViewDelegate  {

    @IBOutlet var sceneView: ARSCNView!

    let configuration = ARWorldTrackingConfiguration()

    struct Images {
        var title: String
        var info: String
    }

    var imageArray: [Images] = []
```

```swift
override func viewDidLoad() {
    super.viewDidLoad()
    // Do any additional setup after loading the view,
    typically from a nib.
    sceneView.debugOptions = [ARSCNDebugOptions.
    showWorldOrigin, ARSCNDebugOptions.showFeaturePoints]
    sceneView.delegate = self

    guard let storedImages =  ARReferenceImage.
    referenceImages(inGroupNamed: "AR Resources",
    bundle: nil) else {
        fatalError("Missing AR Resources images")
    }

    configuration.detectionImages = storedImages

    getData()

    sceneView.session.run(configuration)
}

func renderer(_ renderer: SCNSceneRenderer, nodeFor anchor:
ARAnchor) -> SCNNode? {
    guard let imageAnchor = anchor as? ARImageAnchor else {
    return nil }

    let plane = SCNPlane(width: imageAnchor.referenceImage.
    physicalSize.width, height: imageAnchor.referenceImage.
    physicalSize.height)

    plane.firstMaterial?.diffuse.contents = UIColor.clear

    let planeNode = SCNNode()
    planeNode.geometry = plane
```

```swift
let ninetyDegrees = GLKMathDegreesToRadians(-90)
planeNode.eulerAngles = SCNVector3(ninetyDegrees, 0, 0)

switch imageAnchor.referenceImage.name {
case "CRS-15":
    print("1st image")
    let item = SCNScene(named: "ship.scn")
    let itemNode = item?.rootNode.childNode
    (withName: "ship", recursively: true)

    let rotateMe = SCNAction.rotateBy(x: 0.5, y:
    0.1, z: 0.2, duration: 1)
    let repeatMe = SCNAction.repeatForever(rotateMe)
    itemNode?.runAction(repeatMe)

    itemNode?.position = SCNVector3(anchor.transform.
    columns.3.x, anchor.transform.columns.3.y,anchor.
    transform.columns.3.z)
    sceneView.scene.rootNode.addChildNode(itemNode!)
case "SaturnV":
    print("2nd image")

    guard let currentFrame = sceneView.session.
    currentFrame else { return nil }

    let videoNode = SKVideoNode(fileNamed:
    "SaturnV.mov")
    videoNode.play()

    let videoScene = SKScene(size: CGSize(width: 640,
    height: 480))
    videoScene.scaleMode = .aspectFit
    videoScene.addChild(videoNode)
```

```
        videoNode.position = CGPoint(x: videoScene.size.
        width/2, y: videoScene.size.height/2)

        let videoPlane = SCNPlane(width: imageAnchor.
        referenceImage.physicalSize.width, height:
        imageAnchor.referenceImage.physicalSize.height)
        videoPlane.firstMaterial?.diffuse.contents =
        videoScene

        videoPlane.firstMaterial?.isDoubleSided = true

        let tvPlaneNode = SCNNode(geometry: videoPlane)

        var translation = matrix_identity_float4x4
        translation.columns.3.z = -1.0

        tvPlaneNode.simdTransform = matrix_
        multiply(currentFrame.camera.transform,
        translation)
        tvPlaneNode.eulerAngles = SCNVector3
        (Double.pi, 0, 0)

        tvPlaneNode.position = SCNVector3(0,0,0)
        planeNode.addChildNode(tvPlaneNode)
    default:
        print("Nothing found")
    }

    let node = SCNNode()
    node.addChildNode(planeNode)

    return node
}
```

```swift
func getData() {
    let item1 = Images(title: "CRS-15 SpaceX rocket", info:
    "Commercial Resupply Service")
    let item2 = Images(title: "Saturn V rocket", info:
    "Apollo moon launch vehicle")

    imageArray.append(item1)
    imageArray.append(item2)
}

}
```

To test this code, follow these steps:

1.  Connect an iOS device to your Macintosh through its USB cable.

2.  Click the Run button or choose Product ➤ Run.

3.  Display one of the images, stored in the app's AR Resources folder, on to your computer screen.

4.  Point the iOS device's camera at one of the images stored in the app's AR  Resources folder.

5.  Your video starts playing over the detected image. Notice that the video is the same size as the detected image.

6.  Click the Stop button or choose Product ➤ Stop.

# Summary

Image detection can identify recognized images, but your app still needs a way to respond to the user who provides more information. Displaying text can be suitable in many cases, but two other ways to provide additional information is by displaying virtual objects or by playing video.

405

Displaying a virtual object can provide a three-dimensional view of an item while also using animation to make an augmented reality view come to life. Displaying video can make a detected image change from a static image to a video that provides further information.

Virtual objects and video are just two more ways an augmented reality can respond to detected images and provide additional information about a particular image.

# CHAPTER 16

# Image Tracking and Object Detection

In previous chapters, we learned about image detection. That's where an app can detect an image, stored in its AR Resources folder, and then respond when the iOS device camera recognizes that image in the real world. Image detection works with two-dimensional items such as pictures and photographs, but ARKit 2.0 and iOS 12 offer two additional features that expand on image detection: image tracking and object detection.

Right now, image detection works by linking text, a virtual object, or a video to the location of a detected image. However, if that detected image moves, then the displayed text, virtual object, or video won't move. That's why ARKit 2.0 offers image tracking, which allows text, a virtual object, or video to move if the detected image also moves.

While image detection might be impressive, it's limited to two-dimensional items such as pictures or photographs. To overcome this limitation, ARKit 2.0 offers object detection. First, you can scan in a three-dimensional object. Then you can store this three-dimensional object scan in your augmented reality app.

As soon as the user scans the same item, the augmented reality app can recognize the three-dimensional object and respond by displaying text, virtual objects, or video, just like image detection. Where image detection works with two-dimensional, flat items, object detection works

© Wallace Wang 2018
W. Wang, *Beginning ARKit for iPhone and iPad*,
https://doi.org/10.1007/978-1-4842-4102-8_16

with three-dimensional objects, allowing the user to get information about that object no matter which position or angle of the iOS camera.

For this chapter, let's create a new Xcode project by following these steps:

1.  Start Xcode. (Make sure you're using Xcode 10 or greater.)

2.  Choose File ➤ New ➤ Project. Xcode asks you to choose a template.

3.  Click the iOS category.

4.  Click the Single View App icon and click the Next button. Xcode asks for a product name, organization name, organization identifiers, and content technology.

5.  Click in the Product Name text field and type a descriptive name for your project, such as ImageTracking. (The exact name does not matter.)

6.  Click the Next button. Xcode asks where you want to store your project.

7.  Choose a folder and click the Create button. Xcode creates an iOS project.

Now modify the Info.plist file to allow access to the camera and to use ARKit by following these steps:

1.  Click the Info.plist file in the Navigator pane. Xcode displays a list of keys, types, and values.

2.  Click the disclosure triangle to expand the Required Device Capabilities category to display Item 0.

3.  Move the mouse pointer over Item 0 to display a plus (+) icon.

4. Click this plus (+) icon to display a blank Item 1.

5. Type `arkit` under the Value category in the Item 1 row.

6. Move the mouse pointer over the last row to display a plus (+) icon.

7. Click on the plus (+) icon to create a new row. A popup menu appears.

8. Choose Privacy – Camera Usage Description.

9. Type `AR needs to use the camera` under the Value category in the Privacy – Camera Usage Description row.

Now it's time to modify the `ViewController.swift` file to use ARKit and SceneKit by following these steps:

1. Click on the `ViewController.swift` file in the Navigator pane.

2. Edit the `ViewController.swift` file so it looks like this:

```
import UIKit
import SceneKit
import ARKit

class ViewController: UIViewController,
ARSCNViewDelegate {

let configuration = ARImageTrackingConfiguration()

    override func viewDidLoad() {
        super.viewDidLoad()
        // Do any additional setup after loading the
        view, typically from a nib.

    }

}
```

The most important line to notice is the one that defines an
ARImageTrackingConfiguration:

```
let configuration = ARImageTrackingConfiguration()
```

Previously, we've only defined an ARWorldTrackingConfiguration but
we need ARImageTrackingConfiguration to let our augmented reality app
track a detected image when it moves.

To view augmented reality in our app, add a single ARKit SceneKit
View (ARSCNView) so it fills the entire view. After you've designed your
user interface, you need to add constraints. To add constraints, choose
Editor ➤ Resolve Auto Layout Issues ➤ Reset to Suggested Constraints at
the bottom half of the menu under the All Views in Container category.

The next step is to connect the user interface items to the Swift code in
the ViewController.swift file. To do this, follow these steps:

1.  Click the Main.storyboard file in the Navigator
    pane.

2.  Click the Assistant Editor icon or choose View ➤
    Assistant Editor ➤ Show Assistant Editor to display
    the Main.storyboard and the ViewController.
    swift file side by side.

3.  Move the mouse pointer over the ARSCNView,
    hold down the Control key, and Ctrl-drag under the
    class ViewController line.

4.  Release the Control key and the left mouse button.
    A popup menu appears.

5.  Click in the Name text field and type sceneView,
    then click the Connect button. Xcode creates an
    IBOutlet as shown here:

    ```
    @IBOutlet var sceneView: ARSCNView!
    ```

6. Edit the `viewDidLoad` function so it looks like this:

```
override func viewDidLoad() {
    super.viewDidLoad()
    // Do any additional setup after loading the
    view, typically from a nib.
    sceneView.debugOptions = [ARSCNDebugOptions.
    showWorldOrigin, ARSCNDebugOptions.
    showFeaturePoints]
    sceneView.delegate = self

    sceneView.session.run(configuration)
}
```

Remember, ARKit can only recognize physical objects in the real world after you have stored images of those items in your app. In addition to storing an image, you must also specify the width and height of that real-world object. That way, when ARKit spots that actual item through the iOS device's camera, it can compare that image with its stored image. If they match in both appearance and size, then ARKit can recognize that real-world item.

First, you must capture an image of the item you want to detect. Since these images need to be high resolution, you can capture public domain images off the Internet, such as at NASA (www.nasa.gov). Then you can display these images on your laptop or iPad screen for your iOS device to recognize.

To store one or more images that you want ARKit to recognize, follow these steps:

1. Click the `Assets.xcassets` folder in the Navigator pane.

2. Click the plus (+) icon in the bottom of the pane.
   A popup menu appears.

3. Choose New AR Resource Group. Xcode creates an AR Resources folder.

4. Drag and drop the images you want ARKit to recognize in the real world. Xcode displays a yellow alert icon in the bottom-right corner of your images.

5. Click the Attributes Inspector icon or choose View ➤ Inspectors ➤ Show Attributes Inspector. An AR Reference Image pane appears, as shown in Figure 16-1.

***Figure 16-1.*** *Defining the width and height of the item to recognize*

6. Click in the Width and Height text fields and type the actual width and height of the real item. You can also click the Units popup menu to change the default measurement unit from meters to something else, such as inches or centimeters.

Once we've added one or more images of the real objects we want ARKit to recognize, we need to write actual Swift code to recognize the image when spotted through an iOS device's camera.

First, we need to access the folder containing the images of items to recognize. This folder can be called anything, such as AR Resources. This means using a guard statement to verify that the image folder even exists like this:

412

```
guard let storedImages = ARReferenceImage.
referenceImages(inGroupNamed: "AR Resources",
bundle: nil) else {
        fatalError("Missing AR Resources images")
}
```

This code looks for a folder named AR Resources. If it fails to find it, it ends the program and displays "Missing AR Resources images". If it finds an AR Resources folder, then we can define where the detected images are stored, like this:

```
configuration.trackingImages = storedImages
```

Notice that this line of code uses trackingImages instead of detectionImages. With detectionImages, an app will recognize an image only if it stays in one place. With trackingImages, the app can follow the detected image if it moves.

Finally, we need to use the didAdd renderer function, which runs every time the camera updates its view. If the camera detects a recognized image (ARImageAnchor) then we want to display a virtual object that appears near the detected image.

In our earlier examples, we would display a virtual object to the detected image by attaching it to the rootnode of the scene like this:

```
sceneView.scene.rootNode.addChildNode(objectNode)
```

However, this ties the virtual object to a specific location in the augmented reality view. What we want is to tie the virtual object to the detected image like this:

```
node.addChildNode(objectNode)
```

Now if the detected image moves, the virtual object will move as well. To detect and track the stored image, we need to use the didAdd renderer function. First, we need to make sure we detected a stored image as an ARImageAnchor like this:

```
func renderer(_ renderer: SCNSceneRenderer, didAdd node:
SCNNode, for anchor: ARAnchor) {
    if anchor is ARImageAnchor {

    }
}
```

Then we can create a virtual object to appear over the detected image. In this example, we'll create text as follows:

```
let movingImage = SCNText(string: "Moving Text",
extrusionDepth: 0.0)
movingImage.flatness = 0.1
movingImage.font = UIFont.boldSystemFont(ofSize: 10)
```

Next, we'll need to store this SCNText in a node, so we need to define a node by defining its color and scale:

```
let titleNode = SCNNode()
titleNode.geometry = movingImage
titleNode.geometry?.firstMaterial?.diffuse.contents =
UIColor.white
titleNode.scale = SCNVector3(0.0015, 0.0015, 0.0015)
```

Then we just need to add the node containing our SCNText to the detected image:

```
node.addChildNode(titleNode)
```

The entire ViewController.swift file should look like this:

```
import UIKit
import SceneKit
import ARKit

class ViewController: UIViewController, ARSCNViewDelegate {
```

```swift
@IBOutlet var sceneView: ARSCNView!

let configuration = ARImageTrackingConfiguration()

override func viewDidLoad() {
    super.viewDidLoad()
    // Do any additional setup after loading the view,
    typically from a nib.
    sceneView.debugOptions = [ARSCNDebugOptions.
    showWorldOrigin, ARSCNDebugOptions.showFeaturePoints]
    sceneView.delegate = self

    guard let storedImages =  ARReferenceImage.
    referenceImages(inGroupNamed: "AR Resources",
    bundle: nil) else {
        fatalError("Missing AR Resources images")
    }

    configuration.trackingImages = storedImages

    sceneView.session.run(configuration)
}

func renderer(_ renderer: SCNSceneRenderer, didAdd node:
SCNNode, for anchor: ARAnchor) {
    if anchor is ARImageAnchor {
        let movingImage = SCNText(string: "Moving Text",
        extrusionDepth: 0.0)
        movingImage.flatness = 0.1
        movingImage.font = UIFont.boldSystemFont(ofSize: 10)

        let titleNode = SCNNode()
        titleNode.geometry = movingImage
        titleNode.geometry?.firstMaterial?.diffuse.contents =
        UIColor.white
```

```
        titleNode.scale = SCNVector3(0.0015, 0.0015, 0.0015)

        node.addChildNode(titleNode)
      }
   }
}
```

To test this app, place the item that you took a picture of and stored in the AR Resources folder and display that item on a laptop or iPad placed on a table or floor. Then follow these steps:

1. Connect an iOS device to your Macintosh through its USB cable.

2. Click the Run button or choose Product ➤ Run. The first time you run this app, it will ask permission to access the camera so give it permission.

3. Using the picture on your you stored in your project's AR Resources folder, display this same picture on a laptop or iPad screen.

4. Aim the iOS device's camera at the screen that displays the picture you want ARKit to recognize. When ARKit recognizes the image, it displays the text "Moving Text" over the detected image, as shown in Figure 16-2.

***Figure 16-2.*** *Text appears over the detected image even when you move the detected image*

5.  Move the laptop or iPad screen that's displaying the detected image. Notice that as you move the detected image, the virtual object ("Moving Text") moves along to maintain its distance and orientation with the detected image at all times.

6.  Click the Stop button or choose Product ➤ Stop.

# Detecting Objects

With image detection, we had to store the actual images we want the app to detect in a special AR Resources folder. Object detection works in a similar way except instead of storing a single image to detect, object detection stores the three-dimensional spatial features of an object in the AR Resources folder. To get these three-dimensional spatial features of an object we want to detect in the future, we have to scan that image ahead of time and store that scanned representation of the image in our app.

To enable object detection in your app, you must follow these steps:

1.   Scan the object you want your app to detect using Apple's scanning app. This stores the three-dimensional spatial representation of that object in an .arobject file format.

2.   Store this .arobject file in the AR Resources folder of your own app.

3.   Write Swift code to make your app respond when it detects the object defined by the .arobject file.

# Scanning an Object

The quality of your app's ability to detect an object depends on accurate scanning of that object beforehand. Scanning requires a device capable of running iOS 12 with at least an A9 processor (iPhone 6s, iPhone 6s Plus, iPhone SE, and iPad 2017). The more current the device (higher resolution camera, faster processor, etc.), the better the reference data the scanning will capture.

To increase the accuracy of your scanning, place the object you want to detect on a flat surface free of any additional items. That way the scanning can focus solely on the object you want to detect.

First, you need to install Apple's ARKit Scanner app on an iOS 12 device. To get this ARKit Scanner app, follow these steps:

1. Visit `https://developer.apple.com/documentation/arkit/scanning_and_detecting_3d_objects` and download the ScanningApp, which includes the Swift source code.

2. Open this ScanningApp project into Xcode.

3. Connect an iOS 12 device to your Macintosh using a USB cable.

4. Click the Run button or choosing Product ➤ Run. This installs the ARKit Scanner app on your iOS device.

5. Click the Stop button or choose Product ➤ Stop. At this point, you can disconnect the iOS 12 device from your Macintosh.

Once you have Apple's ARKit Scanner installed on an iOS 12 device, you can start scanning objects. To scan an item, follow these steps:

1. Place the object you want your app to detect on a flat, well-lit surface that's free of any other objects.

2. Run the ARKit Scanner app on your iOS 12 device.

3. Point the iOS device's camera at the object until a cartoon bounding box encloses the object you want to detect, as shown in Figure 16-3.

*Figure 16-3.* *A bounding box defines the area of the object to detect*

4.  When the object appears centered inside the
    bounding box, tap the Next button. The ARKit
    Scanner app displays the bounding box around your
    object along with measurement information about
    that object, as shown in Figure 16-4.

*Figure 16-4.* *The bounding box encloses the object you want to detect*

5.  Tap the Scan button and move around the object.
    As you move, the app displays yellow planes along
    the sides and top of the bounding box to let you
    know which angles it can detect, as shown in
    Figure 16-5. The goal is to move your iOS device's
    camera along all sides and the top of the object until
    yellow planes completely cover the bounding box.

**Figure 16-5.** *As you scan the object, yellow planes show you which areas you've already scanned*

6.    When yellow planes completely cover all sides of the bounding box, tap the Finish button. The ARKit Scanner app now displays the origin of the detected object that you can move if you wish, as shown in Figure 16-6.

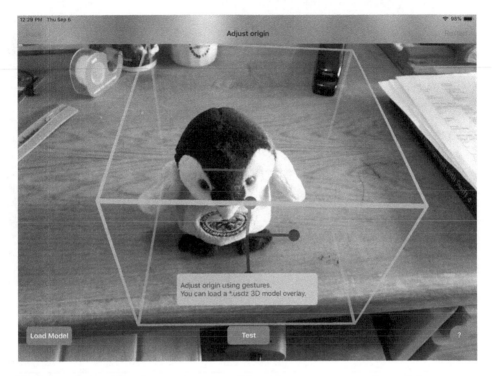

*Figure 16-6.* *After scanning an object, you can move its origin*

7.  Move the origin by swiping your finger on the origin and then tap the Test button.

8.  Move the object to a new location and aim the iOS device's camera at it to make sure the ARKit Scanner app can recognize the object, as shown in Figure 16-7.

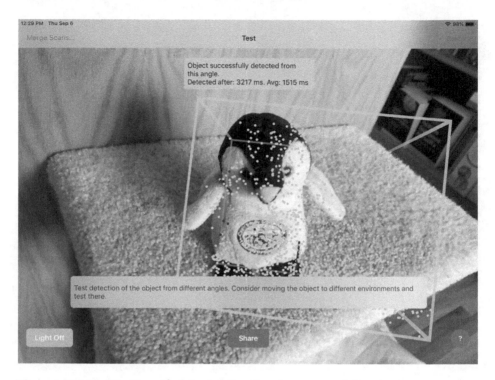

*Figure 16-7.* *Testing if object detection is successful or not*

9.  On your Macintosh, open a Finder window and
    choose Go ➤ AirDrop to open an AirDrop window,
    as shown in Figure 16-8.

***Figure 16-8.*** *Turning on AirDrop on a Macintosh*

10.  Tap the Share button in the ARKit Scanner screen.
     A popup window appears, letting you choose how
     you want to share the .arobject file, as shown in
     Figure 16-9.

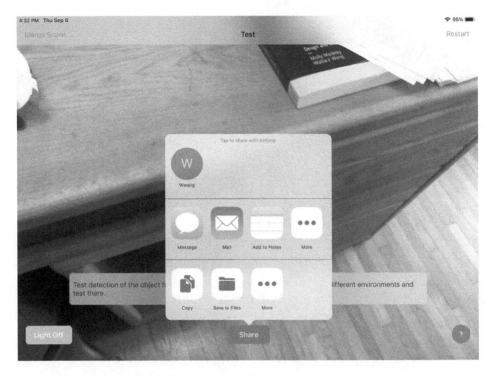

*Figure 16-9.*  *Accessing AirDrop from an iOS device*

11.  Tap the top gray circle that represents your
     Macintosh to transfer the .arobject file to the
     Downloads folder of your Macintosh.

# Detecting Objects in an App

Once you've transferred the .arobject file to your Macintosh, you need to
create an app that can detect the object captured in that .arobject file. To
detect objects, let's create a new Xcode project by following these steps:

1.  Start Xcode. (Make sure you're using Xcode 10 or greater.)

2.  Choose File ➤ New ➤ Project. Xcode asks you to
    choose a template.

3.  Click the iOS category.

4.  Click the Single View App icon and click the Next button. Xcode asks for a product name, organization name, organization identifiers, and content technology.

5.  Click in the Product Name text field and type a descriptive name for your project, such as ObjectDetection. (The exact name does not matter.)

6.  Click the Next button. Xcode asks where you want to store your project.

7.  Choose a folder and click the Create button. Xcode creates an iOS project.

Now modify the Info.plist file to allow access to the camera and to use ARKit by following these steps:

1.  Click the Info.plist file in the Navigator pane. Xcode displays a list of keys, types, and values.

2.  Click the disclosure triangle to expand the Required Device Capabilities category to display Item 0.

3.  Move the mouse pointer over Item 0 to display a plus (+) icon.

4.  Click this plus (+) icon to display a blank Item 1.

5.  Type arkit under the Value category in the Item 1 row.

6.  Move the mouse pointer over the last row to display a plus (+) icon.

7.  Click on the plus (+) icon to create a new row.
    A popup menu appears.

8.  Choose Privacy – Camera Usage Description.

9.  Type AR needs to use the camera under the Value
    category in the Privacy – Camera Usage Description row.

Now it's time to modify the ViewController.swift file to use ARKit
and SceneKit by following these steps:

1.  Click on the ViewController.swift file in the
    Navigator pane.

2.  Edit the ViewController.swift file so it looks like this:

```swift
import UIKit
import SceneKit
import ARKit

class ViewController: UIViewController,
ARSCNViewDelegate {

let configuration = ARWorldTrackingConfiguration()

    override func viewDidLoad() {
        super.viewDidLoad()
        // Do any additional setup after loading the
        view, typically from a nib.

    }

}
```

To view augmented reality in our app, add a single ARKit SceneKit
View (ARSCNView) so it fills the entire view. After you've designed your
user interface, you need to add constraints. To add constraints, choose
Editor ➤ Resolve Auto Layout Issues ➤ Reset to Suggested Constraints at
the bottom half of the menu under the All Views in Container category.

The next step is to connect the user interface items to the Swift code in the ViewController.swift file. To do this, follow these steps:

1. Click the Main.storyboard file in the Navigator pane.

2. Click the Assistant Editor icon or choose View ➤ Assistant Editor ➤ Show Assistant Editor to display the Main.storyboard and the ViewController. swift file side by side.

3. Move the mouse pointer over the ARSCNView, hold down the Control key, and Ctrl-drag under the class ViewController line.

4. Release the Control key and the left mouse button. A popup menu appears.

5. Click in the Name text field and type sceneView, then click the Connect button. Xcode creates an IBOutlet, as shown here:

    **@IBOutlet var** sceneView: ARSCNView!

6. Edit the viewDidLoad function so it looks like this:

```
override func viewDidLoad() {
    super.viewDidLoad()
    // Do any additional setup after loading the
    view, typically from a nib.
    sceneView.debugOptions = [ARSCNDebugOptions.
    showWorldOrigin, ARSCNDebugOptions.
    showFeaturePoints]
    sceneView.delegate = self

    sceneView.session.run(configuration)
}
```

ARKit can only recognize physical objects in the real world after you have stored .arobject files of those items in your app. To store one or more .arobject files that you want ARKit to recognize, follow these steps:

1. Click the Assets.xcassets folder in the Navigator pane.

2. Click + icon in the bottom of the pane. A popup menu appears.

3. Choose New AR Resource Group. Xcode creates an AR Resources folder.

4. Drag and drop the .arobject file into the AR Resources folder, as shown in Figure 16-10.

***Figure 16-10.*** *Displaying an .arobject file in the AR Resources folder*

Once we've added one or more .arobject files of the real objects we want ARKit to recognize, we need to write actual Swift code to recognize the object when spotted through an iOS device's camera.

First, we need to access the folder containing the images of items to recognize. This folder can be called anything, such as AR Resources. This means using a guard statement to verify that the AR Resources folder even exists like this:

```
guard let storedObjects = ARReferenceObject.
referenceObjects(inGroupNamed: "AR Resources",
bundle: nil) else {
    fatalError("Missing AR Resources images")
}
```

This code looks for a folder named AR Resources. If it fails to find it, it ends the program and displays "Missing AR Resources images". If it finds an AR Resources folder, then we can define where the detected .arobject files are stored like this:

```
configuration.detectionObjects = storedObjects
```

Notice that this line of code uses detectionObjects and the guard statement uses ARReferenceObject.referenceObjects.

Finally, we need to use the didAdd renderer function, which runs every time the camera updates its view. If the camera detects a recognized object (ARObjectAnchor), then we want to display a virtual object that appears near the detected object.

First, we need to make sure we detected a stored .arobject as an ARObjectAnchor like this:

```
func renderer(_ renderer: SCNSceneRenderer, didAdd node:
SCNNode, for anchor: ARAnchor) {
    if let objectAnchor = anchor as? ARObjectAnchor {

    }
}
```

Then we can create a virtual object to appear over the detected image. In this example, we'll create text as follows:

```
let movingImage = SCNText(string: "Object Detected",
extrusionDepth: 0.0)
movingImage.flatness = 0.1
movingImage.font = UIFont.boldSystemFont(ofSize: 10)
```

Next, we'll need to store this SCNText in a node, so we need to define a node by defining its color and scale:

```
let titleNode = SCNNode()
titleNode.geometry = movingImage
titleNode.geometry?.firstMaterial?.diffuse.contents =
UIColor.white
titleNode.scale = SCNVector3(0.0015, 0.0015, 0.0015)
```

Then we just need to add the node containing our SCNText to the detected image:

```
node.addChildNode(titleNode)
```

The entire ViewController.swift file should look like this:

```
import UIKit
import SceneKit
import ARKit

class ViewController: UIViewController, ARSCNViewDelegate{

    @IBOutlet var sceneView: ARSCNView!

    let configuration = ARWorldTrackingConfiguration()

    override func viewDidLoad() {
        super.viewDidLoad()
        // Do any additional setup after loading the view,
        typically from a nib.
        sceneView.debugOptions = [ARSCNDebugOptions.
        showWorldOrigin, ARSCNDebugOptions.showFeaturePoints]
        sceneView.delegate = self

        guard let storedObjects =  ARReferenceObject.
        referenceObjects(inGroupNamed: "AR Resources",
        bundle: nil) else {
            fatalError("Missing AR Resources images")
        }
```

```
    configuration.detectionObjects = storedObjects
    sceneView.session.run(configuration)
}

func renderer(_ renderer: SCNSceneRenderer, didAdd node:
SCNNode, for anchor: ARAnchor) {
    if let objectAnchor = anchor as? ARObjectAnchor {
        let movingImage = SCNText(string: "Object
        Detected", extrusionDepth: 0.0)
        movingImage.flatness = 0.1
        movingImage.font = UIFont.boldSystemFont(ofSize: 10)

        let titleNode = SCNNode()
        titleNode.geometry = movingImage
        titleNode.geometry?.firstMaterial?.diffuse.contents =
        UIColor.white
        titleNode.scale = SCNVector3(0.0015, 0.0015, 0.0015)

        node.addChildNode(titleNode)
    }
  }
}
```

To test this app, place the item that you scanned and stored in the AR Resources folder as an .arobject file and put that item on a table or floor. Then follow these steps:

1. Connect an iOS device to your Macintosh through its USB cable.

2. Click the Run button or choose Product ➤ Run. The first time you run this app, it will ask permission to access the camera so give it permission.

3. Place the object you want to detect on a flat surface.

433

4.  Aim the iOS device's camera at the object you want
    ARKit to recognize. When ARKit recognizes the
    object, it displays the text "Object Detected" near
    the detected object, as shown in Figure 16-11.

*Figure 16-11.* *Detecting an object*

5.  Click the Stop button or choose Product ➤ Stop.

# Summary

Image tracking lets your app not only recognize an image and display a virtual object nearby, but also keep that virtual object linked to that image even if that image moves. Object detection lets your app detect a pre-scanned object and display virtual objects around it, such as text.

When using image tracking, make sure you use `ARImageTracking Configuration` (not `ARWorldTrackingConfiguration`) like this:

```
let configuration = ARImageTrackingConfiguration()
```

Then use a guard statement to look for stored images in a special AR Resources folder:

```
guard let storedImages =  ARReferenceImage.
referenceImages(inGroupNamed: "AR Resources", bundle: nil)
else {
        fatalError("Missing AR Resources images")
}
```

Finally, use `trackingImages` to access the stored images in the AR Resources folder:

```
configuration.trackingImages = storedImages
```

When using object detection, use a `guard` statement to define stored .arobject files in the `AR  Resources` folder. Make sure you use `ARReferenceObject.referenceObjects` like this:

```
guard let storedObjects =  ARReferenceObject.reference
Objects(inGroupNamed: "AR Resources", bundle: nil) else {
    fatalError("Missing AR Resources images")
}
```

This code looks for a folder named `AR Resources`. If it fails to find it, it ends the program and displays `"Missing AR Resources images"`. If it finds an `AR Resources` folder, then we can define where the detected .arobject files are stored like this:

```
configuration.detectionObjects = storedObjects
```

With both image tracking and object detection available in ARKit 2.0, augmented reality apps can become far more versatile than ever before.

# CHAPTER 17

# Persistence

Up until now, every augmented reality view project we've created has had one problem. While you might be able to add virtual objects to an augmented reality view, the moment you close the app and start it again, any virtual objects you added would now be gone.

In many cases, this is exactly what you want, so starting the app again creates a blank augmented reality view for the user. However, sometimes you may want to retain any virtual objects placed in the view. To save an augmented reality view so it appears in another person's app or in your own app if you start it up again at a later time, you need to use *persistence.*

Persistence simply saves any virtual objects placed in an augmented reality view in a world map. By saving this world map, you can retain the placement of virtual objects. By loading this world map later, you can restore an augmented reality view to a previous state.

To learn about persistence, let's create a new Xcode project by following these steps:

1. Start Xcode. (Make sure you're using Xcode 10 or greater.)

2. Choose File ➤ New ➤ Project. Xcode asks you to choose a template.

3. Click the iOS category.

© Wallace Wang 2018
W. Wang, *Beginning ARKit for iPhone and iPad,*
https://doi.org/10.1007/978-1-4842-4102-8_17

4.   Click the Single View App icon and click the Next button. Xcode asks for a product name, organization name, organization identifiers, and content technology.

5.   Click in the Product Name text field and type a descriptive name for your project, such as Persistence. (The exact name does not matter.)

6.   Click the Next button. Xcode asks where you want to store your project.

7.   Choose a folder and click the Create button. Xcode creates an iOS project.

Now modify the Info.plist file to allow access to the camera and to use ARKit by following these steps:

1.   Click the Info.plist file in the Navigator pane. Xcode displays a list of keys, types, and values.

2.   Click the disclosure triangle to expand the Required Device Capabilities category to display Item 0.

3.   Move the mouse pointer over Item 0 to display a plus (+) icon.

4.   Click this plus (+) icon to display a blank Item 1.

5.   Type arkit under the Value category in the Item 1 row.

6.   Move the mouse pointer over the last row to display a plus (+) icon.

7.   Click on the plus (+) icon to create a new row. A popup menu appears.

8.  Choose Privacy – Camera Usage Description.

9.  Type AR needs to use the camera under the
    Value category in the Privacy – Camera Usage
    Description row.

Now it's time to modify the ViewController.swift file to use ARKit
and SceneKit by following these steps:

1.  Click on the ViewController.swift file in the
    Navigator pane.

2.  Edit the ViewController.swift file so it looks
    like this:

```swift
import UIKit
import SceneKit
import ARKit

class ViewController: UIViewController,
ARSCNViewDelegate , ARSessionDelegate  {

let configuration = ARWorldTrackingConfiguration()

    override func viewDidLoad() {
        super.viewDidLoad()
        // Do any additional setup after loading the
        view, typically from a nib.

    }

}
```

The most important line to notice is the one that adds the
ARSCNViewDelegate because this contains the functions we need to save
and restore a world map.

To view augmented reality in our app, add the following to the Main. storyboard, as shown in Figure 17-1:

- A single ARKit SceneKit view (ARSCNView)

- Three UIButtons

- A single UILabel

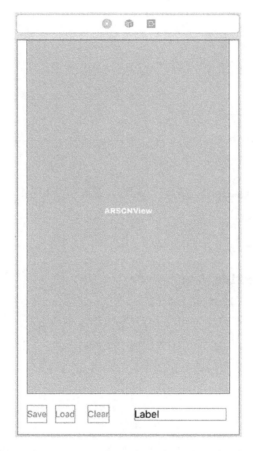

*Figure 17-1.* *Three buttons, a label, and an ARKit SceneKit view on the user interface*

After you've designed your user interface, you need to add constraints. To add constraints, choose Editor ➤ Resolve Auto Layout Issues ➤ Reset to Suggested Constraints at the bottom half of the menu under the All Views in Container category.

The next step is to connect the user interface items to the Swift code in the `ViewController.swift` file. To do this, follow these steps:

1. Click the `Main.storyboard` file in the Navigator pane.

2. Click the Assistant Editor icon or choose View ➤ Assistant Editor ➤ Show Assistant Editor to display the `Main.storyboard` and the `ViewController.swift` file side by side.

3. Move the mouse pointer over the ARSCNView, hold down the Control key, and Ctrl-drag under the `class ViewController` line.

4. Release the Control key and the left mouse button. A popup menu appears.

5. Click in the Name text field and type `sceneView`, then click the Connect button. Xcode creates an IBOutlet as shown here:

   **@IBOutlet var** `sceneView: ARSCNView!`

6. Move the mouse over the label, hold down the Control key, and Ctrl-drag under the IBOutlet you just created.

7. Release the Control key and the left mouse button. A popup menu appears.

8. Click in the Name text field and type lblMessage, then click the Connect button. Xcode creates an IBOutlet as shown here:

```
@IBOutlet var lblMessage: UILabel!
```

9. Underneath the two IBOutlets, type the following:

```
let configuration = ARWorldTrackingConfiguration()
```

10. Edit the viewDidLoad function so it looks like this:

```
override func viewDidLoad() {
    super.viewDidLoad()
    // Do any additional setup after loading the
    view, typically from a nib.
    sceneView.debugOptions = [ARSCNDebugOptions.
    showWorldOrigin, ARSCNDebugOptions.
    showFeaturePoints]
    sceneView.delegate = self
    sceneView.session.delegate = self
    configuration.planeDetection = .horizontal

    let tapGesture = UITapGestureRecognizer(target:
    self, action: #selector(handleTap))
    sceneView.addGestureRecognizer(tapGesture)

    self.lblMessage.text = "Tap to place a virtual
    object"
    sceneView.session.run(configuration)
}
```

At this point, we defined a tap gesture but we need to create a function to handle this tap gesture. Underneath the viewDidLoad function, add the following function called handleTap:

```
@objc func handleTap(sender: UITapGestureRecognizer) {
    guard let sceneView = sender.view as? ARSCNView else {
        return
    }

    let touch = sender.location(in: sceneView)
    let hitTestResults = sceneView.hitTest(touch, types:
    [.featurePoint, .estimatedHorizontalPlane])
    if hitTestResults.isEmpty == false {
        if let hitTestResult = hitTestResults.first {
            let virtualAnchor = ARAnchor(transform:
            hitTestResult.worldTransform)
            self.sceneView.session.add(anchor: virtualAnchor)
        }
    }
}
```

Each time the user taps on the screen, it adds an ARAnchor to the augmented reality view. That also triggers the didAdd renderer function, which we'll need to write to display a blue box on the screen. Underneath the handleTap function, write the didAdd renderer function as follows:

```
func renderer(_ renderer: SCNSceneRenderer,
didAdd node: SCNNode, for anchor: ARAnchor) {
    if anchor is ARPlaneAnchor {
        return
    }

    let newNode = SCNNode(geometry: SCNBox(width: 0.05,
    height: 0.05, length: 0.05, chamferRadius: 0))
```

```
    newNode.geometry?.firstMaterial?.diffuse.contents =
    UIColor.blue
    node.addChildNode(newNode)
}
```

Finally, add a `viewWillDisappear` function as follows:

```
override func viewWillDisappear(_ animated: Bool) {
    sceneView.session.pause()
}
```

# Saving a World Map

At this point, the app will simply allow the user to tap the screen and place blue boxes in the augmented reality view. However, you cannot save the augmented reality view yet. To save an augmented reality view, we need to store the current augmented reality view as a world map.

We can save the world map to any database, but since the world map represents a small amount of data, we're going to store it in the User Defaults database, which is typically used to store app settings. To save a world map, follow these steps:

1. Click the `Main.storyboard` file in the Navigator pane.

2. Click the Assistant Editor icon or choose View ➤ Assistant Editor ➤ Show Assistant Editor to display the `Main.storyboard` and the `ViewController. swift` file side by side.

3. Move the mouse pointer over the button displaying Save on the user interface, hold down the Control key, and Ctrl-drag under the `class ViewController` line.

4.  Release the Control key and the left mouse button. A popup menu appears.

5.  Make sure the Connection popup menu displays Action, then click in the Name text field and type saveButton.

6.  Click in the Type popup menu and choose UIButton, then click the Connect button. Xcode creates an IBAction method as shown here:

```
@IBAction func saveButton(_ sender: UIButton) {

}
```

7.  Edit this saveButton IBAction method as follows:

```
@IBAction func saveButton(_ sender: UIButton) {
    saveMap()
}
```

Each time the user taps the Save button, the Save button runs the saveMap() function, which we'll need to write as follows:

```
func saveMap() {

}
```

The first step to saving the world map is to get the current state of the augmented reality view:

```
self.sceneView.session.getCurrentWorldMap { worldMap,
error in
}
```

This code either retrieves the current state (`worldMap`) or shows an error. In case there's an error saving the current augmented reality state, we need to display an error message and stop trying to save the world map:

```
if error != nil {
    print(error?.localizedDescription ?? "Unknown error")
    return
}
```

If we're successful in retrieving the current state (`worldMap`), then we can create a "map" variable to represent our current world map:

```
if let map = worldMap {

}
```

Next we need to archive this world map as follows:

```
let data = try! NSKeyedArchiver.archivedData(withRootObject: map, requiringSecureCoding: true)
```

Now we need to save this data in the User Defaults database and give it an arbitrary string as a key so we can retrieve it later:

```
let savedMap = UserDefaults.standard
savedMap.set(data, forKey: "worldmap")
savedMap.synchronize()
```

Finally, we need to send a message to the user that we saved the world map:

```
DispatchQueue.main.async {
    self.lblMessage.text = "World map saved"
}
```

The entire saveMap function should look like this:

```
func saveMap() {
    self.sceneView.session.getCurrentWorldMap { worldMap,
    error in

        if error != nil {
            print(error?.localizedDescription ??
            "Unknown error")
            return
        }

        if let map = worldMap {

            let data = try! NSKeyedArchiver.
            archivedData(withRootObject: map,
            requiringSecureCoding: true)

            // save in user defaults
            let savedMap = UserDefaults.standard
            savedMap.set(data, forKey: "worldmap")
            savedMap.synchronize()
            DispatchQueue.main.async {
                self.lblMessage.text = "World map saved"
            }
        }
    }
}
```

# Loading a World Map

After we've saved a world map, the next step is to load that world map back into the augmented reality view. This requires using the user defaults key (defined as worldmap). To retrieve the stored world map, we need to connect the Load button on the user interface to an IBAction method and then write code to retrieve any data stored in the user defaults database.

To load a world map, follow these steps:

1.  Click the Main.storyboard file in the Navigator pane.

2.  Click the Assistant Editor icon or choose View ➤ Assistant Editor ➤ Show Assistant Editor to display the Main.storyboard and the ViewController. swift file side by side.

3.  Move the mouse pointer over the button displaying Load on the user interface, hold down the Control key, and Ctrl-drag under the class ViewController line.

4.  Release the Control key and the left mouse button. A popup menu appears.

5.  Make sure the Connection popup menu displays Action, then click in the Name text field and type saveButton.

6.  Click in the Type popup menu and choose UIButton, then click the Connect button. Xcode creates an IBAction method as shown here:

    ```
    @IBAction func loadButton(_ sender: UIButton) {

    }
    ```

7.  Edit this saveButton IBAction method as follows:

    ```
    @IBAction func loadButton(_ sender: UIButton) {
        loadMap()
    }
    ```

Each time the user taps the Load button, the Load button runs the loadMap() function, which will need to either retrieve a previously saved world map or simply start an ordinary augmented reality session in case no previous world map has been stored.

First, create the loadMap function like this:

```
func loadMap() {

}
```

Now we need to retrieve the data stored in the user defaults database:

```
let storedData = UserDefaults.standard
```

Next, we need an if-else statement where if a world map is found (using the arbitrary worldmap key), one set of code runs, and if a world map is not found, a second set of code runs:

```
    if let data = storedData.data(forKey: "worldmap") {

    } else {

    }
```

If a worldmap key is found, then we need to retrieve and unarchive it:

```
if let unarchived = try? NSKeyedUnarchiver.
unarchivedObject(ofClasses: [ARWorldMap.
classForKeyedUnarchiver()], from: data), let worldMap =
unarchived as? ARWorldMap {

}
```

Then we can store the previously saved world map into the initialWorldMap property and display a message to the user that the world map has been loaded. Finally we can run that configuration:

```
    let configuration = ARWorldTrackingConfiguration()
    configuration.initialWorldMap = worldMap
```

```
configuration.planeDetection = .horizontal
self.lblMessage.text = "Previous world map loaded"
sceneView.session.run(configuration)
```

If a world map has not been found using our arbitrary worldmap key, we just need to load a regular configuration for the augmented reality view so the entire loadMap function looks like this:

```
func loadMap() {
    let storedData = UserDefaults.standard
    if let data = storedData.data(forKey: "worldmap") {
        if let unarchived = try? NSKeyedUnarchiver.
        unarchivedObject(ofClasses: [ARWorldMap.
        classForKeyedUnarchiver()], from: data), let
        worldMap = unarchived as? ARWorldMap {
            let configuration =
            ARWorldTrackingConfiguration()
            configuration.initialWorldMap = worldMap
            configuration.planeDetection = .horizontal
            self.lblMessage.text = "Previous world map
            loaded"
            sceneView.session.run(configuration)
        }
    } else {
        let configuration = ARWorldTrackingConfiguration()
        configuration.planeDetection = .horizontal
        sceneView.session.run(configuration)
    }
}
```

# Clearing an Augmented Reality View

At this point, our app can save a world map and load it again, but let's make one final adjustment and create a Clear button. When the user taps the Clear button, we need to remove any virtual objects so we can create and save a new augmented reality view.

To clear an augmented reality view, follow these steps:

1. Click the `Main.storyboard` file in the Navigator pane.

2. Click the Assistant Editor icon or choose View ➤ Assistant Editor ➤ Show Assistant Editor to display the `Main.storyboard` and the `ViewController.swift` file side by side.

3. Move the mouse pointer over the button displaying Clear on the user interface, hold down the Control key, and Ctrl-drag under the `class ViewController` line.

4. Release the Control key and the left mouse button. A popup menu appears.

5. Make sure the Connection popup menu displays Action, then click in the Name text field and type `saveButton`.

6. Click in the Type popup menu and choose UIButton, then click the Connect button. Xcode creates an IBAction method as shown here:

```
@IBAction func clearButton(_ sender: UIButton) {

}
```

7.   Edit this saveButton  IBAction method as follows:

```
@IBAction func clearButton(_ sender: UIButton) {
    clearMap()
}
```

Each time the user taps the Clear button, the Clear button runs the clearMap() function, which resets tracking and removes any existing anchors where planes and virtual objects exist, essentially clearing the augmented reality view. Add the following clearMap function as follows:

```
func clearMap() {
    let configuration = ARWorldTrackingConfiguration()
    configuration.planeDetection = .horizontal
    self.lblMessage.text = "Tap to place a virtual object"
    sceneView.debugOptions = [.showWorldOrigin,
    .showFeaturePoints]
    let options: ARSession.RunOptions = [.resetTracking,
    .removeExistingAnchors]
    sceneView.session.run(configuration, options: options)
}
```

The entire ViewController.swift file should look like this:

```
import UIKit
import SceneKit
import ARKit

class ViewController: UIViewController, ARSCNViewDelegate ,
ARSessionDelegate {

    @IBOutlet var sceneView: ARSCNView!
    @IBOutlet var lblMessage: UILabel!
```

```swift
let configuration = ARWorldTrackingConfiguration()

override func viewDidLoad() {
    super.viewDidLoad()
    // Do any additional setup after loading the view,
    // typically from a nib.
    sceneView.debugOptions = [ARSCNDebugOptions.
    showWorldOrigin, ARSCNDebugOptions.showFeaturePoints]
    sceneView.delegate = self
    sceneView.session.delegate = self
    configuration.planeDetection = .horizontal

    let tapGesture = UITapGestureRecognizer(target: self,
    action: #selector(handleTap))
    sceneView.addGestureRecognizer(tapGesture)

    self.lblMessage.text = "Tap to place a virtual object"
    sceneView.session.run(configuration)
}

@objc func handleTap(sender: UITapGestureRecognizer) {
    guard let sceneView = sender.view as? ARSCNView else {
        return
    }

    let touch = sender.location(in: sceneView)
    let hitTestResults = sceneView.hitTest(touch, types:
    [.featurePoint, .estimatedHorizontalPlane])
    if hitTestResults.isEmpty == false {
        if let hitTestResult = hitTestResults.first {
            let virtualAnchor = ARAnchor(transform:
            hitTestResult.worldTransform)
```

```
            self.sceneView.session.add(anchor:
            virtualAnchor)
        }
    }
}

func renderer(_ renderer: SCNSceneRenderer, didAdd node:
SCNNode, for anchor: ARAnchor) {
    if anchor is ARPlaneAnchor {
        return
    }

    let newNode = SCNNode(geometry: SCNBox(width: 0.05,
    height: 0.05, length: 0.05, chamferRadius: 0))
    newNode.geometry?.firstMaterial?.diffuse.contents =
    UIColor.blue
    node.addChildNode(newNode)
}

func saveMap() {
    self.sceneView.session.getCurrentWorldMap { worldMap,
    error in

        if error != nil {
            print(error?.localizedDescription ??
            "Unknown error")
            return
        }

        if let map = worldMap {

            let data = try! NSKeyedArchiver.
            archivedData(withRootObject: map,
            requiringSecureCoding: true)
```

```
            // save in user defaults
            let savedMap = UserDefaults.standard
            savedMap.set(data, forKey: "worldmap")
            savedMap.synchronize()
            DispatchQueue.main.async {
                self.lblMessage.text = "World map saved"
            }
        }
    }
}

override func viewWillDisappear(_ animated: Bool) {
    sceneView.session.pause()
}

func loadMap() {
    let storedData = UserDefaults.standard
    if let data = storedData.data(forKey: "worldmap") {
        if let unarchived = try? NSKeyedUnarchiver.
        unarchivedObject(ofClasses: [ARWorldMap.
        classForKeyedUnarchiver()], from: data), let
        worldMap = unarchived as? ARWorldMap {
            let configuration =
            ARWorldTrackingConfiguration()
            configuration.initialWorldMap = worldMap
            configuration.planeDetection = .horizontal
            self.lblMessage.text = "Previous world map
            loaded"
            sceneView.session.run(configuration)
        }
    } else {
        let configuration = ARWorldTrackingConfiguration()
```

```
            configuration.planeDetection = .horizontal
            sceneView.session.run(configuration)
        }
    }

    @IBAction func saveButton(_ sender: UIButton) {
        saveMap()
    }

    func clearMap() {
        let configuration = ARWorldTrackingConfiguration()
        configuration.planeDetection = .horizontal
        self.lblMessage.text = "Tap to place a virtual object"
        sceneView.debugOptions = [.showWorldOrigin,
        .showFeaturePoints]
        let options: ARSession.RunOptions = [.resetTracking,
        .removeExistingAnchors]
        sceneView.session.run(configuration, options: options)
    }

    @IBAction func clearButton(_ sender: UIButton) {
        clearMap()
    }

    @IBAction func loadButton(_ sender: UIButton) {
        loadMap()
    }
}
```

To test this app, follow these steps:

1. Connect an iOS device to your Macintosh through its USB cable.

2. Click the Run button or choose Product ➤ Run.

3.  Aim your iOS device's camera at a flat surface with plenty of distinctive features and tap the screen to place blue boxes in the augmented reality view, as shown in Figure 17-2.

Save  Load  Clear   World map saved

***Figure 17-2.*** *Placing virtual objects on a distinctive flat surface*

4.  Press the Home button twice on your iOS device to display a list of currently running apps (or swipe up on the Home screen and pause on an iOS device without a Home button). All currently running apps appear as thumbnail images, as shown in Figure 17-3.

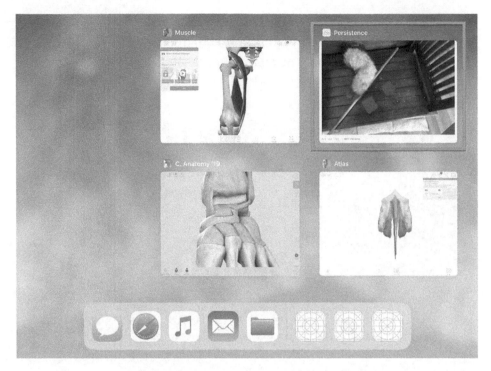

***Figure 17-3.*** *Displaying currently running apps as thumbnail images*

5.  Swipe up on the Persistence app thumbnail (or firmly press on the Persistence app thumbnail and tap the minus sign inside a red circle on an iOS device without a Home button).

6.  Return to the Home screen and tap on the Persistence icon to load the app again, as shown in Figure 17-4.

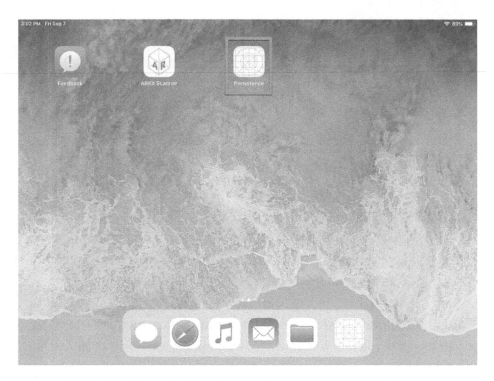

***Figure 17-4.*** *Finding the Persistence icon on the iOS device screen again*

7.  Tap the Load button on the Persistence app. The message `Previous world map loaded` appears.

8.  Aim your iOS device's camera at the flat surface where you had previously placed one or more blue boxes in the augmented reality view. As soon as the app recognizes the same area, it displays the virtual objects you placed earlier. (You must place your virtual objects on a flat surface with lots of distinctive features to make it easy for ARKit to recognize the same area and display the saved virtual objects in the same location again. If ARKit cannot recognize the area, it won't be able to display the saved world map.)

459

9.  Tap the Clear button to remove all virtual objects from the augmented reality view. At this point, you can repeat Steps 3–8 again.

10. Click the Stop button or choose Product ➤ Stop.

# Summary

Persistence gives your app a way to save the current augmented reality view so the user can load it and view it again. This can be handy if an augmented reality session can take place over an extended period of time, such as an augmented reality game where users can save the game and return to it at another time.

Saving a world map in the user defaults is the simplest way to store an augmented reality view. The key is simply giving the user the ability to save a world map, load it at a later time, and clear the augmented reality view.

# APPENDIX A

# Converting 3D Model Files

To display virtual objects in an augmented reality app, you have several options. First, you can create virtual objects out of common geometric shapes (box, sphere, torus, pyramid, etc.). The problem with this approach is that it's time-consuming and clumsy. Trying to create sophisticated images like a dinosaur, medieval castle, or jungle river can only create chunky figures that don't look realistic.

A second approach is to draw the virtual object yourself using a 3D modeling program. While this can create more realistic and sophisticated images, it's beyond the skill of all but the most experienced graphic artists.

A third solution is to simply download and use a 3D model that someone else has already created. Several sites that offer 3D models for free (or for a fee) include:

- TurboSquid (`www.turbosquid.com`)
- Free3D (`https://free3d.com`)
- Poly (`https://poly.google.com`)

However, ARKit can only accept two types of files: SceneKit (.scn) and COLLADA (.dae). You won't find too many SceneKit (.scn) images available, but you will find many COLLADA (.dae) images available. Of course, many 3D models are stored in other file formats so if you want to

© Wallace Wang 2018
W. Wang, *Beginning ARKit for iPhone and iPad*,
https://doi.org/10.1007/978-1-4842-4102-8

use them, you'll have to convert them into a COLLADA (.dae) file first. Then you can use them with ARKit or convert them to a SceneKit (.scn) file as well.

# Converting COLLADA (.dae) to SceneKit (.scn)

If you have a COLLADA (.dae) file, you can drag and drop it into the Navigator pane of Xcode and then use the file with no further need of conversion. However, if you want to convert a COLLADA (.dae) file into a SceneKit (.scn) file, follow these steps:

1. Drag and drop the COLLADA (.dae) file into the Navigator pane of Xcode.

2. Choose Editor ➤ Convert to SceneKit scene file format (.scn), as shown in Figure A-1. A dialog box appears, letting you know that SceneKit (.scn) files may not be compatible with some applications.

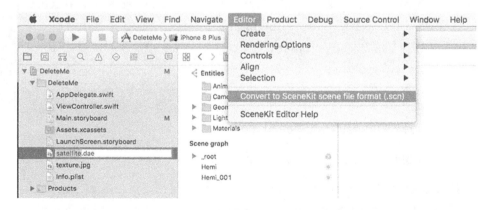

***Figure A-1.*** *The Editor menu displays the Convert to SceneKit Scene File Format command*

3.  Click the Convert button. Xcode converts your
    COLLADA (.dae) file into a SceneKit (.scn) file.

# Convert 3D Models into a COLLADA (.dae) File

Since there are many 3D models available that are not saved in either the
SceneKit (.scn) or COLLADA (.dae) file format, you won't be able to use
those files unless you convert them into a COLLADA (.dae) file first. While
there are numerous 3D modeling programs that offer the capability of
importing a 3D model and exporting it as a COLLADA (.dae) file, most of
these programs are expensive.

For a free option, download Blender (www.blender.org), which is an
open source 3D modeling program that runs on Windows, Linux, and
MacOS. After you download and install Blender on your computer, you'll
be able to use Blender to import 3D models stored in other file formats and
export them as COLLADA (.dae) files.

To use Blender to convert 3D models into COLLADA (.dae) files, follow
these steps:

1.  Start Blender. Blender will create a 3D model that
    includes a camera, cube, and lamp, which appear
    in both the 3D model and as names listed in the
    upper-right corner of the Blender window, as shown
    in Figure A-2.

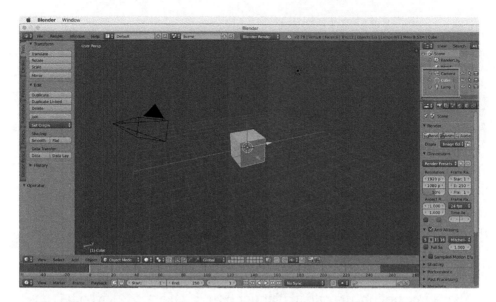

***Figure A-2.*** *Blender creates a basic 3D model that includes a camera, cube, and lamp*

2.  Right-click on the Camera, Cube, and Lamp listed in the upper-right corner of the Blender window. A popup menu appears, as shown in Figure A-3.

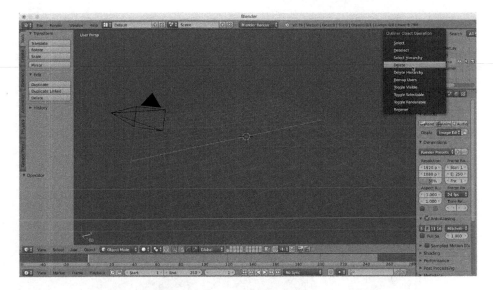

**Figure A-3.** *The popup menu displays the Delete command*

3.  Choose Delete.

4.  Repeat Steps 2-3 until you've deleted the Camera, Cube, and Lamp.

5.  Choose File ➤ Import. Blender displays a menu of all 3D model file formats it can import, as shown in Figure A-4.

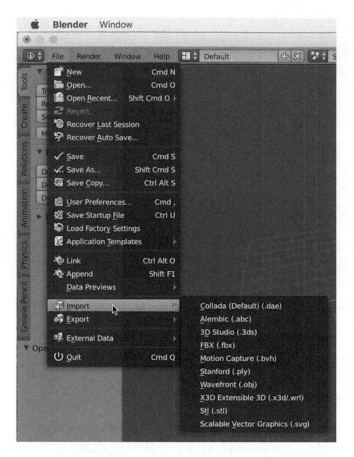

***Figure A-4.*** *The File ➤ Import menu displays all 3D model file formats Blender can open*

6.  Choose the 3D file format of the 3D model that you want to open, such as 3D Studio (.3ds) or Wavefront (.obj). Blender displays a list of folders.

7.  Navigate to the folder that contains the 3D model you want to import.

8.  Click on the 3D model you want to import and click the Import button in the upper-right corner of the Blender window, as shown in Figure A-5.

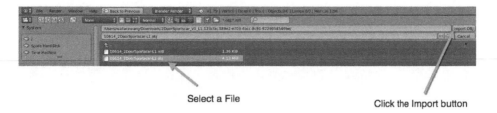

Select a File                                    Click the Import button

***Figure A-5.*** *Importing a 3D model file*

9.  Choose File ➤ Export ➤ COLLADA (default) (.dae).
    Blender displays all the folders on your computer.

10. Choose a folder to store your COLLADA (.dae) file.

11. Click on the untitled.dae default filename and give
    your file a more descriptive filename.

12. Click the Export button in the upper-right corner of
    the Blender window. Blender stores your COLLADA
    (.dae) file in your chosen folder. Now you can
    drag and drop this COLLADA (.dae) file into the
    Navigator pane of Xcode.

# APPENDIX B

# Creating Virtual Objects Visually

There are often two ways to accomplish almost everything in Xcode. One way is programmatically, where you write Swift code to do something. The second way is visually, where you drag and drop items to do something.

When creating virtual objects to display in an augmented reality view, this book mostly focused on creating virtual objects programmatically using Swift code similar to the following:

```
let boxNode = SCNNode()
boxNode.geometry = SCNBox(width: 0.08, height: 0.08,
length: 0.08, chamferRadius: 0)
boxNode.geometry?.firstMaterial?.diffuse.contents =
UIColor.green
boxNode.position = SCNVector3(x, y, z)
sceneView.scene.rootNode.addChildNode(boxNode)
```

While writing Swift code to create virtual objects is fine, it can get cumbersome when creating multiple virtual objects. As an alternative to writing so much Swift code to create virtual objects, Xcode gives you the option of adding virtual objects and storing them in a SceneKit (.scn) file. Then all you need to do is add and arrange as many virtual objects as you

© Wallace Wang 2018
W. Wang, *Beginning ARKit for iPhone and iPad*,
https://doi.org/10.1007/978-1-4842-4102-8

wish and store them as a SceneKit (.scn) file. When you load this SceneKit (.scn) file in an augmented reality view, all the virtual objects appear without you having to define each one individually.

# Creating a SceneKit Assets Folder

The first step to using a SceneKit (.scn) file is to create an assets folder by following these steps:

1. Choose File ➤ New ➤ File. A template window appears.

2. Scroll down to the Resource category and click the SceneKit Catalog icon, as shown in Figure B-1.

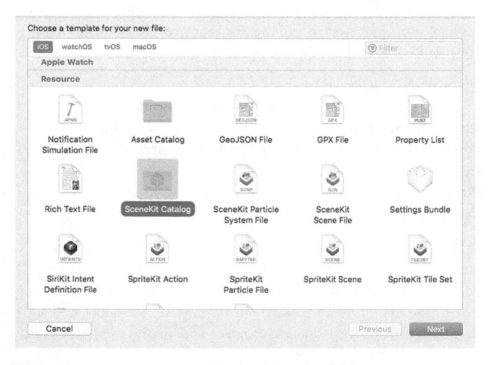

*Figure B-1.* *Creating a SceneKit Asset Catalog folder*

3. Click the Next button. Xcode displays a Save As dialog.

4. Click the Create button. Xcode creates a SceneKit Asset Catalog.scnassets folder in the Navigator pane.

5. Click on the SceneKit Asset Catalog.scnassets folder and press Return. Edit this name to something shorter, such as scene.scnassets.

# Creating a SceneKit (.scn) File

Once you've created a SceneKit Assets folder, you need to create a SceneKit (.scn) file to store in this SceneKit Assets folder. To create a SceneKit (.scn) file, follow these steps:

1. Choose File ➤ New ➤ File. A template window appears.

2. Scroll down to the Resource category and click the SceneKit Scene File icon, as shown in Figure B-2.

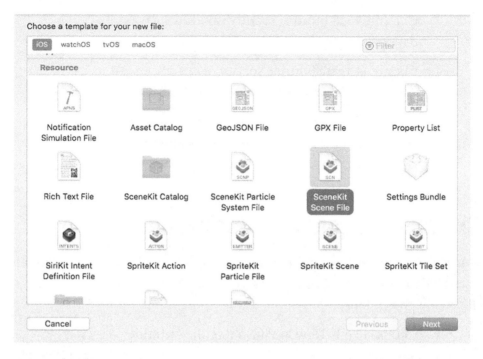

*Figure B-2.* *Creating a SceneKit Scene File*

3.  Click the Next button. Xcode displays a Save As
    dialog.

4.  Click the Create button. Xcode creates a SceneKit
    Scene.scn file in the Navigator pane.

5.  Click on the SceneKit Scene.scn file and press
    Return. Now you can edit this filename to something
    more descriptive if you want.

6.  Drag and drop this SceneKit Scene.scn file into
    the SceneKit Assets folder. The SceneKit Scene.scn
    file is inside the folder when it appears indented
    underneath the SceneKit Assets folder, as shown in
    Figure B-3.

*Figure B-3.* *Placing a SceneKit file inside the SceneKit assets folder*

# Adding Virtual Objects to a SceneKit (.scn) File

After you've created a SceneKit (.scn) file and stored it into your SceneKit Assets folder, the next step is to add virtual objects to that SceneKit (.scn) file through the Object Library by following these steps:

1. Click on the SceneKit (.scn) file stored inside your SceneKit assets folder. Xcode displays a blank scene.

2. Click the Object Library icon to display the Object Library window.

3. Scroll down to find the different geometric shapes available such as Box, Cylinder, or Pyramid, as shown in Figure B-4.

Object Library icon

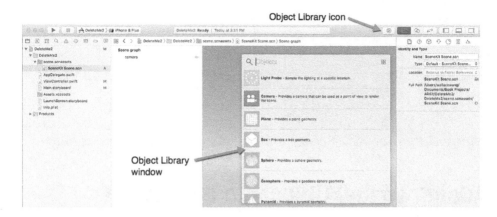

Object Library
window

***Figure B-4.*** *The Object Library window*

4.  Drag and drop one or more geometric shapes, such
    as a Box, Sphere, or Torus from the Object Library
    window on to the SceneKit, as shown in Figure B-5.

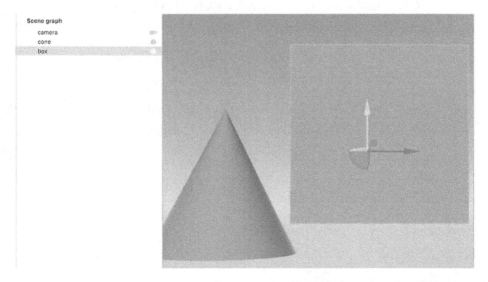

***Figure B-5.*** *Placing virtual objects on to the SceneKit (.scn) file*

# Customizing Virtual Objects

Once you've placed one or more virtual objects in a SceneKit (.scn) file, you can customize that virtual object through one of the following inspectors:

- Node inspector—Defines the position, scale, and Euler angle

- Attributes inspector—Defines the dimensions

- Materials inspector—Defines the outer appearance

- Physics inspector—Defines how the virtual object responds to physics

- Scene inspector—Defines the background illumination

To view an inspector pane for a virtual object, follow these steps:

1. Click on the virtual object that you want to modify.

2. Choose View ➤ Inspectors and then choose the inspector pane you want to view, such as Materials or Node, or click on the appropriate icon at the top of the inspector pane, as shown in Figure B-6. Each time you open a different inspector pane, you'll be able to modify various properties of your selected virtual object.

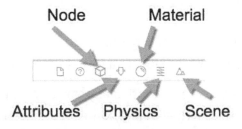

*Figure B-6.* *The inspector pane for a virtual object*

# Linking Virtual Objects

Each time you drag and drop a virtual object into a SceneKit (.scn) file, it acts independently of any other virtual objects in that same SceneKit file. However, you may want to keep two or more virtual objects linked together. That way if you modify the position of one virtual object, all linked virtual objects will move to maintain their relative position to the other virtual objects.

To link one virtual object with another, follow these steps:

1. Click on the Show/Hide Scene Graph View icon to open the Scene Graph View. The Scene Graph View lists all the names of the virtual objects displayed in a SceneKit (.scn) file such as box or cone, as shown in Figure B-7.

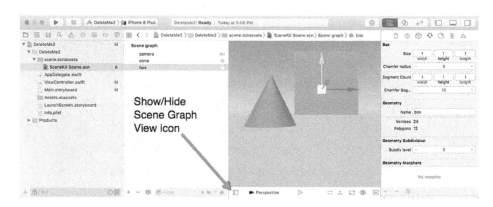

***Figure B-7.*** *The Show/Hide Scene Graph View icon*

2. Click on the virtual object name in the Scene Graph View that you want to link to another virtual object.

3. Drag the virtual object until it appears underneath under another virtual object name. Xcode displays a blue horizontal line.

4.  Drag the virtual object to the right underneath the name of another virtual object. The blue horizontal line appears indented, as shown in Figure B-8.

***Figure B-8.*** *Indenting a virtual object name under another one*

5.  Release the left mouse button. Xcode now displays the virtual object name indented underneath the other virtual object name, which displays a gray disclosure triangle that you can click to hide or show all linked virtual objects, as shown in Figure B-9.

***Figure B-9.*** *The Scene Graph View displays linked virtual objects by indenting*

# Displaying a SceneKit (.scn) File in Augmented Reality

After you've modified any virtual objects by defining their position, size, scale, or Euler rotational angle, you can finally display your entire SceneKit (.scn) file in an augmented reality view. First, you must know the folder name (such as scene.scnassets) and the SceneKit filename (such as myScene.scn).

Then you can create a variable to hold your scene such as:

```
let item = SCNScene(named: "scene.scnassets/myScene.scn")!
```

This code assumes the SceneKit assets folder is called `scene.scnassets` and that the SceneKit (.scn) file is called `myScene.scn`.

Now you can add this item to your augmented reality view like this:

```
sceneView.scene = item
```

Assuming your user interface contains an ARKit SceneKit View and its IBOutlet is defined as sceneView, displaying a SceneKit (.scn) file can be as simple as this entire `ViewController.swift` file:

```swift
import UIKit
import SceneKit
import ARKit

class ViewController: UIViewController, ARSCNViewDelegate {

    @IBOutlet var sceneView: ARSCNView!

    let configuration = ARWorldTrackingConfiguration()

    override func viewDidLoad() {
        super.viewDidLoad()
        // Do any additional setup after loading the view,
        // typically from a nib.
        sceneView.debugOptions = [ARSCNDebugOptions.
        showWorldOrigin, ARSCNDebugOptions.showFeaturePoints]
        sceneView.delegate = self
        let item = SCNScene(named: "scene.scnassets/myScene.scn")!

        sceneView.scene = item
        sceneView.session.run(configuration)

    }

}
```

# Index

## A, B

Aiming point, 192–196
ARKit
    Apple's free Xcode compiler, 15
    augmented reality app
        iOS device's camera, 23–25
        Macintosh, 19
        options, 21
        SceneKit, 22
        target, 22–23
        virtual airplane, 24–25
        Xcode project template, 20
    COLLADA, 27
    definition, 19
    IKEA, Metaio's technology, 8
    iOS 12, 16
    iPhone 6s/6s Plus or iPad Pro, 15
    Macintosh, 15–16
    Objective-C, 14–15
    simulator program, 15
    Swift, 14–15
    Swift code (*see* Swift code)
    Xcode, 19
ARKit coordinate system, 49
ARKit SceneKit View (ARSCNView),
        148, 185, 367, 440
Augmented reality (AR)

Apple
    Akonia Holographics, 14
    ARKit (*see* ARKit)
    Flyby Media's technology, 14
    IKEA Place app, 8–9
    SensoMotoric instruments, 14
    VRvana, 14
ARSCNView object, 29
Berlin Wall app, 10–11
camera privacy setting, 29–30
device capabilities setting, 31
Disney corporation, 13
Ferrari, app, 9–10
HUD, 3–4
hunting scope, 2–3
IKEA, Metaio's technology, 8–9
Info.plist file, 29–31
iOS devices, 5–6, 15
    high resolution cameras, 5
    high-resolution displays, 5–6
    motion tracking, 6
    powerful processors, 5
measuring cup, 2
Pepsi promotional prank, 11–12
Pokemon GO, 6–7
TAC, 12–13
user interface, ARSCNView
    object, 29

© Wallace Wang 2018
W. Wang, *Beginning ARKit for iPhone and iPad*,
https://doi.org/10.1007/978-1-4842-4102-8

CPSIA information can be obtained
at www.ICGtesting.com
Printed in the USA
LVHW032145130219
607434LV00007B/146/P